STANISLAVSKY AND MINDFULNESS

Stanislavsky and Mindfulness synthesises the two disciplines of acting and mindfulness focusing on elemental concepts from Stanislavsky's System. Following mindfulness from East to West, this collection explores how Stanislavsky used techniques of mindfulness to create a way for actors to portray truthful characters.

Using elements of neuroscience and wellbeing, Ingleson and her team of diverse authors share how mindfulness creates more believable and affective acting from a modern perspective. They discuss active, engaged performance and self-care and share workshop and rehearsal exercises that readers can take away and use in their own practice. British, American, African, European and Asian heritage voices come together to explore an inclusive and kind theatre-making and share new approaches to life in the industry and actor training. The contributors to this book, introduced by a foreword from Professor, director and author Anne Bogart, comprise theatre professors, directors and actors, Buddhists, Yoginis, academics, arts psychotherapists and mindfulness teachers.

Part of the "Stanislavsky And..." series, *Stanislavsky and Mindfulness* is an accessible resource for theatre students, drama teachers and academics and readers with an interest in acting and how to apply mindfulness to different areas of our lives.

Dawn Ingleson is Head of Creative Producing at Mountview Academy of Theatre Arts, London, UK. She was formerly a Senior Lecturer and Course Leader of *Acting and Performance* at London South Bank University (LSBU), has worked as a guest lecturer at Goldsmiths University and was a Producer and the *War Horse* Education Manager for the National Theatre, London. She is a Fellow of the Higher Education Academy (FHEA).

Stanislavsky And...
Series Editor: Paul Fryer

Stanislavsky And... is a ground-breaking new series of edited collected essays, each of which explores Stanislavsky's legacy in the context of issues of contemporary relevance and impact.

Drawing upon a unique series of webinars, symposia and study events presented as part of The S Word research project, each volume will focus upon a specific topic, utilising the expertise of a wide range of scholars and practitioners. A variety of written forms are supplemented by suggestions for studio work and exercises encouraging the widest possible practical exploration of the topic.

The series presents topics in a highly accessible form. It will appeal to students, teachers and practitioners at all levels, as well as those who wish to expand upon their knowledge of contemporary theatre practice and will positively encourage the development of new scholarship in the field.

Volumes currently available in the series are:

Stanislavsky and Intimacy
Joelle Ré Arp-Dunham

Stanislavsky and Gender
Mark Shields

Stanislavsky and Mindfulness
Being in the Moment
Dawn Ingleson

For more information about this series, please visit: www.routledge.com/Stanislavsky-And/book-series/STAS

"*Stanislavsky and Mindfulness* is a compelling antidote to screen-learning, digital isolation and the misconception that Stanislavsky's system is 'trauma-informed'. His commitment to well-being and communion is celebrated in this *must-have* volume by sincerely mindful practitioners and educators. What a joy!"

Bella Merlin, *Actor and Distinguished Professor, University of California, Riverside*

"Integrating mindfulness into Stanislavsky's System facilitates richer, more authentic performances. Whether you're new to acting or needing a refresher *Stanislavsky and Mindfulness* brings together the knowledge of a diverse mix of practitioners allowing for a varied and thought-provoking read."

Golda Rosheuvel, *NAACP and Screen Actors Guild Award-nominated actor*

"Human interaction, mindfulness and self-care are crucial to the wellbeing of actors in rehearsal, on set and in all areas of practice. *Stanislavsky and Mindfulness* addresses this and much more, comprehensively. It is essential reading."

Tom Goodman-Hill, *Emmy Award-nominated actor*

"Breath and mindfulness not only calms us, fosters our imagination and intuition but connects us to each other and the audience. *Stanislavsky and Mindfulness* is a powerful instrument and supplies us with oxygen in the pursuit of a shared experience."

Kate Fleetwood, *Tony and Olivier Awards-nominated actor*

"Informative, thought-provoking and inspiring, *Stanislavsky and Mindfulness* is both a deep dive analysis and much-needed practical guide into Stanislavsky's system and how through that we may hold actors and artists in training mindfully."

Lisa Spirling, *Artistic Director, Theatre Royal Stratford East, London*

STANISLAVSKY AND MINDFULNESS

Being in the Moment

Edited by Dawn Ingleson

Routledge
Taylor & Francis Group
LONDON AND NEW YORK

Designed cover image: Photography by Nico Heugh Simone and Design by Nigel Hook.

First published 2026
by Routledge
4 Park Square, Milton Park, Abingdon, Oxon OX14 4RN

and by Routledge
605 Third Avenue, New York, NY 10158

Routledge is an imprint of the Taylor & Francis Group, an informa business

British Library Cataloguing-in-Publication Data
A catalogue record for this book is available from the British Library

Library of Congress Cataloging-in-Publication Data
Names: Ingleson, Dawn editor
Title: Stanislavsky and mindfulness : being in the moment / edited by Dawn Ingleson.
Description: Abingdon, Oxon ; New York, NY : Routledge, 2025. | Series: Stanislavsky and... | Includes bibliographical references and index.
Identifiers: LCCN 2025012747 (print) | LCCN 2025012748 (ebook) | ISBN 9781032853703 hardback | ISBN 9781032847603 paperback | ISBN 9781003517856 ebook
Subjects: LCSH: Stanislavsky, Konstantin, 1863-1938--Criticism and interpretation | Acting--Study and teaching | Mindfulness (Psychology) | LCGFT: Essays
Classification: LCC PN2728.S78 S754 2025 (print) | LCC PN2728.S78 (ebook) | DDC 792.02/8071--dc23/eng/20250422
LC record available at https://lccn.loc.gov/2025012747
LC ebook record available at https://lccn.loc.gov/2025012748

ISBN: 978-1-032-85370-3 (hbk)
ISBN: 978-1-032-84760-3 (pbk)
ISBN: 978-1-003-51785-6 (ebk)

DOI: 10.4324/9781003517856

Typeset in Galliard
by SPi Technologies India Pvt Ltd (Straive)

CONTENTS

FIGURES

NOTES ON CONTRIBUTORS

Benjamin Askew is an acting teacher, writer/director with experience as a professional actor. He received his PhD from the University of the Arts London and is currently Lecturer in Acting and Research for Performance, Leeds Conservatoire, UK, having previously taught at schools, including Manchester School of Theatre and Drama Centre London, where he led the teaching of Theatre Analysis. He originated the *ACT for Acting* project and is founder and director of *The Working Action Group*, a theatre company and creative research community exploring links between contemporary psychology and psychophysical theatre. He became the inaugural Stanislavsky Research Centre research fellow in 2024.

Anne Bogart is a theatre and opera director and a Professor at Columbia University where she runs the Graduate Directing Program. Author of *A Director Prepares*; *The Viewpoints Book*; *And Then, You Act*; *Conversations with Anne*; *What's the Story*; and *The Art of Resonance*. Recent theatre productions include *Existentialism*; *Eastland*; *The Beautiful Lady*: *Radio Christmas Carol*; *Falling & Loving*; *The Bacchae; Chess Match No. 5*; *Lost in the Stars*; *The Theater is a Blank Page*; *Persians*; *Steel Hammer*; *A Rite*; *Café Variations*; *Trojan Women (After Euripides)*; *American Document*; *Antigone*; and *Under Construction*. Recent operas include Bartok's *Bluebeard's Castle*, Wagner's *Tristan and Isolde*, Ruders' *The Handmaid's Tale*, Handel's *Alcina*, Dvorak's *Dimitrij*, Verdi's *Macbeth*, Bellini's *Norma* and Bizet's *Carmen*.

Philippe Bosher is an actor, director and actor trainer specialising in Meisner. He freelances at UK drama schools, including LAMDA, Italia Conti and the Royal Central School of Speech and Drama. He recently left teaching at

LAMDA fulltime, after three years, during two of which he led and directed the acting faculty as the Head of Acting. He founded an actor training company called *Drama Lab*, successfully making conservatoire-level actor training more accessible to young people. Philippe is a graduate of the MA in Actor Training & Coaching at the Royal Central School of Speech and Drama. Before that he was an actor.

Gabriela Curpan is a Senior Lecturer and Course Leader (acting) at the University for the Creative Arts, (UCA) London, UK. She was awarded her PhD practice as research from Goldsmiths, University of London, in 2019. Her research interest combines Stanislavski and Demidov's techniques to explore acting for both stage and screen. In addition, Gabriela is a Romanian professional female actor, trained mainly in the UK, with over twenty-five years of stage, screen, and voice-over experience.

David Gilbert is a director and theatre-maker from Zimbabwe who has worked with leading London theatres for almost a decade. David has worked on projects and shows with Kiln Theatre, the National Theatre, the Young Vic, the Unicorn Theatre, the Almeida Theatre and Trafalgar Studios. He has a passion for new writing, devised and ensemble theatre. He does this holistically in his role as New Work Producer at Talawa Theatre Company and as Associate Director at Trybe House Theatre. He is one of Frantic Assembly's Learn & Train Practitioners delivering devising workshops and residencies across the UK and was associate director on their touring shows – 2022/23 *Othello* and 2023/24 *Metamorphosis.*

Max Harrison is Artistic Director of Lidless Theatre, London, U.K. He trained at LAMDA, under Mike Alfreds, and on the National Theatre Directors Course, 2024. His plays have been nominated for multiple Off-West End Awards, including Best Production, Best Ensemble, and Best Lead Performer. Credits include *Miss Julie*, *Leaves of Glass* (Park Theatre), *Vesper Monologues* (Arcola Theatre), *Tender Napalm* (King's Head Theatre), *In Place of Fear*, *Moonfleece* (Pleasance Theatre), *Little Pieces of Gold* (Southwark Playhouse), and *Festen*, *The Oresteia*, and *Copper Beeches* (East 15).

Associate Work: *Waiting for Godot* (West End, James MacDonald), *Five Characters in Search of a Good Night's Sleep* (Southwark Playhouse, Mike Alfreds).

Dawn Ingleson is the Head of Creative Producing, Mountview Academy of Theatre Arts, London, and was formerly Course Leader, *Acting and Performance* and *Drama and Applied Theatre*, London South Bank University (LSBU), UK. Before then, she worked at Goldsmiths, University of London and was a Producer and *War Horse* Education Manager, National Theatre, London.

She has worked in theatres across the UK and in New York, Toronto and Tokyo. Her research started with conflict resolution and she now studies mindfulness and pedagogy. Dawn's work on *Stanislavsky and Mindfulness* started with an introductory article on Stanislavski training and mindfulness. In 2023, she convened a symposium hosted by LSBU in partnership with The S Word.

Abigail Killeen is Professor of Theater at Bowdoin College, USA and an actor. A career highlight is her adaptation of Isak Dinesen's *Babette's Feast*, which premiered at Portland Stage, transferred Off-Broadway, and was nominated by the Off-Broadway Alliance for the "Most Unique Theatrical Experience". With Karin Coonrod's Compagnia de'Colombari, Abigail has performed Shakespeare, Walt Whitman, and Flannery O'Connor. Rooted in her New England home, she has performed with Connecticut Free Shakespeare (of which she is a founding member), Portland Stage, Good Theater, Dramatic Rep, Fenix, and Portland Shakespeare. Recent publications include a piece on pedagogical inclusivity in *Ecumenica: Performance and Religion*, and two contributions to the forthcoming *Karin Coonrod's Transnational Theatre*.

Elisa Lewis is a Senior Lecturer in Psychology at London South Bank University (LSBU), UK. Elisa completed her PhD focused on the mental health of students aiming for careers at a high risk of suicide at the Royal Veterinary College and Birkbeck, University of London. Her research interests are in mental health and well-being within specific occupational groups, and she has published widely in this area. Elisa is currently researching the mental health of professional actors and fostering resilience in student actors.

Edward McGurn teaches and trained as an actor at the Royal Conservatoire of Scotland, UK where he also completed his Master's in Education.

Before moving into teaching, he worked in many major theatres throughout the British Isles.

Edward has two decades of experience in engaging with Nadine George Voice Work and has studied psychophysical acting practices in diverse locations such as Mexico, Denmark, Poland and Romania.

Additionally, Edward is an early career researcher, with publications in the *Stanislavski Studies* journal and *Anthropocosmic Theatre* by Nicolás Nuñez. He has also acted as a reviewer for *Stanislavski Studies*, reviewing areas relating to the crossovers between Stanislavski and Shakespeare.

Inga Romantsova is a Siberian/Australian actress and academic. Currently she is PhD candidature at Flinders University. She also holds MA and MPhil degrees in Theatre and Film and lectures at the Actors Centre Australia. Inga is a graduate of Russian State Institute of Performing Arts. She began her career as an actress in St. Petersburg and continued in Australia as an award-winning actress (*Petrol*, 2023; *I Want to Make a Film about Women*, 2019). She has shared her research at several international conferences, including The S-Word Symposia held in Malta, Prague, London, Athens, and Perth, Australia. Inga has been published in the *Stanislavsky Studies* journal and contributed chapters to a few books in the *Stanislavsky And...* series, commissioned by Routledge.

Laura Smiley, Associate Professor and Head of BFA Acting at Slippery Rock University, USA, is a certified teacher of Cognitive-Based Compassion Training. She focuses on utilising these protocols to foster compassion as a foundation for resilience with Kristin Neff's self-compassion work to promote wellness for actors. She is proactive in sharing the boundary practice work developed by *Theatrical Intimacy Education*. A teacher of Uta Hagen, Laura also teaches Acting Shakespeare, Fundamentals of Directing, Voice for the Actor and Acting Technique. Recent SRU projects include a regional premiere of *ASTRONOTS* by Mora V. Harris and Kate Hamill's *Pride & Prejudice*.

Hitendra Kanji Solanki is the Mindfulness & Wellbeing Adviser for *Simply Mindful*, a mindfulness and well-being consultancy for the humanitarian sector. He teaches at London South Bank University, UK where he was Course Director for MSc Development Studies. Hitendra has been active in the humanitarian sector for over 21 years and led a 3-year Mindfulness & Wellbeing project for the Start Network's Transforming Surge Capacity programme, funded by the then named UK government Department for International Development (DFID) under their Disasters & Emergencies Preparedness Programme. Hitendra is a qualified mindfulness teacher, having received his award from the Centre for Mindfulness Research & Practice, Bangor University, and also has been a Training Assistant with the Center for Mindfulness, University of Massachusetts.

Evi Stamatiou is a practitioner-researcher in actor training with two decades of international experience as actor and creative. She has received awards and funding from the Arts Council of England, the Stavros Niarchos Foundation and the British Science Festival. Currently a Senior Lecturer, Acting for Stage and Screen at the University of East London, UK, she holds a PhD from The Royal Central School of Speech and Drama. A Senior Fellow of the Higher Education Academy, she is chair of the Acting Program at the Association for Theatre in Higher Education (ATHE). Recent publications include *Bourdieu in the Studio* and *Critical Acting Pedagogies* (co-editor).

Georgina Sowerby trained at Drama Centre London. As an actor, her work includes: National Theatre, Almeida, Royal Court, National Theatre Scotland, and The Wrestling School. She is co-founder and co-director of dirtymarket.

co.uk, making imaginative, immersive work in unusual places. Dirty Market Theatre use *Bricolage* technique, incorporating discarded materials of all kinds. Their recent Wellcome-funded project – omageni.com – created with obstetricians and midwives, involves a game, podcast and film installation, all exploring complex dilemmas in medication and pregnancy.

Georgina has taught acting for 25 years. She is currently Head of MFA Professional Acting, Bristol Old Vic Theatre School, UK.

Polly Teale was Artistic Director of Shared Experience Theatre. Productions she wrote and directed transferred to the West End and toured internationally. These included the award-winning trilogy *Bronte*, *Jane Eyre* and *After Mrs Rochester* (Best Director Evening Standard Awards, Time Out Best West End Production) published by Nick Hern and now on the school syllabus.

Polly has an MA in Arts Psychotherapy from the Institute for the Arts in Therapy and Education where she teaches. She works in drama schools and believes that psychological understanding can deeply enrich the student's practice, as well as supporting creative freedom and personal growth.

James Thompson is Professor of Applied Theatre at the University of Manchester, UK and co-Director of The Care Lab. He was one of the founders of the TiPP Centre, and the founder and former Director of *In Place of War*, which researched and developed arts programmes in conflict zones. He was Editor of *RiDE: The Journal of Applied Theatre and Performance* (2019–24) and has written widely on applied theatre and socially-engaged arts. His most recent books are *Performance Affects* (2009), *Humanitarian Performance* (2014) and, edited with Amanda Stuart Fisher, *Performing Care* (2020). His most recent publication, *Care Aesthetics*, was published in summer 2022.

ACKNOWLEDGMENTS

Thanks go to Paul Fryer, who invited me to edit this book and supported me throughout with timely guidance and care. Thank you to Elena Marchevska, my colleague and research mentor during my time at LSBU, who had great confidence in me throughout. Thanks to Dan Barnard for his support and to my students at LSBU, who have worked with me with great fun and kindness in class (some of whom are pictured in this book), and to those who attended the symposium. You all know who you are. Thank you to Tassia, Claire and Lucia from Routledge for their understanding and collegiality and also to the contributors of this book, who, with patience and compassion, answered my never-ending questions. Thank you to Alan Power for his creativity and support, to Nico Heugh Simone for the use of his production photos for the front cover, and to Nigel Hook for his design expertise. I also want to thank my friends who have been fabulous with their love and advice, especially Lisa, Amy, Aimée and Jo. Lastly, I want to thank my family, who have been by my side all the way through. Therefore, I dedicate this book to them: my mum and late dad, my husband and soul mate, Theo, and my two loving and creative sons, Oli and Ezra.

FOREWORD

Anne Bogart

Why now? What makes a book exploring the integration of yoga and mindfulness into the acting techniques of the famous Russian theater practitioner Konstantin Stanislavsky particularly noteworthy at this moment? Why is this book necessary right now? For so many years, the focus on Stanislavsky's work was primarily on its psychological elements, with less attention paid to the physical and spiritual components influenced by yoga. Here I will attempt to address this question, beginning with a personal perspective.

I meditate daily, and for the past 50 years the practice of Tai Chi Chuan has been a constant companion in my life. For a long time, I regularly attended yoga and Aikido classes. All these disciplines are, for me, in service of mindfulness and towards an embodied connection with the world. And yet, and yet, in the current highly digitised world that we inhabit, I find it increasingly difficult to maintain attention. And I understand that attention is what is required to thrive, function, and produce. But throughout the day, I am drawn irresistibly to my iPhone. I scroll through social media more than I read books. All of this causes me shame, but I recognise that I am part of a wave, a cultural drift.

This drift is also occurring in wider social circles, driving us further and further from one another, into a vortex of solipsism, information overload, and anonymity. People are becoming more isolated and polarised in their digital cocoons, making it harder to find common ground or engage in productive dialogue. Social media algorithms tend to show us content that aligns with our existing beliefs, creating "filter bubbles" that reinforce our views and limit our exposure to diverse perspectives. The constant online competition for our attention can lead to information overload, making it difficult to focus on meaningful connections or engage deeply with important issues. As people spend more time in online spaces, traditional local communities and face-to-face interactions suffer, leading to an erosion in meaningful community engagement.

But if you look closely, there is also a growing resistance to this fracturing of attention. As a response to the challenges posed by digital communication, people are showing increased appreciation for in-person human interaction. Suddenly, bookstores everywhere are reporting increased sales as people seek ways to escape the tyranny of the digital world. Many organisations are incorporating mindfulness practices into their culture, encouraging employees to be present and engaged during interactions. Companies are implementing initiatives to enhance human connection, creating a supportive environment that values interpersonal relationships. The Democratic Convention during the week of August 19 2024 promoting Kamala Harris and Tim Walz was a cry in the dark for warmth, joy, and communion. These examples are a testament to the enduring value of physical spaces that offer unique, engaging experiences and foster community connections, serving as a counterbalance to the digital world.

In the theater we also seem to be undergoing a massive cultural shift. The field is waking up to re-examine our shared assumptions about the habitual way that things have been done in the past. There is a heightened sensitivity around sexual harassment and assault as people speak up about abusive practices. What was once tolerated or overlooked is no longer deemed acceptable and new policies and procedures are being put into place to prevent inappropriate behavior and sexual misconduct. With this increased awareness and accountability comes a heightened sensitivity to rehearsal dynamics and a deliberate empowerment of victims. The behavior of directors and producers and other theater workers is being called into question. Rather than seeing acting training as a kind of boot camp where trauma and cruelty is encouraged, a new consciousness, yes, mindfulness about how people are being treated, is becoming the norm. The changes in industry practices include Diversity Equity and Inclusion (DEI) initiatives, intimacy training, and more humane working hours. This cultural reckoning is profoundly affecting our practices and our behaviors in the rehearsal hall. We are becoming more mindful of our own circumstances.

In this spirit, I am not surprised that theater scholars and practitioners are turning to Konstantin Stanislavsky's long-term interest in mindfulness in relation to the theater and the techniques that he developed to achieve it. The publication of *Stanislavsky and Mindfulness* and the enthusiasm of its many contributors is an expression of this interest and curiosity.

Stanislavsky recognised that the craft of acting depends upon an actor's ability to fully occupy the present moment. He began to incorporate yoga into his acting system and his studios as early as 1906. Drawing from Eastern mysticism and spiritualism, he applied yogic practices and Buddhist meditative techniques to actor training. He was particularly influenced by the book *Hatha Yoga*, written by Ramacharaka (the pen name of William Walker Atkinson), and he studied other concepts of yoga practice seriously, particularly *pranayama* (breathing exercises). He incorporated these principles and practices into his acting methodology, using it as a tool for actors to develop focus and self-awareness, and to access higher creative states.

The most detailed connection between Stanislavsky's System and yoga is found in notes from his classes with Moscow Art Theater artists in 1919 when he began to incorporate structural principles of yoga into his understanding of an actor's creative and individual development. Through his study and application of yogic exercises, he started to connect breathing principles to actors' attention, noting that calm breathing led to healthy thoughts, more embodied feelings, and a heightened focus. He also adapted specific yoga exercises to help actors transcend their physical limitations and access higher levels of creative consciousness. He emphasised that achieving self-knowledge was not an intellectual exercise, but rather a visceral and sensual one.

Acting is the art of conscious action in the present moment. Being in the moment is the key necessity for every actor. Stanislavsky's research aimed to help the actor to arrive at that place, the present moment, fully and consciously. When an actor is in a heightened state of mindfulness, their interaction with other actors is also significantly heightened. I believe that Stanislavsky's adaptation of embodied mindfulness not only had an immense impact upon the quality of the Moscow Art Theater productions, but also became a significant bedrock in the notion of ensemble, which, at the time, was still a new concept in the theater and, ultimately, became foundational for many ensemble theaters around the world. The idea of theater as a collaborative art form, rather than a vehicle for stars, gained prominence thanks to the example of Stanislavsky and the Moscow Art Theater.

The theater is ultimately about social systems and the human interactions within them. Every play asks the question "How are we getting along?" For this reason, the qualitative presence of a group of actors working together upon the stage has an enormous impact on an audience's experience and their reception of the play. Their shared presence and sensitivity help to create a more qualitative communion between the actors and the audience.

Although he was intensely interested in yoga, Stanislavsky did not mention mindfulness specifically. In our current cultural and political environment, however, it is natural that we make a link between Stanislavsky's research and our culture's current quest for mindfulness and attentiveness within the needs of a radically changing social system. This book is a group meditation upon the importance of mindfulness in actor training, locating an anchor in Stanislavsky's interests, findings, and training methods.

The entire theater field is asking for increased mindfulness in the rehearsal hall. There is a great cry for rooms that are co-operative, supportive, and kind, rather than accepting of domineering and frightening behavior. In previous times, those who were being abused tended to keep quiet. No longer. Gone is any tolerance for abusive and exploitative behavior. The #MeToo movement managed to profile and put abuse onto display for the world to see, leading to the dismissal of many abusers from their positions, removing them from the very system that once harbored them. High-profile figures in the theater have faced consequences for alleged misconduct, including removal from positions of power, cancellations of projects, public disgrace and setbacks. This new consciousness, this mindfulness, has changed the nature of mentorship, teaching and professional relationships. In addition to attention to the ethical behavior of our rehearsal rooms, there is a growing mindfulness to issues of diversity and equality in the light of a previous lack of both.

Systemic change takes time. Naturally, there are concerns about false accusations and the potential for an overreaction to allegations. The full extent of its long-term impact is still unfolding. I do wish that we could institute a system of and truth and reconciliation for those who have been accused and excluded. There is work to do. And this is why I believe that this book is necessary. We turn back to Stanislavsky to move forwards effectively.

INTRODUCTION

Dawn Ingleson

My journey with mindfulness began in 2018 when I participated in a workplace Mindfulness-Based Stress Reduction (MBSR) course. I was simply interested in it and wanted to give it a go. I had no idea at that point how much research had already gone into mindfulness and performance. I know now, and although there has been a lot of discussion about the parallels between mindfulness and acting approaches and some practitioners use it in their teaching, directing and indeed acting, there has not been a dedicated collection of explorations of Stanislavsky and the contemporary relationship to mindfulness itself. Relevant research has been carried out by colleagues, including incisive work from Daniel Plá from the Federal University of Santa Maria, Brazil and Deborah Middleton and Franc Chamberlain from the University of Huddersfield, UK.[1] We have also discussed his use of yoga, particularly with the knowledge provided by Sergei Tcherkasski in his book *Stanislavsky and Yoga*,[2] which many of us reference in our chapters. We also know about Stanislavsky's borrowing from Eastern traditions and his sense of spirituality, which have been discussed in other writing from Sharon Marie Carnicke,[3] Bella Merlin,[4] R. A. White,[5] and Rose Whyman,[6] among others. However, in this volume, I wanted to explore more specifically how those documented ideas, alongside a collective greater knowledge of neuroscience, now translate into a mindfulness practice in actor training and how that can help actors with both their well-being and their craft and how that is essential to the here and now.

Bringing together a new group of academics and practitioners in the spirit of the series *Stanislavsky And* ... who have not spoken about this before in this way but have been practising it or reflecting on it in their own work for years, culminated in part in an international symposium I convened in 2023 at

DOI: 10.4324/9781003517856-1

London South Bank University. The contributors in this book comprise theatre professors, practising Buddhists and Yoginis, directors, actors, academics, arts psychotherapists and mindfulness teachers. The relationship between their teaching, acting and directing experience and practice to the writing of these chapters is key to this project and to our sharing of the work with you, the reader.

This book synthesises the two disciplines of acting and mindfulness focusing on elemental concepts from Stanislavsky's System. The collection embraces these two methodologies exploring the histories of their relationship starting with an introduction of the journey mindfulness has been on, from East to West, by Hitendra Kanji Solanki. We explore how Stanislavsky used techniques of 'mindfulness', as we now know it, to create a way for actors to portray truthful characters through various discussions of how we teach and with Gabriela Curpan's description of her mirror exercises we can see ways in which we can take actors quickly into the creative state. It also discusses contemporary mindful ways of being in the rehearsal room and in performance, a kindness and care for oneself and each other in this private and shared work, and how a non-judgmental approach can help to achieve more believable acting without scarring the actor. We practice voice work through dynamic meditation with Edward McGurn and discuss the outcomes with students. We explore the current changes in values and ways of working in Western actor training and in the professional rehearsal room with Georgina Sowerby and Benjamin Askew, with Benjamin taking mindfulness as a further tool to support his approach of Acceptance and Commitment Training (ACT) in acting. Georgina's provocations complement those of Abigail Killeen and Philippe Bosher, as they discuss the recent history of actor training and where it has left us as a sector in both the UK and the USA. We share our practice and our own work to fuel this discussion while Philippe asks us to take a moment and then develops Stanislavsky's practice and explores it further through Meisner's sense of mindfulness. We invite you to share our findings and our offers of practical exercises to develop this work further in your own rehearsal spaces and classrooms.

Each contributor brings a unique perspective from their own experience of working in performance and with Stanislavsky's System. We have new translations from Inga Romantsova, as she re-investigates Stanislavsky's own writings. They examine how their use of mindfulness can improve the work in the space and how mindfulness techniques help focus the actor. There are discussions on the histories of directors' relationships with actors and the idea of actor self-care. An actor's preparation and 'de-role-ing' is explored through studies with acting students and professional practitioners alike through thoughts from Elisa Lewis's research and Max Harrison and David Gilbert in conversation. There is a plethora of different voices exploring actor training and ways to use both Stanislavsky's System and mindfulness to create more authentic acting, as well as improving our relationship with the work. Polly Teale, familiar in many UK secondary schools as her plays have become set exam texts, lends us her expertise and leans into her experience and knowledge of arts psychotherapy to touch on these aspects of the work. There are some provocations that test the landscape of training. There are practical ideas, anecdotes and examples from the industry and workshop activities. Each chapter describes in helpful detail, or ends with an example of, practical exercises that can be used in the reader's own practice. An overarching theme is care, framed for us by James Thompson's Note on Care. However, this book does not stray into the realm of full drama therapy. Mindfulness is a useful tool that can provide therapeutic support, but therapy and mindfulness are close relatives, which is not the same thing. We focus on the craft of acting and, in general, leave the practice of therapy to other, appropriately qualified colleagues. We move tentatively into interdisciplinary areas with Laura Smiley's introduction of cognitively-based compassion training and Evi Stamantiou's offer of discussing the wider benefit of studying acting and using mindfulness as a starting point to explore further neuroscientific elements of social cognition. Evi tackles dual awareness, and Gabriela cites Michael Chekhov's double consciousness.

Several of us mention social media and the way it has changed the environment in which we are working in now and how different the present-day notion of 'being in the moment' is, compared with when Stanislavsky was acting, directing and teaching. This is essentially the underpinning of the collection. Coming to terms with what 'being present' means now in our changed world and how we can look after each other and ourselves while aiming for the same quality of Life in Art and Art in Life. As James says in his Note on Care, the rehearsal room 'can have a care aesthetics where the ambition for craft and well-being are indistinguishable from each other.'

Notes

1 See the many articles and editorials written by the authors for *The Journal of Performance & Mindfulness* and these articles below:

F. Chamberlain, D. K. Middleton, & D. Plá (2014). Buddhist mindfulness and psychophysical performance. *Paper presented at International Symposium for Contemplative Studies*, Boston, MA, November.

D. Middleton & D. Plá (2018). Adapting the Dharma: Buddhism and contemporary theatre training. *Journal of Global Buddhism*, *19*, 113–125.

D. Plá, A. P. Gouveia, & M. Bonfitto (2022). Contemplation, performing arts and co-existence. *Journal of Performance and Mindfulness*, *5*(1), 1–4.

D. R. Plá (2019). Mindfulness, meditation and dharma art: Clues for the pedagogy of the actor. *Journal of Performance and Mindfulness*, *2*(1), 1–12.

2 S. Tcherkasskiĭ (2016) *Stanislavsky and Yoga*, V. Farber, V. (trans.). Holstebro, Denmark: Icarus Publishing Enterprise; London: Routledge.

3 See S. M. Carnicke (2023) *Dynamic Acting Through Active Analysis: Konstantin Stanislavsky, Maria Knebel, and Their Legacy*. 1st ed. London: Bloomsbury

Publishing Plc and S. M. Carnicke (2009) *Stanislavsky in Focus*. 2nd ed. New York: Routledge.

4 See, in particular, B. Merlin, (2014) *The Complete Stanislavsky Toolkit*. London: Nick Hern Books and B. Merlin (2014) *Beyond Stanislavsky: A Psycho-Physical Approach to Actor Training*. 1st ed. South Yarra: Taylor and Francis. DOI:10.4324/9781315059839.

5 See R. A. White (2006) Stanislavsky and Ramacharaka: The Influence of Yoga and Turn-of-the-Century Occultism on the System. *Theatre Survey*, 47 (1), pp. 73–92. DOI:10.1017/S0040557406000068.

6 See R. Whyman, (2016) Explanations and Implications of 'Psychophysical' Acting. *New Theatre Quarterly*, 32 (2), pp. 157–168. DOI:10.1017/S0266464X16000051.

1

THE CAREFUL REHEARSAL

A Note on the Aesthetics of Care

James Thompson

In 2012 I was hosting a colleague from the Democratic Republic of Congo who was undergoing treatment in the UK for a bullet wound to his elbow. After the initial orthopaedic and plastic surgery, he undertook six months of physiotherapy to help him recover the movement in his arm, and, in particular, in his hand and fingers. This was painstaking treatment that required commitment on his behalf, and the responsive, skilled dedication of the physiotherapist on hers. I was present at many of these sessions and, not being a health care professional, started to frame their encounter in my own terms. Rather than the language of health or well-being, I felt that I was witnessing *something beautiful.*

To say that a caring relationship was a thing of beauty, of course, raises as many questions as it answers. And it is enquiring exactly what it might mean to speak of *the aesthetics of a caring relationship* that has motivated my research on this area since that time.[1] It had led me to study care workers, mental health nurses and family carers and learn about the qualities and inequalities shaping their work. It has also allowed me to learn from those involved in my own field of theatre studies, and from individuals working across other art forms, for example dance and the visual arts. The aim of this short piece, as a contribution to *Stanislavsky and Mindfulness*, is to ask what this relationship between care and aesthetics might mean for those involved more specifically in the training and rehearsing of and with actors. If I am arguing that care – in a hospital context – had a certain craft, virtuosity or artfulness, what am I saying about its relation to a context where *craft* is already assumed to be an objective.

One place to start is by noting that the claim that care can have an aesthetic is immediately a claim of the opposite. That is, if care can be an aesthetic experience, aesthetic practices perhaps themselves can be caring. This is not only in

DOI: 10.4324/9781003517856-2

the narrow sense that we think generally about taking care when we commit to a certain practice, but an argument that in certain circumstances during an arts activity an act of care is also completed. A person, actor or student has their care needs met as the artform unfolds. In an account of care aesthetics, therefore, it is not that care is the safety net, the risk assessment, or the well-being policy encompassing the work, but rather that in the doing of the work – in rehearsals, in workshops, in performances – care takes place. Of course, the sub-text of this argument is that the opposite is also true – so that for some participants an art process can be experienced as deeply uncaring. My interest is that given this, how do we as arts professionals aim to maximise the chances that care is the outcome, rather than resorting to the minimal ambition that no harm is done.

Of course, assertions linking art and care are nothing new. In her foundational definition of nursing, Florence Nightingale argued that it 'is an art [...] it requires an exclusive devotion, as hard a preparation, as any painter's or sculptor's work' (1859, quoted in Chinn and Watson, 1994, xv). While this may not be a full enough account of the complex range of skills and attributes that a nurse brings to her or his work, it demonstrates that the craft *and graft* of nursing has long been recognised. When Jean Benedetti writes that Stanislavsky was searching for an actor who 'has developed a virtuoso technique, trained his body, voice, facial expressions, had understood the theory of art, painting and literature and anything else an actor needs' (Benedetti, 2016, 30) we see a curious overlap. The point is not that nursing has *borrowed from* the fine arts, or, alternatively, that actor training is drawing on a body of work more associated with health care professionalism. Rather, each works within a sensory, embodied and crafted realm which could learn from each other, in much the same way that Mindfulness and Stanislavsky studies learn from each other in this edition. Care aesthetics, in this argument, is embedded in moments of care and in artistic practice – wherever they are found.

Nursing scholars Peggy Chinn and Jean Watson defined the aesthetic work of care in the following way:

> [It] includes intentional auditory, visual, sensory, olfactory, and tactile art or acts [...] Among these are purposive movement, touch, sound, color, form, nature, and so on. [...] the aesthetic character of the expressive form of caring, as revealed in the perception and action of the nurse, includes direction, force, balance, and rhythm.
>
> *(Chinn and Watson, xvi)*

The most accomplished health care professionals exhibit these proficiencies to different degrees in the multiple encounters that make up their daily work. These are certainly the attributes I noticed in the physiotherapist treating my colleague. This is not to say that this is an easy practice or one that is not also constrained by multiple institutional and social pressures that work against this ideal, but there is an ambition amongst many health care workers to draw on these different expressive forms of caring as they develop their work. Jean Benedetti, in his account of Stanislavsky's ***method of physical action***,[2] notes in a similar language that it is 'precisely [the] capacity to reflect back, to respond to and judge other people's thoughts and feelings that is at the root of art' (Benedetti, 2013, 3). Here Chinn and Watson's nurse and Stanislavsky's artist share some common attributes.

So, what are the implications of this argument? On the one hand, care aesthetics is making a broad claim. We live in a world where quality care and positive caring relations are diminished through multiple factors, and creating processes through which we learn how to connect with others, meet needs and have needs met, is vital. The extraordinary capacity of the physiotherapist to create an intimate, beautiful relationship with my colleague was one example of this human capacity. But similarly, at the level of our professional practice, as artists and teachers we can create experiences for our students, participants or actors where the very act of making also sustains, nurtures and enables them to thrive. We teach them to lift a colleague in a movement piece and the aim is for them to do so with elegance ***and*** care. We support them as they use, in Chinn and Watson's words, 'purposive movement, touch, sound' that meets their collaborators in an environment of mutual respect. The artful rehearsal is a careful one because it develops the aesthetic experience through which we 'reflect back' and 'respond to' others. It can have a care aesthetics where the ambition for craft and well-being are indistinguishable from each other.

Notes

1 See Thompson (2015, 2022).
2 See Benedetti (2013).

References

Benedetti, J. (2013) *Stanislavski and the Actor: The Method of Physical Action*. London: Routledge.

Benedetti, J. (2016) *Stanislavski: An Introduction (Performance Books)*. London: Bloomsbury Publishing.

Chinn, P. and Watson, J. eds. (1994) *Art and Aesthetics in Nursing*. New York: National League for Nursing Press.

Thompson, J. (2015) Towards an aesthetics of Care, *RiDE*: The Journal of Applied Theatre., 204, pp. 1–12.

Thompson, J. (2022) *Care Aesthetics: For Artful Care and Careful Art*. London: Routledge.

2

AN OVERVIEW OF MEDITATION & MINDFULNESS

From Traditional East to Contemporary Uses in the West

Hitendra Kanji Solanki

Journeys Intertwined

Unfolding across several millennia, the story of meditation and mindfulness, and its journey from its ancient traditional spiritual roots in the East to its present-day renaissance in the West, weaves a beautifully ornate tapestry.

Given its vast panoramic nature, and the intricacies of a myriad strands interwoven throughout history, of people, places, and influences, conveying its colour and grandeur in full would, probably, necessitate an epic work of theatrical storytelling in its own right. However, for this volume of *Stanislavsky and Mindfulness*, a few choice threads may yet offer compelling glimpses and insights into these vibrant characters, momentous events, and the twists and turns interwoven into the fabric of this epic tale.

It is hoped, therefore, in understanding the richness of the journey of meditation and mindfulness from East to West, that it may provide clarity on the historical and spiritual relationship between Stanislavsky, the development of his system, and, ultimately, the flourishing of mindfulness itself.

Timeless Beginnings, Ancient Insights

From its earlier timeless beginnings, the elemental roots of mindfulness were first recorded in the writings of the *Vedas*, the oldest compilation of Indian spiritual philosophy and metaphysical practices, dating back to the *Vedic* age, around 5000–2000 BCE.[1,2] This sacred esoteric knowledge, known as *Vedanta*, was incorporated in the *Upanishads*, the culminating scriptures within the four main texts that comprise the *Vedas*, the foundational scriptures of Hinduism.[3,4]

DOI: 10.4324/9781003517856-3

One of the earliest forms of meditation, richly elaborated upon within these *Upanishads*, is a form of concentration upon an object, known as *Upasana*. Buddhist scholar Bhikku Sujato describes this cultivation of concentration, noting that, 'in this immersion of awareness in one's actions we can discern a precursor to the Buddhist emphasis on mindfulness through all one's activities' (Sujato 2012, 155).

As the *Vedic* age unfolded over the following centuries, these practices evolved and branched into other forms of meditative traditions.[5] Chief amongst these was the system of metaphysical practices and teachings led by one Siddhartha Gautama, an Indian prince who became a wondering ascetic, and who eventually became known as the historical *'Buddha'*, around 500–400 BCE.[6]

Of these, the *Satipatthana Sutta*, translated as the 'The Discourse on the Foundations of Mindfulness', essentially forms the esoteric heart of the Buddha's teachings, and outlines the way for ending suffering, understanding the true nature of reality, and ultimately achieving liberation, or '*Nibbana*' (Nirvana), through the four-fold approach of establishing mindful awareness of the body, feelings (sensations), mind (consciousness), and mental contents.[7,8]

This path of *Satipatthana* also became known as *Vipassana*, meaning to 'see clearly' (Giommi and Barendregt 2014, 2), and laid the foundations for Buddhist insight meditation, or mindfulness, as it is popularly known today.[9,10]

However, as *Vipassana* began to flourish, earlier forms of *Vedic* meditation also continued to evolve, and around 200 BCE, the Indian sage Patanjali composed his famous treatise, the *Yoga Sutra*.[11] Here, Patanjali revealed eight stages, which he termed *Ashtanga* (meaning eight-fold), required to achieve '*Sat Chit Ananda*' (meaning truth, consciousness, and bliss) through the liberation of the soul[12] (Wani 2021, 327).

These eight limbs of *Ashtanga Yoga* consist of the following – *Yama* (ethics), *Niyama* (discipline), *Asanas* (physical postures), *Pranayama* (control of life force, *Prana*, in the body via breath), *Pratyahara* (sense withdrawal), *Dharana* (mental concentration), *Dhyana* (meditation), and finally, achieving *Samadhi* (transcendental consciousness).[13,14] Given its supreme goal of achieving transcendental consciousness, *Ashtanga Yoga* became known, more popularly, as *Raj Yoga* (meaning 'King Yoga' in Sanskrit).[15,16]

As yoga continued evolving over the centuries, further experiential insights were also written into later scriptures (between 500 to 1400 CE). Of these, the *Hatha Yoga Pradipika*, written by Yogi Swatmarama, is considered as the authoritative text on the *Asanas*, or postures, covering the third limb of *Ashtanga Yoga*, and provides metaphysical guidance on the manipulation of *Prana* within the body.[17]

Indeed, this control of *Prana* through mastery of the *Asanas*, within *Hatha Yoga*, is a foundational stage towards *Samadhi*, or transcendental consciousness, the ultimate goal of *Raja Yoga*. As such, the *Hatha Yoga Pradipika* explicitly clarifies, it is the 'knowledge of *Hatha Yoga* which shines forth as a stairway for those who wish to ascend to the highest stage of yoga, *Raja Yoga*' (Muktibodhananda 1998, 23).

It is from these ancient esoteric insights, especially from *Hatha* and *Raja Yoga*, that Stanislavsky would discover, and, ultimately, draw his spiritual inspiration for his 'system'.

Stanislavsky at the Crossroads (1200–1900 CE)

As the wealth of these ancient metaphysical discourses continued flourishing throughout the East, some of the earliest glimpses of this knowledge arriving in the West can also be traced through a variety of historical writings.

One of the very earliest is recorded in the romantic writings of Marco Polo, following his travels in China and Sri Lanka (1292 and 1295 CE), chronicling the life of the Buddha, whom he compared to the saintliness of Christ.[18]

However, it was from 1600 CE onwards, as the great maritime trade routes of the East India Company opened, and the 'civilising mission' of colonial Western powers began to spread, that the first translations of Hindu and Buddhist scriptures appeared in Europe[19] (Said 1979, 254).

These included the first English translation of the *Bhagavad Gita* in 1785, by Charles Wilkins,[20,21] and, in 1805, Henry Thomas Colebrooke (1765–1837), published his *Essay on the Vedas*, followed by a translation of Patanjali's *Yoga Sutra* in 1823, in which he curiously describes yogis as 'sorcerers' (Rocher and Rocher 2014, 170, 192). By 1824, the first original Buddhist manuscripts had also arrived in Europe for study by such Orientalist Western scholars.[22,23]

As Orientalist writings continued flourishing in the late 1800s and early 1900s, popular writings began appearing across Europe and the United States. Notable works included *The Light of Asia* in 1879, by Edwin Arnold (1832–1904), poetically narrating the life of the Buddha, and selling over a million copies, with a Russian translation published in 1890.[24] Additionally, Friedrich Max Muller (1823–1900) published a collection of *Vedic* fables known as the *Hitopadesa*, in 1844.[25]

Bolstered by such popular publications, early esoteric movements also flourished, such as the Theosophical Society, founded by spiritualist Helena Petrovna Blavatsky (1831–1891) in 1875. Blending the occult, with Buddhist and Hindu esoteric practices, Blavatsky published several international best-sellers, including *The Secret Doctrine* (1888), and by 1908 had founded the Russian Theosophical Society. However, Blavatsky soon became controversial, with credible allegations of fraudulently concocting fabulous journeys to learn secret wisdom from enlightened masters in hidden Himalayan caves.[26]

Whether Stanislavsky was directly influenced by Blavatsky's work remains unclear. Regardless, it is estimated that as early as 1913, there were already some 35 active occult organisations, with at least 30 journals on esoteric issues published between 1881 and 1918, providing a potentially rich backdrop of influences available to him.[27]

However, several of Stanislavsky's contemporaries are known to have been influenced by Blavatsky, including writer Maxim Gorky (1868–1936), and Leopold Antonovich Sulerzhitsky (1873–1916), the artistic director of Stanislavsky's First Studio of the Moscow Art Theatre in 1912.[28,29] Indeed, Bella Merlin suggests that Sulerzhitsky's 'most profound contribution to Stanislavsky's development was his introduction of *Hatha Yoga* into the actor-training programme' (Merlin 2003, 21). Additionally, artist and poet Nikolai Konstantinovich Roerich (1874–1947), a member of the Russian Theosophical Society, worked as a set designer for Stanislavsky in 1912. Later, Roerich, accompanied by his wife Helena, travelled across India and Tibet, between 1923 and 1928, to learn directly from meditation and yoga masters in the Himalayas.[30]

Along with these potential influences upon Stanislavsky personally, in parallel, the grander journey of Eastern metaphysics and its journey West continued to unfold.

One of the most momentous milestones in this journey was the World Parliament of Religions, held in Chicago in 1893, and the arrival of 'the eloquent' Swami Vivekananda to the West (Kittelstrom 2009, 244). A disciple of the highly revered Indian mystic Ramakrishna, Vivekananda's lectures reportedly made a profound impression on audiences, attracting unprecedented media attention. Ultimately, this historical moment is considered to be the first authentic exposition of *Vedic* knowledge of yoga and meditation to lay audiences in the West. By 1896, Vivekananda had established the Vedanta Society of New York, and had delivered lectures on 'The Philosophy of the Vedanta' to students at Harvard University. He also published several bestselling books until his death in 1902, including *Karma Yoga* (1896), and *Raja Yoga* (1899).[31]

Of particular significance to our story, *and we can only speculate*, one individual that may possibly have attended Vivekananda's lectures at the World Parliament of Religions, was a magazine writer named William Walker Atkinson (1862–1932). Previously a lawyer in Pennsylvania, Atkinson moved to Chicago around 1900, where he began writing for several magazines.[32] Joining the Theosophical Society in 1903, Atkinson soon thereafter became a prolific writer on Eastern mysticism, mysteriously using a string of pseudonyms, for his almost 700 magazine articles, and the almost 100 books he wrote in the three decades before his death.[33] Whilst some pseudonyms were banal, such as *'Theron Q. Dumont'*, some were clearly influenced by his interest in Eastern mysticism. These included, *'Swami Panchadasi'*, *'Swami Bhakta Vishita'*, and, eventually, his most well-known pseudonym, *'Yogi Ramacharaka'* (Theosophy Wiki, 2022). However, problematically, there is no evidence that Atkinson actually met Vivekananda, or that he was ever ordained as a monk and given such a name, ***and more troublingly***, whether he actually practiced yoga or meditation himself.

Nonetheless, with increasing public interest in Eastern mysticism, Atkinson's books, written as Yogi Ramacharaka, which included *The Hindu-Yogi Science of Breath* (1903), *Hatha Yoga* (1904), *Raja Yoga* (1906), and *Gnani Yoga* (1907), went on to become international bestsellers. Indeed, three of Atkinson's books were found in Stanislavsky's personal library collection (*Hatha Yoga*, *Raja Yoga*, and *Teachings of Yoga about the Mental World of the Person*), and these seem to be the primary sources from which Stanislavsky drew his inspiration in devising his acting 'system'.[34,35] Whilst it remains unclear whether Stanislavsky was ever aware of Atkinson's real identity, it seems that the knowledge contained therein was accepted as authentic, and taken in good faith by him regardless.

However, some clearly did question Atkinson's authenticity. In a letter dated September 1935, and following their long sojourn in India and Tibet, Helena Roerich, the wife of Nikolai Roerich, wrote, 'let us bear in mind that the so-called yogi, Ramacharaka (an American by the name of Atkinson), certainly was never a yogi even if he was amongst the listeners of Vivekananda' (Roerich 2017, 22). Carnicke also adds, 'however bastardized the Ramacharaka books might seem to true disciples of Yoga, Stanislavsky and the members of his First Studio found them exceedingly valuable' (Carnicke 2009, 175). Remarkably, despite their imperfections and questionable provenance, Atkinson's books remain in print to this day.

A Metaphysical Wild West

As the 20th century arrived, with the popularity of Eastern mysticism blossoming, a new and equally colourful cohort of characters began to emerge, including some authentic, and some not. In many ways, the early 1900s resembled a veritable metaphysical 'wild west' for truth seekers.

Vividly describing this carnival-like landscape in the United States, Deslippe elaborates that at this time yoga was, 'primarily seen not as physical and postural, but as mental and magical. This was largely due to a stream of fantastic and influential stories of Indian wonder-workers that reached the American public.' As a result, the 'general public, aided by legions of vaudeville stage performers and fortune tellers, saw Indians as holders of supernatural and psychic abilities' (Deslippe, 2018, 7).

Nonetheless, authentic Eastern teachers slowly began to establish themselves, and, by 1933, more than 20 genuine lineage swamis from India were already teaching in various *Vedanta Society* branches across the United States.[36]

More significantly, the arrival, in 1920, of Indian yogi Paramahansa Yogananda (1893–1952), can be considered to be a watershed moment in the transmission of authentic yoga and meditation practices to the West.

Speaking at the International Congress of Religious Liberals held in Boston, on 'The Science of Religion', and subsequent lecture tours, gained him widespread popularity throughout the country, and by 1925, Yogananda had founded the Self Realization Fellowship in Los Angeles. By 1927, his influence growing, Yogananda was invited to the White House by President Coolidge, 'making him the first Swami to meet with a U.S. President' (Self-Realization Fellowship 2018). However, Yogananda's greatest influential legacy was the publication of his *Autobiography of a Yogi* in 1946.

With its deeply personal and compelling glimpses of Eastern mysticism, *Autobiography of a Yogi* became a global bestseller, and, over the following decades, became highly influential in mainstreaming meditation into the realm of popular culture.

A striking example of this can be found on the cover of the 1967 Beatles album, *Sgt. Pepper's Lonely Hearts Club Band*, which features a collage of historical figures and celebrities, including Yogananda, along with both his own guru, Sri Yukteswar, and also his guru's guru, Lahiri Mahasaya.[37] By 1968, clearly influenced by Yogananda, the Beatles travelled to India to learn meditation under the guidance of their guru, Maharishi Mahesh Yogi. As Goldberg jovially articulates, 'it may have been the most momentous spiritual retreat since Jesus spent those forty days in the wilderness. The media frenzy over the Fab Four made known to the sleek, sophisticated West that meek, mysterious India had something of value. Our understanding of spirituality would never be the same' (Goldberg 2010, 7).

Importantly, the preface for *Autobiography of a Yogi* was written by distinguished anthropologist and Tibetan Buddhist scholar and Theosophist, Walter Yeeling Evans-Wentz (1878–1965). As a friend of celebrated analytical psychologist Carl Jung (1875–1961), he was a notable influence on Jung's work.[38] Jung was also deeply influenced by other Eastern teachers, including Japanese Zen Buddhist master Daisetz Teitaro Suzuki (1970 1966), Ramana Maharishi (1879–1950), and Ramakrishna (1836–1886).[39,40] Inevitably, Jung's metaphysical and psychological writings, which generously cite Buddhism, the *Upanishads*, and the *Vedas*, through the lens of academic scrutiny, began to slowly usher in a greater scientific appreciation and respectability for meditation and yoga in the West.[41]

Authenticity, Science, and the Rise of Mind–Body Medicine (1945–Present Day)

The re emergence of international travel, after the end of World War Two (1939–1945), witnessed a flurry of genuine meditation and yoga teachers arriving in the West, beginning a steady revival of authentic spiritual teachings and practices.

Most notably, following the brutal Chinese invasion of Tibet in 1959, the Dalai Lama (1935–present) escaped into exile in India. As a Buddhist monk, and the spiritual leader of Tibet, his first book, *My Land and My People* published in 1962, in contrast to the earlier romanticised Orientalist writings, provided an unvarnished insight into the reality of Tibet. Receiving a Nobel Peace Prize in 1989, helped raise his profile further, providing a greater and eminently faithful awareness of Buddhist spiritual practices around the world.[42]

Additionally, other Buddhist and Hindu teachers were also significantly instrumental in the transmission of authentic meditation practices. Japanese Zen Master Shunryu Suzuki (1904–1971), who founded the San Francisco Zen Center in 1959, and whose book *Zen Mind Beginner's Mind* (1970), continues to be one of the most widely read books on Zen meditation in the world. From Vietnam, Zen Master Thich Nhat Hanh (1926–2022), travelled to the United States in 1961 as a peace activist against the Vietnam War (1955–1975). His book, *The Miracle of Mindfulness*, published in 1975, remains a bestseller to this day. Additionally, Tibetan Buddhist monk, Chogyam Trungpa Rinpoche (1939–1987), was hugely influential, and his books, *Born in Tibet* (1966), and *Meditation in Action* (1969), were among the first authentic teachings on mindfulness meditation. In 1970, he also founded Naropa University in Colorado, which became regarded as the birthplace of the modern mindfulness movement.[43] Similarly, from India, Hindu teachers also played a significant role in the flourishing of yoga. These included, Swami A.C. Bhaktivedanta Prabhupada (1896–1977), founder of the '*Hare Krishna*' movement, and Swami Satchidananda Saraswati (1914–2002), iconically photographed addressing the 400,000 strong crowd attending the Woodstock Music & Art Fair in 1969.[44]

Indeed, during this volatile period, amidst the backdrop of the Vietnam War, the heady mix of counterculture, civil rights, the hippie movement, and birth of psychedelic drugs, that many began to turn towards alternative ways to support their mental wellbeing. Thus, as Eastern spirituality and meditation became further intertwined with psychology, and in addressing anxiety and stress, the first clinical studies on meditation and yoga also began to appear.

Two of the first medical professionals to study the effects of meditation were Harvard-trained cardiologist Dr. Herbert Benson (1935–2022), and PhD researcher, Robert Keith Wallace (n.d.) at the University of California. Their papers, published between 1970 and 1972, on the physiological responses of Transcendental Meditation were groundbreaking. Openly citing *Patanjali* and *Vedic* sources, they scientifically demonstrated its 'practical therapeutic value in the alleviation of mental and physical tension' (Wallace 1970, 1754).

Undoubtedly, it was Benson's book, *The Relaxation Response*, published in 1975, that firmly established the beginnings of mind–body medicine. Becoming an international bestseller, with over four million copies sold, it catalysed a breakthrough in the acceptance of meditation as a credible and acceptable form of stress reduction and for enhancing mental and physical wellbeing.[45] Indeed, following its publication, the, 'Transcendental Meditation movement claimed more than 400,000 adherents, studying at more than 300 centers in the United States alone' (Risen, 2022).

However, the most prominent phase in the flourishing of meditation and mind–body science can be attributed to Professor Jon Kabat-Zinn (1944–present) from the University of Massachusetts Medical School. Kabat-Zinn had been practicing meditation as early as 1966, having been taught the techniques by his teacher, Korean Zen Master Seung Sahn.[46] In 1979, following a meditation retreat, Kabat-Zinn realised that he should 'use the insights he'd gained from Buddhism to help Americans suffering from chronic health conditions and stress' (Parade 2020). As a result, Kabat-Zinn founded the Stress Reduction Clinic at the University of Massachusetts Medical Center, offering patients an eight-week experiential course in mindfulness meditation and *Hatha Yoga* that developed into the Mindfulness-Based Stress Reduction (MBSR) course. Following extensive research confirming the beneficial findings of MBSR, Kabat-Zinn published *Full Catastrophe Living* in 1990, his seminal work on mindfulness. Since its publication, more than 700 hospitals around the world now offer MBSR courses to their patients. Additionally, MBSR Teacher Training university degree courses are now training thousands of mindfulness teachers globally, allowing mindfulness to be mainstreamed further into society.[47]

Within this field of mind–body science, a significant insight into the efficacy of meditation and yoga has been the increasing evidence from neuroscientists, such as Dan Siegal (1957–present), and Richard Davidson (1951–present). Being at the forefront of research into mindfulness and meditation, their books, including Davidson's *The Science of Meditation: The expert guide to the neuroscience of mindfulness and how to harness it* (2018), and Siegel's *The Mindful Brain* (2007), have become global bestsellers.

As such, scientific research into meditation has exploded exponentially, and the number of scientific papers that now generously, and confidently, quote the *Upanishads*, *Yoga Sutra*, and the *Satipatthana Sutta* have become increasingly accepted. Of 15,764 papers identified as relating to mindfulness published between 1916 and 2019, over 96.3% were published after 2000.[48]

Leveraging this scientific evidence, many corporations are now also acknowledging its benefits for employee wellbeing, and in nurturing self-awareness for improving management and leadership skills. Google, for example, launched its Search Inside Yourself Leadership Institute (SIYLI) in 2007, offering mindfulness to all its employees.[49] Similarly, programmes such as the InnerMBA, organised by major corporations such as *LinkedIn* and *Patagonia*, are also popular.[50] Indeed, in 2022, *Harvard Business Review* noted that 'more than half of American employers offer some form of mindfulness training to their workers' (Cameron & Hafenbrack, 2022).

Importantly, mindfulness is also becoming increasingly commonplace in everyday life. For example, Oprah Winfrey's popular *Super Soul Sunday* television series (2011–2021), regularly hosted Buddhist meditation masters and experts, including Thich Nhat Hanh, Jon Kabat-Zinn, and Pema Chodron. Moreover, mindfulness is now commonly taught in schools globally, through initiatives such as the Mindfulness in Schools Project (MISP) in the UK,[51] and is even being taught on popular children's programmes, such as *Sesame Street*.[52] Additionally, popular mobile meditation apps, such as *Headspace*, launched in 2012, claim to have '*touched*' over a hundred million lives, and are now providing greater access to meditation practices than at any other time in history.[53]

And so, with that reflection, just like the practice of mindfulness itself, the journey of mindfulness and meditation, from East to West, gently brings us to the present moment. To the here and now.

Here & Now, Reflections, and a Way In

On reflecting on the few threads from this vast tapestry, from these small glimpses of the historical journey they have offered, the author has been struck by humanity's deep fascination and yearning for achieving higher consciousness and self-knowledge, and for a means to express this experience and transcend the human condition.

From the ancient insightful poetry of the *Upanishads*, the colourfully spacious and hypnotic landscapes painted by Nikolai Roerich, the lush vividness within Edwin Arnold's prose, to the psychedelic and spiritually inspired lyrics of the Beatles, artistic expression has played a pivotal role in the transmission and flourishing of meditation and yoga throughout history. Indeed, Stanislavsky's own aspiration for '*experiencing*' such a state of transcendental consciousness in his art, for himself and his actors, is eloquently articulated by Carnicke, who expresses, 'at such a moment, the artist feels something akin to that of a yogi who has reached a higher state of consciousness' (Carnicke 2009, 130).

Importantly, despite Atkinson's 'secondhand' and 'diluted' writings (White 2006, 83), Stanislavsky, in his yearning to reach this higher state of consciousness, seems to have genuinely and wholeheartedly endeavoured to embody the spirit of *Hatha* and *Raja Yoga* into his system regardless. Nonetheless, with genuine respect and acknowledgment, *perhaps it does not matter*, as both Atkinson and Stanislavsky, can still be regarded, given the dedication to their art, even if inadvertently and imperfectly, as colourful and significant catalysts contributing to the historical flourishing of yoga and meditation in its journey to the West.

Significantly, whilst mindfulness, in the true Buddhist tradition of the *Satipatthana Sutta*, does not appear to have influenced Stanislavsky during his lifetime, *perhaps this also does not matter*? Indeed, given our unique perspective, here and now, with an eminently authentic knowledge of ancient mindfulness practice, interwoven with increasing technological and scientific evidence of its efficacy, that the threads of this ornately unfolding tapestry have, *only now*, led us to observe this perfect moment for the renaissance of genuine mindfulness.

As such, perhaps, this moment presents an invaluable opportunity for actors and artists to finally, *retrospectively*, help fulfil Stanislavsky's esoteric vision. In essence, mindfulness may finally complete the metaphysical heart of the 'system' he began, whereby 'an actor turns to his spiritual and physical creative instrument. His mind, will and feelings combine to mobilize all of his inner elements' (Stanislavski 1989, 261). Indeed, as Ingleson eloquently argues, 'mindfulness in both its Buddhist and Yogic origins and the mindful-based approaches that have been popularized by Jon Kabat-Zinn should be integral now, in some part, to an actor's contemporary relationship with Stanislavsky's teachings' (Ingleson 2022, 172).

The author, being of Indian heritage, with dual experience of traditional Hindu and Buddhist meditation, and as a qualified teacher of Kabat-Zinn's scientific and secular Mindfulness-Based Stress Reduction (MBSR) training, ardently concurs that Ingleson's argument is genuinely compelling. Having successfully jointly delivered an exploratory mindfulness module at London South Bank University, the author, together with Ingleson, observed a variety of beneficial impacts of such dedicated mindfulness training with a cohort of undergraduate acting students. Certainly, as this volume will explore further, our initial findings suggest that introducing mindfulness-based acting pedagogies, in complementarity with Stanislavsky's 'system', may potentially have innumerable benefits for enhancing authenticity, in safely 'de-role-ing', improving practice, and, undoubtedly, in supporting self-care and wellbeing for actors.

And so, perhaps, as we come full circle, it may be that as we revisit and appreciate Stanislavsky's original vision, and, equally, envision a flourishing of a new age for acting, that the ancient art of mindfulness, just might be, *finally*, the way in.

Notes

1 Saraswati 2018, 1.
2 Kak 1994, 3.
3 Jha 2020, 2422.
4 Davis 2015, 55.
5 Jamison and Witzel 1992, 85.
6 Cousins 1996, 112.
7 Chavan 2007, 249.
8 Thera 2005, 8.
9 Chavan, 2007, 249.
10 Goenka and Given-Wilson 1998, 1.
11 Sumertini 2021,42.
12 Razzaq 2021, 2–3.
13 Saraswati 2018, 25–26.
14 Maehle 2006, 2–5.
15 Saraswati 2018, 229.

16 White 2014, 115.
17 Muktibodhananda 1998, 4.
18 Almond 2022.
19 Dodson 2007, 1.
20 Dodson 2007, 22.
21 Said 1979, 78.
22 Almond 2022.
23 Dodson 2007, 1.
24 Ober 2020, 1–2.
25 Davis & Nicholls 2016, 71.
26 White 2006, 77.
27 White 2006, 77.
28 Wegner 1976, 89.
29 White 2006, 79.
30 White 2006, 77.
31 Nikhilananda 1953, 96, vi.
32 White 2006, 82.
33 Deslippe 2012, 41–42.
34 White 2006, 82.
35 Carnicke 2009, 172.
36 Deslippe 2018, 17.
37 Foxen 2017, 19.
38 McGuire 2003, 439, 442.
39 Lee et al. 2021, 1850.
40 Jung 1969, 548.
41 Jung 1917, 178, 273, 367.
42 The Office of His Holiness the Dalai Lama 2024.
43 Singleton & Goldberg 2013, 227.
44 Goldberg 2010, 178–180, 198–201.
45 Benson 2000, 14, 50.
46 Kabat-Zinn 2011, 286, 289.
47 jonkabat-zinn.com 2022.
48 Lee et al. 2021, 1851–1852.
49 SIYLI 2024.
50 InnerMBA 2024.
51 Mindfulness in Schools Project 2024.
52 Sesame Street: Elmos's Mindfulness Spectacular! 2024.
53 Headspace 2024.

References

Almond, P.C. (2022). *How the West discovered the Buddha through literature*. Scroll.in. Available at: https://scroll.in/article/1023855/how-the-west-discovered-the-buddha-through-literature (Accessed 15.08.24).

Benson, H., (2000). *The relaxation response*. New York: Harper Collins.

Cameron, L.D. and Hafenbrack, A. (2022) Research: When mindfulness does – and doesn't – help at work. *Harvard Business Review*. Available at: https://hbr.org/2022/12/research-when-mindfulness-does-and-doesnt-help-at work#:~:text=More%20than%20half%20of%20American,valued%20at%20over%20%2450%20billion (Accessed 15.08.24).

Carnicke, S.M. (2009). *Stanislavsky in Focus*. 2nd ed., London and New York: Routledge.

Chavan, D.V., 2007. Vipassana: the Buddha's tool to probe mind and body, *Progress in Brain Research*, 168, 247–253.

Cousins, L.S. (1996). The dating of the historical Buddha, *Journal of the Royal Asiatic Society*, 6, 105–112.

Davis, J.R. and Nicholls, A. (2016). Friedrich Max Müller: The Career and Intellectual Trajectory of a German Philologist in Victorian Britain, *Publications of the English Goethe Society*, 85(2–3), 67–97.

Davis, R.H. (2015). *The Bhagavad Gita a biography*. Princeton, NJ and Oxford: Princeton University Press.

Deslippe, P. (2012). The Swami of Baltimore: The life and legacy of William Walker Atkinson. *Maryland Life*. Available at: https://www.academia.edu/5261386/The_Swami_of_Baltimore_The_Life_and_Legacy_of_William_Walker_Atkinson (Accessed 09.08.24).

Deslippe, P. (2018). The Swami Circuit: Mapping the terrain of Early American Yoga, *Journal of Yoga Studies*, 1, 5–44.

Dodson, M.V. (2007). *Orientalism, Empire, and National Culture*. Basingstoke and New York: Palgrave Macmillan.

Foxen, A.P., (2017). *Biography of a Yogi: Paramahansa Yogananda and the Origins of Modern Yoga*. New York: Oxford University Press.

Giommi, F. and Barendregt, H., (2014). Vipassana, insight and intuition: Seeing things as they are, In Nirbhay N. Singh (ed.), *Psychology of Meditation*, Paris: Nova Press. 129–146.

Goenka, S.N. and Given-Wilson, P., (1998). *Satipaṭṭhāna Sutta Discourses: Talks from a Course in Mahā-Satipaṭṭhāna Sutta*. Pariyatti: Onalaska.

Goldberg, P., (2010) *American Veda: From Emerson and the Beatles to yoga and meditation how Indian spirituality changed the West*. New York: Three Rivers Press.

Headspace (2024). *Your everyday mental health app*. Available at: https://www.headspace.com/about-us?origin=navigation (Accessed 15.07.24).

Ingleson, D., (2022). Stanislavski training and mindfulness – being in the moment, *Stanislavski Studies*, 10(2), 161–176.

InnerMBA (2024) *The inner path to success: Grow yourself to grow your career and your business*. Available at: https://innermba.soundstrue.com/ (Accessed 15.08.24).

Jamison, S.W. and Witzel, M. (1992). *Vedic Hinduism*. Harvard University, Available at: https://sites.harvard.edu/witzel/features/vedic-hinduism/. (Accessed 15.08.24).

Jha, S. (2020). Reflection of spiritualism: An interpretation of Vedanta by Max Mueller and Aurobindo, *International Journal of English Literature and Social Sciences*, 5(6), 2422–2424.

jonkabat-zinn.com (2022). *About Jon Kabat-Zinn*. Available at: https://jonkabat-zinn.com/about/jon-kabat-zinn/ (Accessed 15.07.24).

Jung, C. G. (1917). *Psychology of the Unconscious: A Study of the Transformations & Symbolisms of the Libido, a Contribution to the History of the Evolution of Thought*. London: Kegan Paul, Trench, Trubner & Co Ltd.

Jung, C.G. (1969). *Collected Works of C.G. Jung, Volume 11: Psychology and Religion: West and East*. Princeton University Press, 720. Available at: https://www.jstor.org/stable/j.ctt5hhr4b. (Accessed 15.08.24).

Kabat-Zinn, J. (2011). Some reflections on the origins of MBSR, skillful means, and the trouble with maps, *Contemporary Buddhism*, 12(1), 281–306.

Kak, S. (1994). The evolution of early writing in India. *Indian Journal of History of Science*, 28, 375–388.

Kittelstrom, A. (2009). The international social turn: Unity and brotherhood at the world's parliament of religions, Chicago, 1893, *Religion and American Culture: A Journal of Interpretation*, 19(2), 243–274.

Lee, J., Kim, K.H., Webster, C.S. and Henning, M.A., (2021). The evolution of mindfulness from 1916 to 2019, *Mindfulness*, 12, 1849–1859.
Maehle, G. (2006). *Ashtanga Yoga Practice and Philosophy*. Novato, CA: New World Library.
McGuire, W. (2003). Jung, Evans-Wentz and various other gurus, *Journal of Analytical Psychology*, 48(4), 433–445.
Merlin, B. (2003). *Konstantin Stanislavsky*. London and New York: Routledge.
Mindfulness in Schools Project (2024) *Providing evidenced-based mindfulness for educators since 2009*. Available at: https://mindfulnessinschools.org/ (Accessed 15.08.24).
Muktibodhananda, S. (1998). *Hatha Yoga Pradipika*. Bihar, India: Yoga Publications Trust.
Nikhilananda, S. (1953). *Vivekânanda, a Biography*. New York: Ramakrishna-Vivekananda Center.
Ober, D. (2020). Translating the Buddha: Edwin Arnold's Light of Asia and its Indian publics, *Humanities*, 10(1), 3.
Parade (2020). *Meet Mr. Mindfulness: How Jon Kabat-Zinn Brought Mindfulness to the Masses*. Available at: https://parade.com/717983/parade/meet-mr-mindfulness-how-jon-kabat-zinn-brought-mindfulness-to-the-masses/ (Accessed 15.07.24).
Razzaq, T., (2021). An analytical comparison of meditation between Hinduism & Buddhism, *Al Sirat-Journal of Islamic and Social Sciences*, 1(2), 1–6.
Risen, C. (2022). *Dr. Herbert Benson, Who Saw the Mind as Medicinal, Dies at 86*. The New York Times. 17 Feb. Available at: https://www.nytimes.com/2022/02/17/health/dr-herbert-benson-dead.html (Accessed 15.07.24).
Rocher, R. and Rocher, L. (2014). *The Making of Western Indology*. London and New York: Routledge.
Roerich, H. (2017). *Letters of Helena Roerich II: 1935–1939*. New York: Agni Yoga Society, Incorporated.
Said, E. (1979). *Orientalism*. New York: Random House.
Saraswati, S.S. (2018). *Yoga Darshana Upanishad*. Amazon: CreateSpace Independent Publishing Platform.
Search Inside Yourself Leadership Institute (2024). *About*. Available at: https://siyli.org/about/(Accessed 15.08.24)
Self-Realization Fellowship (2018). *January 5, 2018 Marks 125th Birth Anniversary of Father of Yoga. In the West*. Available at: https://yogananda.org/press/press-january-5-2018-marks-125th-birth-anniversary-of-father-of-yoga-in-the-west. (Accessed 15.07.24).
Sesame Street (2024) *Elmo's Mindfulness Spectacular*. Available at: https://youtu.be/I85gpjErUVw (Accessed 15.07.24).
Singleton, M. and Goldberg, E. eds., (2013). *Gurus of Modern Yoga*. New York: Oxford University Press.
Stanislavski, C. (1989). *An Actor Prepares*. Reynolds Hapgood, E. (trans.). New York and London: Routledge.
Sujato, B. (2012). *A History of Mindfulness*. Taiwan: Santipada.
Sumertini, N. W. (2021). The philosophy of liberation in the Patanjali Yoga Sutra, *International Journal of Multidisciplinary Research and Publications (IJMRAP)*, 45, 42–47.
The Office of His Holiness the Dalai Lama (2024). *The 14th Dalai Lama*. Available at: https://www.dalailama.com/the-dalai-lama/biography-and-daily-life/brief-biography (Accessed 14.07.24).
Thera, N. (2005). *The Heart of Buddhist Meditation: A Handbook of Mental Training Based on the Buddha's Way of Mindfulness: With an Anthology of Relevant Texts Translated from the Pāli and Sanskrit*. Kandy: Buddhist Publication Society.

Wallace, R.K. (1970). Physiological effects of transcendental meditation, *Science*, 167(3926), 1751–1754.
Wani, A.M., (2021). Hindu spiritualism: A study of Upanishads and Yoga Sutras, *International Journal of Philosophy*, *9*(1), 5.
Wegner, W.H. (1976). The creative circle: Stanislavski and Yoga, *Educational Theatre Journal*, 28(1), 85.
White, D.G. (2014). *The Yoga Sutra of Patanjali: A Biography*. Princeton, NJ: Princeton University Press.
White, R.A. (2006). Stanislavsky and Ramacharaka: The influence of Yoga and turn-of-the-century occultism on the system, *Theatre Survey*, 47(1), 73.
Wiki, T. (2022). *William Walker Atkinson*. Available at: https://theosophy.wiki/en/William_Walker_Atkinson (Accessed 14.07.24).

3

A RESCUE MISSION

Reversing Legacies of Harm in Actor Training

Abigail Killeen

In June of 2022 the *New York Times* published an article by one of its lead theater critics, Jesse Green. In it, he names giants from the theatrical teaching tradition in the United States, rooted in early Stanislavsky, known as the American Method. He also names prolific directors and producers in the American commercial theater, some of which were sanctioned and even deified by the same American Method. Green goes on to recount now-legendary stories of the cruelty inflicted on actors in classrooms and rehearsal halls and writes, 'without monstrousness, we do not have what we have been conditioned to think of as the theater itself' (Green, 2022).

Mr. Green's article is focused on men, and it is largely men who have been empowered to inflict this cruelty. But women are not exempt from dubious behavior in the American acting space. Montgomery Clift, one of the American Method's shining stars who pledged to become 'the greatest actor in the world' (Bosworth, 1980, 270), had a Method acting coach who allowed – even cultivated – such a dependence on her insight that he could barely complete a take without her approval.[1]

Why was cruelty allowed to flourish in the name of the Method and actor training in the United States? Stories like this cut to my bone. In the early 1990s I studied a version of the American Method at one of its most celebrated conservatories. I spent three very difficult but instructive years deep in study, just three degrees from Stanislavsky himself. Thirty years later, I can't say I'm not grateful. But it was cruel. Must American theater training be synonymous with monstrousness?

If you asked me soon after I completed my degree I would say yes, believing that trauma in training is part of becoming an actor. And in fact, that is how I survived it: I told myself that surviving in the face of the cruelty was the

DOI: 10.4324/9781003517856-4

only way to develop in the art. But in the last number of years the importance of trauma-informed practices in education has taken center stage.[2] It is now common knowledge that students who feel unsafe cannot learn.[3] Resistance within the professional acting field against bullying behaviors has become commonplace, and regulations in the United States like Title IX, a federal law prohibiting discrimination in schools that receive federal funding, now include bullying as harassment, along with sexual harassment and illegal discrimination. An American theater without monstrousness is not only possible, but necessary. As a remedy I suggest highlighting creative processes that allow for parasympathetic response in students and actors in order to heal the residual 'monstrousness' that endures in the American theater field. I offer these suggestions and observations since I believe healed acting classrooms have the ability to change not only the field, but also the wider world. This deliberately provocative claim concludes the chapter. I argue healthy acting classes are uniquely equipped to help rehabilitate the fractured focus that is a by-product of our digital era.

Late Stanislavsky vs the American Method: Effective Pedagogies with Wildly Different Effects on the Student

First, a brief definition: the American Method is an acting pedagogy inspired by teaching from Russian émigrés in the first half of the twentieth century. Highly effective in all its derivations, the Method is a Stanislavsky-rooted panoply of methodologies codified by various teachers who were all part of the Group Theatre in New York in the 1930s. The ensemble-based, political, and complicated Group lasted for only ten years in the United States before finances made the venture unviable. But its members, who had learned early Stanislavsky, used that foundation to create new, radical, and sometimes contradictory acting training methodologies. These approaches became known as 'The Method' and are entrenched in American theater study today. Joanne Woodward called the work of the Group and the schools of acting that grew from it the 'passionate experiment that gave us the foundation from which all [actors] work' (PBS American Masters, 2016). Sharon Marie Carnicke has chronicled how the American Method entered the American university system.[4] And Rosemary Malague further elaborates that while 'The Method' became synonymous with Lee Strasberg's work at the Actors Studio in New York, its genealogy can also be traced to Stella Adler, Sanford Meisner, and Uta Hagen. These four teachers

> became the preeminent American teachers of the twentieth century. And though none of them is still living, their names and techniques remain alive well into the twenty-first century. Their influence began with their respective acting, directing, teaching, and writing careers and it continues

> posthumously today, at the institutions with which they were associated, through their books, videos, and other documentary evidence of their work, as well as through their own disciples, who continue to transmit the theories and techniques to new generations...this is the genealogy of Stanislavskian acting in the United States.
>
> *(Malague, 20)*

Different versions of the Method, all inspired by these teachers, are not the only acting pedagogies in American acting classrooms today, but they persist as the most dominant. And while I have seen, taught, and experienced the power and effectiveness of these pedagogies, I wrestle with their history of cruelty. Besides attesting to this anecdotally from my own training, this cruelty has also been recorded by Carnicke and Malague. Carnicke does the yeoman's work of separating Stanislavsky's theory and practice from the American Method in her *Stanislavsky in Focus*, and Malague's *An Actress Prepares: Women and the Method* has documented and examined teachers of American Method with a special focus on their damage to women.

I will begin with the personal. Two experiences in my adult life helped me heal from my years at the conservatory and find new access to flourishing creative energy and expression: cultivating a mindfulness practice as well as encountering late Stanislavsky in acting study. Why? Though Stanislavsky didn't yet have this language, I experience his late work, Active Analysis, as activating my parasympathetic nervous system, an experience I could recognize since it was familiar to me from my own established mindfulness practice. This is in direct contrast to my experience with the Method which, due to the *way* it was taught, forced me to create a performance from the sympathetic nervous system, commonly referred to as a 'flight/fight/freeze/fawn' response.

The parasympathetic invites the possibility of artistry because it encourages relaxation, trust, resilience, creative thought, and ease.[5] An actor in a parasympathetic state can rehearse creatively and effectively. Mindfulness also activates the parasympathetic nervous system. A review of empirical studies of the effects on mindfulness on psychological health concludes 'mindfulness brings about various positive psychological effects' including, among others: 'increased subjective well-being, reduced psychological symptoms and emotional reactivity, and improved behavioral regulation' (Keng et al., 2011a,b, 1041). Other studies suggest the resilience of a growth mindset is another chief feature of mindfulness.[6] For the sake of rigorous acting training and robust theater-making we must be able to cultivate rehearsals and classrooms where parasympathetic systems are in the lead. While relaxation is certainly a stated value of the Method, its teachers' way of communicating, such as shouting, shaming, or intimidating, for example, could not achieve that effect. Rather, it is late Stanislavsky, or Active Analysis, that shows us the way.

I first studied Active Analysis with Sharon Marie Carnicke in 2017 and continue today. In class she often refers to the Stanislavskian concept of 'experiencing' a role that 'resides in the tacit dimension; it can be known but not expressed' (Carnicke, 2009, 130–131). Similarly, it is the work of mindfulness that helps us to know ourselves enough to access tacit knowledge, releasing the need to be seen in a desirable way in favor of being seen in an authentic way.[7] In Active Analysis, the actor learns to first identify, then trust in their 'tacit knowledge', building autonomous, self-reliant artistry.

Contrast this with the teacher most associated with the American Method: Lee Strasberg. Carnicke cites accounts of Strasberg 'testing' actors. 'He might rage, frightening and intimidating them, as readily as he might encourage or comfort them' (Carnicke, 2009, 54). Malague goes further by documenting Strasberg's particular damage to women students. She quotes a female student, 'But it was so awful, with Strasberg…[he] was so intent on getting what he called "real emotion" that he reduced us to a pulp' (Malague, 45) Earlier in the same chapter Malague provides an excellent summary of the problem:

> Acting students are under tremendous pressure to do as they are told – and to *please* the patriarchal authority figure in the room…[O]ne of the overriding concerns of this book – and particularly this chapter on Lee Strasberg – is the extent to which an actor's 'free will' is curtailed in Method acting classrooms. And I am especially concerned about aspects of Method training that were – and may continue to be – 'particularly disabling to women'.
>
> *(Malague, 33)*

Just because this way of teaching was particularly disabling to women students doesn't mean the damage wasn't also done by women teachers. I had a Method acting teacher whom I quote even today in my teaching. Some of her observations were utterly masterful and her conclusions have continued to reveal new depths of understanding to me about the art of acting over the years. But this learning came at a price. On the first day of class, after I performed an exercise, she told me to go home and commit suicide because I was never going to be an actress. She once slapped me to make a point and regularly shamed and shouted as my classmates and I bravely continued to perform exercises for her. Her class was required and cumulative – we met with her twice a week for three years. If we complained to the conservatory's administration, we were told we didn't 'have what it took' to 'make it' as actors. As a result, I learned how to perform terrified, but I *did not* learn to trust myself as an artist. This lack of self-trust is the response I am most interested in disrupting since it is the opposite of what Stanislavsky intended. Without self-trust, it is impossible to engage in, as Dawn Ingleson has coined in her article that links Stanislavsky's techniques to mindfulness practices, 'mindful acting' – a term she calls 'straightforward and inclusive as it encompasses kindness, self-care, and is a social approach as well as a singular practice' (Ingleson, 2022, 169). This is not the Method's legacy. Rather, I am reminded of the account of Stanislavsky's nightmare, described in Sharon Marie Carnicke's most recent book, *Dynamic Acting through Active Analysis*. 'In a recurring nightmare, he would often see a typical acting student of the future standing before a stern teacher, who continually checks the student's work against the "rules" in Stanislavsky's published books...Stanislavsky cries out, "Shred, burn my books, dismiss the students, tell them I have committed a crime!"' (Carnicke, 2022, 18). Student actors are about to enter a profoundly competitive and uncertain field. They must learn to *trust themselves* and their artistry.

This trust can be accomplished by training that permits actors to work parasympathetically, or in a relaxed, thoughtful, and emotionally aware state. This is similar to mindfulness and in line with Stanislavsky's teaching. Again, as Dawn Ingleson has written, '[t]he language used in both mindfulness approaches and Stanislavskian techniques becomes blurred and starts to overlap' (Ingleson, 2022, 168). But this student-centered teaching was lost with the American Method. Dare I suggest that these were teachers that grew to love themselves in the art more than the art in themselves, as Stanislavsky himself cautioned against? The fact that their methodologies were becoming famous because of their students: Al Pacino, Robert DeNiro, Marlon Brando, Marilyn Monroe, James Dean...it must have been intoxicating. And the need to hold onto celebrity resulted in another unfortunate reality of the Method in practice: seeing students with a fixed mindset rather than a growth mindset.

Fixed and Growth Mindsets

Much has been written about psychologist Carol Dweck's work on fixed and growth mindsets. Summarized here, a fixed mindset is the belief that your 'qualities are set in stone', resulting in an 'urgency to prove yourself over and over', versus a growth mindset, or 'the belief that your basic qualities are things you can cultivate through your efforts...everyone can change and grow through application and experience' (Dweck, 2006, 3–4). This is another way of describing effective rehearsal and what we now recognize as effective teaching. This is not what the Method's teachers could create in their classrooms. Rather, they turned their Stanislavsky-based approaches into fixed mindsets, codifying their methodologies as 'brands'. As Carnicke has observed: 'by the mid twentieth century the American Method had made a fetish of terminology and created a kind of dogma out of what should have been a freeing principle' (Carnicke, 2022, xiv). And Stanislavsky's work was never fixed: 'Stanislavsky does not lay out a single right way to act. There is nothing absolute about his compendium of theory and techniques for the ephemeral art of acting that he so loved' (Carnicke, 2009, 3). In the Method teacher's classroom, too often there was one way to do the work – and it needed to be right.

Instead, Active Analysis helps an actor to do it *true*, much in the same way mindfulness practice helps us to observe ourselves honestly and clearly, without judgement. If student mindsets are fixed in the acting classroom, they can become consumed by the need to prove, over and over, that they are special or talented rather than, as Stanislavsky so beautifully said, freed 'to create the human life of the spirit of the role' (Carnicke, 2009, 87).

The vexed notion of 'talent' is another fixed mindset, and I illustrate with a story from my own training. After completing my acting study, I later returned to the conservatory to hold auditions for a touring production I was directing. I ran into a former teacher while setting up the audition room. Learning why I was there, he asked to see my audition list. He then took out a pen and placed check marks next to names. Handing the sheet back to me, he said, 'check mark means talent. No check mark, no talent.' It would behoove us as practitioners to interrogate the use of this word and infuse our rigid definitions with a growth mindset. Consider this definition of Dweck's fixed mindset, but entertain my substitution of the word 'talent' as it can be so cavalierly applied in acting training:

> Individuals with more of a fixed mindset believe that their **talents** are simply fixed. They tend to approach learning with the goal of looking **talented**, and they often shy away from challenges because they believe that having to work hard at something or making mistakes means they don't have **talent**. Those with more of a growth mindset, on the other hand, believe that **talent** can be developed – they are more likely to see effort as something that propels learning and to see setbacks as opportunities to build new **talents**.
>
> *(Armstrong, 2019)*

Fixed mindsets cultivate anxious responses. In contrast, Active Analysis relies on the actor's self-awareness in rehearsal. This is a release, as Bella Merlin has noted, of 'personality acting' in favor of actors 'working from their own raw materials', linking their individual 'living, breathing temperaments…to the circumstances of the play' (Merlin, 2003, 25). That foundation, coupled with 'Here, Today, Now', or, as Bella Merlin further describes, 'whatever the actors have – here, today, now, are the physical and emotional tools from which they work' (Merlin, 2003, 25).

The experience of learning in the Method's tradition is one of great fear: we were certainly asked to work with what we had, but when we presented it, it was castigated as not good enough. 'When you're working, you're right' is a quote from Maria Knebel that Sharon often uses in class, and one I cling to when my habits of self-judgement creep in. Similarly, a mindfulness teacher I admire encourages practitioners of mindfulness to 'persevere in contemplative practice without worrying about where we are on the journey, and without comparing ourselves with others or judging others' gifts as better than ours'

(Keating, 2011, 139). Permission to till the fertile soil of my inner life as the path to authentic performance: it is only in this way I have been able to cultivate the stamina to keep showing up in an art form whose industry is particularly disparaging of aging women. It is only in this way I have begun to really understand the invitation within Stanislavsky's admonition to love the art in myself more than myself in the art.

Redistributing Power to Guard the Parasympathetic Response

Collaboration is a hallmark virtue in the art of making theater: our art form can only exist in community. In addition to training that allows actors the freedom to create their work in a parasympathetic state, actors also require healthy boundaries to guard these creative processes in charged professional environments. The need of a stronger bellwether in support of these boundaries became clear to me after I presented an early version of this paper at the Stanislavsky and Mindfulness Symposium.[8] An acting student asked me how to work parasympathetically while under a contract with a harshly demanding director. I fumbled in my answer. Thankfully my colleague Evi Stamatiou stepped in. She pointed out that with a regular mindfulness practice, safety can always be found within one's own body. I'd like to elaborate on this critical concept using activist and author Starhawk's interrogation of power, first introduced to me in a non-violent direct-action training. Starhawk sorts power into three categories: 'power-over' – a systemic, destructive power that requires compliance to flourish; 'power-with' – the power of community with a shared goal; and 'power-within' – inner strength that results from conviction and clarity (Killeen, 2023). Practicing standing against 'power over' *through* 'power-with' and 'power-within' gave me accessible, clear language for identifying power dynamics in rehearsal, helping me guard my parasympathetic artistic response for the sake of an artistic goal, even in the face of a challenging teacher or director. My answer for that student today is this: the degree to which you practice mindfulness and grow in your artistry you build 'power-within'. The degree to which you connect to the ensemble and the project you are creating together you build 'power-with'. These two powers in collaboration are a very effective force against 'power-over'.

Reclaimed Focus to Change the World

In conclusion, I will address my deliberately provocative assertion that acting classes are uniquely equipped to change the world by rehabilitating fractured focus. It is no secret that our digitized, information-drenched, plugged-in culture has eroded our collective ability to concentrate. We notice it in our daily lives. A simple online search will reveal articles and studies published in major new outlets calling our splintered focus a crisis with many solutions offered: nature bathing, digital detoxing, social media fasts, etc. My family, friends, and colleagues, as well as I, know our behavior with our devices can become compulsive. Yet our daily lives are set up in a way that requires them: it is how we reach our aging parents, our children, mitigate a work issue, check the date/time/schedule, exercise, shop, check on a friend, get driving directions to a new destination, or even figure out what to make for dinner. How do we reclaim our focus when the very thing that steals it is also the tool upon which we've built the functionality of our lives?

I believe the simple structure of a late-Stanislavsky acting class can restore our focus in a way that can begin to remind our exhausted brains what it is to slow down and connect. It accomplishes this restoration on two levels: attention and empathy. The first level is attention. As Sharon Marie Carnicke has observed, a 'hallmark' of Stanislavsky's company was their tremendous *focus*. Carnicke's interrogation of the Russian *perezhivanie*, what she calls Stanislavsky's 'lost term', 'describe[s] an actor's unbroken concentration on the events of the play during performance'. She quotes one Western critic who says the actors 'are wholly concentrated on their job and their acting is sustained the whole time the curtain is up...' (Carnicke, 2009, 133). Simply learning and practicing Active Analysis is practicing fierce focus, and I have begun to name renewed focus as a learning goal in the acting classes I teach.

The second level materialized for me after reading Johann Hari's 2022 book, *Stolen Focus*. In it, Hari travels worldwide to query attention experts on the trend of atrophied attention due to devices. The remedy, he posits, is not simple willpower. The external forces calling us to our devices are simply too great to fight with a short digital detox or trying to look at a phone less. Though Hari offers no quick fixes, he does suggest a series of lifestyle changes, one of which is to regularly immerse oneself in complex narrative. He states, '[f]or many of us, reading a book is the deepest form of focus we experience – you dedicate many hours of your life, coolly, calmly, to one topic, and allow it to marinate in your mind. This is the medium through which most of the deepest advances in human thought over the past four hundred years have been figured out and explained' (Hari, 2022, 80). While on a three-month hiatus from all technology he noticed, 'I wasn't just reading more – I was reading differently. I was becoming much more immersed in the books I had chosen...I felt like I was understanding and remembering more of what I read...' (Hari, 2022, 81).

This observation struck me since I regularly experience the theatrical text I've rehearsed, memorized, and performed twenty and thirty years ago has lodged itself in my mind and heart and can be recalled. Even more remarkably, it comes to mind unbidden when I experience or observe an emotional event similar to the one from the play. As satisfying as it is to be able to face a young person with a broken heart and gently quote *Romeo and Juliet* or *Uncle Vanya* when my own words fail me, I began to consider that this response could be proof that the way actors work with text is an even deeper kind of immersion in narrative. I suggest its effects are exponential to the singular experience of reading a book since the way actors immerse themselves in narrative involves the body in community.

Hari goes on to interview the lead of a fascinating study whose findings linked the reading of fiction to not only better focus, but also higher degrees of empathy. When we read fiction we

> imagine what it is like to be another person…trying to understand the different characters, their motivations, their goals. It's a form of practice…it's a far better virtual reality simulator than machines currently marketed under that name…what would happen if we discovered a drug that boosted empathy as much as reading fiction has been shown to…it would be a very popular drug…empathy is one of the most complex forms of attention we have – and the most precious.
>
> *(Hari, 2022, 88)*

I believe we have a version of that drug. Imagining what it is like to be another person…trying to understand the different characters, their motivations, their goals as a kind of practice…*this is an acting class*, the kind of class I believe Stanislavsky strove to create. The values presented therein have only grown in urgency in the years since his death: an acting class is an environment where we practice being together in a room, sharing the generosity of our full attention. We then read complex fictional narrative and examine the characters so deeply we actually take on their physical characteristics and memorize the words they say. It is indeed a 'far better virtual reality simulator'! It is a workshop for focus and empathy, and I believe this practice can also provide healing – not just from the 'monstrousness' that became synonymous with the American theater, but to the very culture that is splintering our attention and championing a reductive view of human nature. This healing rescues Stanislavsky from the destructive aspects of the Method's legacy, and honors the genius in his life and work.

Notes

1 See pages 127–128 in Bosworth, P. (1980) *Montgomery Clift: A Biography*. Bantam Books: New York.

2 See National Education Association. "Trauma-Informed Practices." (September 2023) https://www.nea.org/professional-excellence/student-engagement/tools-tips/trauma-informed-practices.

3 For safety and relationship to academic performance see Lacoe, Johanna. (December 2020) "Too Scared to Learn? The Academic Consequences of Feeling Unsafe in the Classroom," *Urban Education*, Vol. 55, No. 10. https://files.eric.ed.gov/fulltext/EJ1265973.pdf For the need for emotional safety along with physical safety, see Lewis, Katherine Reynolds. (December 2023) "Students Need Safety to Learn", in Collazo, Julie Schwietert (ed.) "Safe to Learn". www.palabranahj.org https://www.palabranahj.org/archive/students-need-safety-to-learn-pe7h4.

4 See pages 56–67 in Carnicke, S. M. (2009) *Stanislavsky in Focus, 2nd Edition*. New York: Routledge.
5 See E. Boynton (October 26, 2020) "How Meditation Affects Your Brain and Boosts Well-Being". *Right as Rain*, UW Medicine. https://rightasrain.uwmedicine.org/mind/well-being/science-behind-meditation.
6 See Esther Calvete et al. (2022) "A growth mindset intervention to promote resilience against online peer victimization: A randomized controlled trial." *Computers in Human Behavior*, Volume 135 https://doi.org/10.1016/j.chb.2022.107373.
7 See Association for Psychological Science. (March 14, 2023) "Know thyself: How mindfulness can improve self-knowledge." ScienceDaily. Accessed April 17, 2023. www.sciencedaily.com/releases/2013/03/130314180259.htm.
8 An International symposium convened by Dawn Ingleson at London South Bank University, April, 2023.

References

Armstrong, K. (October 29, 2019) "*Carol Dweck on How Growth Mindsets Can Bear Fruit in the Classroom*". Association for Psychological Science. https://www.psychologicalscience.org/observer/dweck-growth-mindsets (Accessed April 25, 2023).

Bosworth, P. (1980) *Montgomery Clift: A Biography*. New York: Bantam Books.

Carnicke, S.M. (2009) *Stanislavsky in Focus*, 2nd Edition. New York: Routledge.

Carnicke, S.M. (2022) *Dynamic Acting through Active Analysis*. New York: Routledge.

Dweck, C. (2006) *Mindset: The Psychology of Success*. New York: Ballantine.

Green, J. (June 8, 2022) "Is It Finally Twilight for Theater's Sacred Monsters?", *The New York Times*. https://www.nytimes.com/2022/06/08/theater/men-american-theater.html (Accessed November 22, 2024)

Hari, J. (2022) *Stolen Focus: Why You Can't Pay Attention – and How to Think Deeply Again*. New York: Crown.

Ingleson, D. (2022) Stanislavski training and mindfulness – being in the moment, *Stanislavski Studies*, 102, 161–176, DOI:10.1080/20567790.2022.2094103 (Accessed November 22, 2024).

Keating, T. (2011) *Invitation to Love: The Way of Christian Contemplation*. London: Bloomsbury.

Keng, S.-L. et al. (2011a) "Effects of mindfulness on psychological health: A review of empirical studies", *Clinical Psychology Review*, vol. 31,6: 1041–1056. doi:10.1016/j.cpr.2011.04.006. https://www.ncbi.nlm.nih.gov/pmc/articles/PMC3679190/?_escaped_fragment_=po=24.2188 (Accessed March 30, 2023).

Keng, S.-L. et al. (May 13, 2011b) "*Effects on Mindfulness on Psychological Health, A Review of Empirical Studies*". National Library of Medicine. https://www.ncbi.nlm.nih.gov/pmc/articles/PMC3679190/?_escaped_fragment_=po=24.2188 (Accessed April 2, 2023).

Killeen, A. (November 18, 2023) "Lecture notes on Non-Violent Direct Action Training", *Spirit-Centered Witness to Gun Violence, Non-Violent Direct Action raining*, Friends School of Portland. Unpublished.

Merlin, B. (2003) *Konstantin Stanislavsky*. New York: Routledge.

PBS American Masters. (July 1, 2016) "Broadway Dreamers: The Legacy of the Group Theatre", YouTube video, 6:45, https://www.youtube.com/watch?v=Zd308_SiF1c&t=300 (Accessed February 2023).

4

THE MINDFULNESS OF MEISNER

An Answer to the Crisis of Stanislavski's 'Experiencing'

Philippe Bosher

Introduction

I believe actor training is in a crisis of identity. A fractured relationship between the 'old school' and the 'new school'. A fraught argument between the rewards of Stanislavski's 'experiential acting' and the need for compassion and student safety. I believe acknowledging the relationship between mindfulness and acting is the solution to bridging the paradigm shift between the old and the new schools of actor training.

The belief that a relationship existed between mindfulness and acting began in my first Meisner Technique class. It was 7:25 p.m. on a Thursday in Bristol, 2018. I'm sitting opposite somebody I've just met, in front of twelve others. I'm stressed. My heart is pounding, and my palms are sweaty. The teacher instructs me to 'move my attention' to the person sitting opposite. To keep it there and always move it back if it drifts. I reply, 'Oh, like mindfulness meditation'. He looks at me quizzically and says, 'Yes, I suppose'. It changes my life forever.

This suspicion has never left me. What felt essential to acting felt similar to what I did for twenty minutes, twice a day. Moving my attention onto a mantra given to me by a meditation teacher, only a twenty-minute walk from where I studied acting. I have since taught acting with the idea that it shares DNA with meditation and mindfulness practices.

This chapter will seek to clarify the relationship between Meisner and mindfulness. To argue that this relationship can provide a sustainable way to pursue the significant emotional demands of Stanislavski's experiential approach to acting. I will clarify this relationship by first defining mindfulness and the Meisner Technique. I will then compare and contrast the two practices to argue that their similarities cause a relationship but that their

DOI: 10.4324/9781003517856-5

differences separate their identities. I will then briefly provide two ways in which mindfulness can benefit actors, leading into how these benefits could form a sustainable hybrid training approach between the old and the new schools of actor training.

What Is Mindfulness?

I will define mindfulness as a skill used to develop the individual's awareness of the stimuli inside and outside of themselves. As Professor Mark Williams puts it: 'knowing directly what is going on inside and outside of ourselves, moment by moment' (Williams, n.d., NHS online). Mindfulness has its roots in Buddhism, which teaches a way of finding presence in connection to external stimuli. This is in order to rebalance an overreliance on being a 'thinker of thoughts in favour of a broader connection to a sense of oneness and integration with all things' (Shonin et al., 2014, 3). I would also emphasise the distinction present in Williams' definition. The first is awareness of an individual's inner sensations; the second the awareness of the outside world. This distinction will play a key part in exploring the relationship between mindfulness and Meisner work:

1 Mindfulness reduces the impacts of stress via *internal* awareness. Watching the transient internal sensations of the body and thoughts of the mind creates a sense of distance between you, the 'watcher' and the sensations you experience. In creating this distance, the individual finds a sense of peace. The equivalent of getting out of the river to watch the flow of water, rather than being carried along by it.
2 Mindfulness reduces the impact of stress via *external* awareness by emphasising external stimuli in the practicing individual's environment, rather than internal thought. By paying more attention to the outside, there is a lessening of attention on our own thoughts and sensations.

In summary, mindfulness is the skill of deliberately placing one's attention on external stimuli or internal sensation. To become aware of what is outside and what is within, as a means to stress reduction and a route to psychological well-being. For the purposes of this chapter, I will focus on the foundational single point of focus form of mindfulness in contrast to the more open focus practices that accompany more advanced forms of mindfulness meditation.

A Mindful Pause

As the writer, I hope that you have felt a profound thrill as you have read this remarkable chapter. But let us pause to experience what I'm talking about. Read these instructions and give it a go, wherever you are:

After you've read this sentence, stop reading and for 60 seconds listen to the world around you. What can you hear? *For 60 seconds at least.*

I heard a plane pass overhead. A few birds chirping and the neighbour's dog barking. I probably would have 'heard' them had I kept writing, but would I have noticed them? For those moments, they were the centre of my experience, before I turned my efforts back to writing a remarkably spellbinding chapter. What did you hear? As you heard and listened, where you thinking much?

This is the heart of mindfulness. Whilst I gave my attention to the birds, it came at the cost of thinking about my thoughts and desires to blow you away with my clever words. It was a nice break. Now, back to this egotistical struggle for your attention, understanding and approval.

From Stanislavski's 'Experiencing' to Meisner's 'Doing'

Before we jump into the delightful world of Sanford Meisner, it is important to recognise the work's roots in Stanislavski's. In common with most western actor-training methods, as well as roots we might also use the following associated words: trunk, leaves, branches, and bark. The heirs of Stanislavski's work are permeated with his philosophy.

I will focus on Stanislavski's belief that acting is the 'art of experiencing' (Stanislavski and Benedetti, 2009, 71). Simply put, to create believable acting the actor 'lives the role without noticing how he is feeling, not thinking about what he is doing and so everything comes out spontaneously, subconsciously' (Stanislavski and Benedetti, 2009, 73). Stanislavski used the word '*perezhivanie*' (pronounced peh-reh-gi-van-yay) to describe this 'process by which an actor experiences the character's emotions afresh in each performance' (Stanislavski and Benedetti, 2009, 25). This is a simple, yet transformative idea that moves actors away from pretending, demonstrating or perhaps showing emotion. Stanislavski-based approaches teach the actor to experience the role, feeling the sensations that the character could have, rather than pretending, deciding or controlling a performance.

Intuitively, this checks out. If I want someone to believe that I'm feeling sad, a way to approach this is to experience sadness. Rather than scrunching my face up and forcing tears to come out of my eyeballs to mimic the external signs of the emotion. Investing in the fictional world of the character and performing the action to achieve the character's goal will result in the actor experiencing the character's emotional life. This works on the premise that if I want something as a human being, I will do something to try to fulfil that want. Depending on how that 'doing' goes, I will have a resulting emotional life. For example, right now I want to write a thrilling chapter that captures the reader's imagination and validates my entire existence. I've been researching, thinking, and now writing to achieve that goal (my action). If the readers write to me in their millions to tell me how wonderful this chapter is, I'll *feel* thrilled.

However, if it's judged as the worst garbage to ever grace paper, I will *feel* embarrassed and ashamed. I will experience these sensations because of how my attempt to achieve that want to impress you goes.

Meisner doubles down on this idea, emphasising Stanislavski's idea of 'communion'. If we wanted to find a simple definition of Meisner work, we might understand it as being connected action, i.e. listening to our partners to adjust the manner in which we carry out our action towards them.

Meisner's Communion

Meisner's work is rooted in Stanislavski's idea of '*Obschenie*' (pronounced ob-shay-ni-yah) or communication; 'the act of being in contact with an object or another person verbally or non-verbally' (Stanislavski and Benedetti, 2009, 714). Meisner used this idea to solve two central problems[1] he witnessed in the actor:

- Actors are self-conscious, too wrapped up in their own considerations and tension to work with authenticity, ease and playfulness.
- Actors don't listen. We could even consider the second problem as an extension of the first, that if an actor is too self-absorbed, they won't be reactive and in communication with their scene partners.

Meisner's student William Esper agrees, stating that 'An actor who makes himself the focus of his attention becomes self-conscious and paralysed. Fortunately, the placement of your concentration can be controlled by your will' (Esper and DiMarco, 2008, 45). Esper refers to the placement of concentration as the antidote to self-consciousness to introduce Meisner's key exercise: 'repetition'.

The Repetition Exercise

Repetition's purpose is to develop the actor's ability to move their attention from themselves and onto their scene partners. 'Repetition forces you into real contact with your partner' (Esper and DiMarco, 2008, 59) and it is this contact that renders them instinctive and free of self-consciousness. As Victoria Hart puts it, 'partners give their full attention to each other, listening and answering, hearing more than the words' (Bartow, 2008, 54). In short, the actor begins to experience their partner as a result of truly listening to the emotional content of the partner's communication rather than pre determining or demonstrating a response. For the purposes of this chapter, I'll discuss a simple variation that captures its essence:

Two actors sit or stand opposite each other. As soon as one of them observes something that inspires the impulse to draw breath and speak an observation, they make a 'call' about the other. The observed partner repeats the observation. A short, imagined interaction between two actors may go something like this:

Actor A: You laughed
Actor B: I laughed
Actor A: You laughed
Actor B: I laughed

The point of repeating what is meaningless text about the other is precisely what Hart refers to when she says, 'they are hearing more than the words'. Although the above interaction is a repeated single observation, if it is spoken by two actors listening to each other and having an honest response to the other, a dynamic interaction will arise. This is an inescapable result of two different people, with two different points of view coming into contact and expressing their points of view.

Let us look at that previous text again, this time imagining what happens if A *perceives* an accusing nature to the way Actor B initially laughed:

You laughed (Actor A *accuses* B)
I laughed (Actor B defies A, enjoying the accusation)
You laughed (Actor A expresses shock at the enjoyment)
I laughed (Actor B expresses a defiant pride)

The text has turned to glass. We see through the 'text' of the observations to observe the behaviour displayed by the two actors. Given that they are two different people with two different points of view, a dynamic interaction is inevitable when those two different points of view express each other. The aim of repetition is to connect two actors into Stanislavski's 'communion' with one another. To be experiencing the authentic emotional life between them, rather than pretending or demonstrating a 'dramatic conversation'. Repetition is just one side of the Meisner coin. If we pursue dynamic acting, just listening isn't enough; it must be coupled with action.

Investing in the Reality of Doing

The action arises as 'the foundation of acting is the reality of doing' (Meisner and Longwell, 1987, 35). This principle simply states that if you want the audience to believe what you're doing, you must really do it. If there is a scene that involves the actor seducing the other in order to achieve their want, the actor must really perform the action of seduction in order to invoke sensations of being seduced in their partner. We hear the echoes of Stanislavski in this idea. That believable acting is only believable in virtue of the actions being committed for a desired result.

Here we reach the Independent Activity exercise, where repetition is coupled with a real, physical, difficult and urgent task under fictional circumstances. If the actor is capable of investing in the reality of doing something under urgent fictional circumstances, their bodies will respond with a strong sensation. A very simple example to understand this exercise is to imagine the following:

You have somewhere very important to be where there is a significant consequence for being late. You are getting ready to leave and learn that there will be considerable transport delays, making it harder to get to your destination on time. You still must finish breakfast, get dressed and instead of 20 minutes to do all these things, you now have 5 minutes.

The above scenario would undoubtedly cause sensation. You want something and you do something to try and achieve that want. Depending on how it goes, you feel sensation. The technique involves mixing the influence of performing a task and listening to your partner and how these stimuli affect your inner life. This provides the impetus for the actor's authentic behaviour. The problem with this Stanislavskian approach is that its benefits are also its greatest costs. If the actor truly experiences their role, they will inevitably experience some difficult sensations. Drama rests upon conflict, so unpleasant, challenging or negative sensations are inevitable. To meet this inevitability, I believe the relationship between Meisner and mindfulness may just hold the keys to sustainable experiencing.

Meisner and Mindfulness

My approach to determining the nature of the relationship between mindfulness and Meisner centres around two key similarities that bring the two practices together. However, it is the differences that accompany these similarities which keep the two practices separate.

The first and perhaps most obvious similarity between the practices is the deliberate moving of one's attention. Meisner work centres on the actor moving their attention deliberately to the other actor's behaviour. This mirrors Williams' definition of mindfulness and the idea of 'knowing what is going on inside and outside of ourselves' in order to 'pay attention on purpose in the present moment without judgement to things as they actually are' (Williams and Penman, 2011, 52). The acting partner is outside of ourselves. It is a dynamic and ever-shifting part of the external environment. Meisner work also links to Williams' definition via the awareness of what is inside the individual. Although there is less obvious emphasis on this part, successful training in the work is heavily reliant on the actor being able to express a 'full point of view'. In other words, it requires the actor to have an awareness of their inner life, and the sensations present in themselves. It is an awareness of what the other actor's behaviour causes you to feel, an experience of inner sensation which then evolves into impulse. For example, upon moving my attention to the window of a Gail's bakery, it is the resulting inner sensation of desire that guides my impulse to enter the bakery and purchase a spinach and feta roll. Victoria Hart puts it perfectly when she states that Meisner work 'sets students on a course to understanding what it means to be truthful when living in the imaginary world. It establishes them in a deepened connection, both to themselves and to their acting partners' (Bartow, 2008, 55). It is this connection to the acting partner and the individual's own point of view that provides the fuel for authentic acting. The observer witnesses their partner's behaviour and the individual's point of view creates sensation which informs the responding behaviour.

The first contrast to this similarity is the need for the actor to have a connection to both their acting partner and their inner life simultaneously. The technique rests upon the actor having the ability to listen to their partner whilst also recognising the affect their partner's behaviour has on their own inner life. For example, they could observe their partner staring at them 'creepily'. Having paid attention to this, it may give the observer a sensation of discomfort. The actor needs to be aware of the external partner and the internal sensations experienced by the observer simultaneously. From my reading of foundational mindfulness practices, attention is guided towards single points of focus. To observe the exterior world in favour of our thoughts and feelings or to witness the inner life's transient sensations. The difference in Meisner work lies in requiring the actor to be aware of the exterior and the interior of the actor at the same time. Foundational mindfulness in contrast encourages single points of focus.

This contrast goes deeper, as mindfulness discourages judgement on the inner life. It is defined as to 'pay attention on purpose in the present moment without judgement to things as they actually are' (Williams and Penman, 2011, 52). In pursuit of better physiological well-being, the idea is to avoid the judgement of one's inner life in the experience of negative sensation or thought. The ideal is to witness negative thoughts and feelings as transient experiences rather than engaging with them or judging them as negative. Mark Williams defines this aspect as 'you come to the profound understanding that thoughts and feelings (including negative ones) are transient. They come and they go, and ultimately, you have a choice about whether to act on them or not' (Williams and Penman, 2011, 19). Although this does offer the idea that acting on them is a choice, Meisner work relies on the actor consistently judging the sensations they experience in order to 'act on them'. If Actor B was employing a Meisner approach to receiving a creepy look from Actor B, they would see the behaviour and pass immediate and spontaneous judgement. The equivalent of Meisner's 'pinch and ouch' principle,[2] that the actor is working towards instinctive non-intellectual responses to the stimuli they perceive.

So, although mindfulness and Meisner share the movement of attention, foundational mindfulness can favour a single focus of attention whilst Meisner requires a simultaneous focus of inner life and outer stimuli. Mindfulness promotes the idea of not judging what is observed whilst Meisner requires judgement to inform behavioural response.

The second similarity between the two practices is the idea that mindfulness is used as a tool to reduce stress and anxiety. Mindfulness works to heighten the awareness of inner sensation to witness its transient nature. It is the very impermanence of thoughts that allow them to be less influential on the individual. The equivalent of saying, 'Well why should I be so influenced by my thoughts if they come and go all the time?' Mindfulness also teaches how to focus on external stimuli to reduce rumination. The idea being that paying attention to external stimuli comes at the cost of emphasis on inner thought.

Meisner work doesn't place an emphasis on watching the impermanence of inner thoughts, although approaching Meisner work with that element could be a benefit in terms of strong experienced sensation, as explored later. However, it does parallel mindfulness' emphasis on external attention at the cost of inner thought. The repetition exercise is designed to reduce the actor's self-consciousness by virtue of moving their awareness onto the 'other'. In simple terms, a negative correlation where the more the actor listens to their partner, the less self-conscious they are and vice versa. In this regard, the two practices share the idea that externally placed attention comes at the cost of inner thought. Attention isn't limitless. The more I place externally, the less I have internally. Resulting in Stanislavski's 'public solitude' (Stanislavski and Benedetti, 2009, 236). The necessary skill for the actor to behave as if they are alone even if being watched by an audience, by virtue of reducing self-consciousness in favour of task specific or partner-based attention.

This parallel is short-lived, as it is the desired outcome of each practice that separates the two practices. Mindfulness is aimed to reduce stress and relax the individual. Meisner work does move an actor towards relaxation and stress reduction, but it is in order to perform action in performance. They are using similar principles for separate aims. Mindfulness is aiming for relaxation and better physiological well-being, there is no emphasis on what you do after the moment of mindfulness. Meisner work, on the other hand, is aiming for authentic action, devoid of self-consciousness and tension. A desire for a highly reactive and playful actor rather than a relaxed and peaceful individual.

In summary, mindfulness practices and Meisner work do share the movement of attention, and both aim for stress and self-consciousness reduction. However, Meisner work requires a dual awareness of inner life and outer stimuli simultaneously. Meisner work also requires the individual to actively judge their inner experience to express their point of view. Mindfulness is aiming for a different result than Meisner work.

After spending time with this relationship, I can agree with my younger self that acting is similar to mindfulness. However, they are by no means identical. Rather, mindfulness is a part of the process rather than an identical practice.

My belief is that this relationship of similarity could lead to greater actor training efficacy if utilised. The rest of this chapter will briefly detail the benefits that mindfulness holds for actors, supporting my classroom observations with related research.

Resilience

I have observed a marked increase in actors' resilience in dealing with the challenging aspects of a role by learning to be non-judgemental towards their experiential acting. This is particularly aimed at more negative experiences because 'it's not the mood that does the damage but how you react to it' (Williams and Penman, 2011, 23). The aim is to harness the actor's ability to tolerate uncomfortable sensation with the knowledge that the experience is transient. In reflection sessions, my students report that practicing access to that relaxed 'place' before acting exercises gives them confidence to then approach more challenging aspects of the fictional worlds they experience. It's as if this base of relaxation promotes more exploration in their work. They can fully experience all the sensations of their work, but their mindful approach allows them to react to it in a far more positive way, there is less 'holding on' and judgement of the sensations that are experienced in the work.

Cognitive Function and Creativity

Since weaving mindfulness elements into my practice, I've observed actors feeling as though the mindfulness foundation allows them greater access to creativity. There is evidence that mindfulness improves cognitive function with 'anxiety, depression and irritability all decreasing with regular sessions of meditation. Memory also improves, reaction times become faster and mental and physical stamina increase' (Williams and Penman, 2011, 19). If cognitive faculties improve, there is also a likely impact on the actor's creativity as 'there is a strong theoretical basis for presuming a relationship between mindfulness and creativity' (Henriksen et al., 2022, 15) with mindfulness having a direct impact on 'creative thinking habits, including: relaxation or flow states (improved concentration), risk-taking (requiring a lack of fear about judgment), and curiosity or open-mindedness/openness to experience (reducing self-conscious experience)' (Henriksen et al., 2020, 109). In short, the actors have more access to creativity as a result of taking the time to find relaxation and operate mindfully. It is a consistent reflection that the relaxation-focused aspects of my classes make 'everything else easier'. I base my emphasis on this work in my classes on Maharishi Mahesh Yogi's observations on the benefits of meditation: 'The art of using one's full potential is the same as the art of shooting an arrow ahead; one begins by pulling the arrow back on the bow. As the arrow is drawn back, it gains the maximum strength for going forward' (Maharishi, 2001, 83).

In other words, mindful practice supports the actor's pursuit of greater creative efficacy and freedom by building them up through mindfulness-based relaxation techniques.

These are just two potential benefits I have witnessed in my classes and chosen to focus on. I have no doubt mindfulness has myriad other benefits. I believe the resilience to more negative and challenging aspects of experiential acting and greater creativity actors may gain from mindfulness may just be the solution through the crisis of Stanislavski's experiential approach to acting.

The Old versus the New School

I studied the Actor Training and Coaching Masters at the Royal Central School of Speech & Drama. It was a programme designed to ensure practitioners could be the compassionate answer to a sector challenged by despotic and cruel teaching. The course was designed to ensure actor training was compassionate, that the student was held and cared for as they progressed through the rigours of training. I call this the 'new school' of actor training. In my opinion, the new school regards Stanislavskian 'experiential' acting with an air of distrust, given its ability to create powerful negative sensation in the training actor. If we are aiming to guide a student to experiencing their work, there is an inevitable consequence that a student will experience negative sensation at some point due to the conflict-driven nature of drama.

In contrast, the old school can be summed up by the cliché 'breaking the student down to build them up', a teaching philosophy that is still wrestling with the echoes of all-knowing and all-powerful teachers of the past. This is an undeniably reductive description, but it serves to introduce the idea that the old school protects the art and craft first, the student second. The student must experience the full spectrum of sensation to truly embody the life of a character. Regardless of whether it is the darker emotions of heartbreak and grief or the lighter colours of joy and bliss. Both schools have their pros and cons. The new school ensures students are happy, supported and cared-for. This is undeniably important for healthy and sustainable educational environments. However, there is the potential for students to not be pushed to their full potential, to keep them away from potentially negative emotional experiences within the work. Speaking from my own experience, it is emotionally easier to congratulate a student for mediocre work than to call them out and push them to go further to reach a true experience.

The old school preserves the pursuit of truth over the comfort of the student. This can and has resulted in traumatised actors, with more painful memories of drama school than are publishable. Although these two definitions of the old and the new school are reductive, I believe this accurately sums up the dilemma of the current training sector. Rigour versus compassion. Safety versus experiencing. The sector is trying to embrace the necessary needs of inclusion, compassion and joy-based practice whilst still trying to produce actors of a high standard who can experience their work. An approach that picks a side doesn't work. We need a hybrid future. One where students are safe yet perhaps not always comfortable to safely explore uncomfortable territory.

My argument is that mindfulness can allow us to embrace the rigour of the old school whilst supporting students with the compassion of the new. I believe that mindfulness practices can strengthen the student, increase their resilience and creativity. To stay calm under pressure, to manage performance anxiety and return to a regulated state after the dysregulation of more difficult content. For the actor, acting can be difficult and challenging as well as uplifting and beautiful. We need to deliberately lean into this, talk about it and prepare students for it rather than avoid it.

We need to move forward by embracing the component of mindfulness in acting, by acknowledging that the very skill parallels the very practices that increase physiological well-being, creativity and resilience. Although my focus has been on the Meisner practice, which is my specialism, the Stanislavskian route means it shares many commonalities with the work of Adler, Strasberg and Hagen to name a few. It is therefore my belief that a mindful actor is a better actor. Mindfulness isn't Meisner work, but the relationship must be acknowledged to empower actors. To move towards a hybrid of the old and new school to form a *better* school.

Conclusion

I believe that actor training is in a crisis of identity. I believe that mindfulness and related meditation practices hold significant similarity to the actor training principles inherent in Meisner work, a progression of Stanislavski's ideas. I believe that acknowledging and utilising this relationship between mindfulness and Meisner work can lead actors and actor trainers towards embracing the necessary rigour of the craft compassionately.

I argued this belief by first defining mindfulness and Meisner work. Using these definitions to compare the practices. The comparison led me to believe that although they are linked by their similarities, they are not identical. It is more accurate to describe mindfulness as a component of Stanislavski based Meisner work. Acknowledging this component, I then briefly detailed the benefits mindfulness holds for the actor's creativity and resilience. I then detailed the distinction between the old and new schools of acting and how mindful practices might just be the way towards a better actor training future. A future where the demands of acting practice are compassionately supported by mindfulness to enable actors to achieve Stanislavski's experiential concept of acting.

Mindfulness Exercise

The exercise below is mindful in the sense that it is developing your metacognitive abilities.

There is no 'desired' result, it is simply the act of witnessing the subject of your attention which develops the mindfulness muscle. The difference between being swept up in the river of day-to-day experience and sitting on the bank to watch its flow.

Breath as Anchor – a warm-up or cool-down.

The objective of the exercise is to promote relaxation, calm and focus through observation of the breath. To increase the mindfulness skill of watching where one's attention rests and goes to.

Example music to use: *Vaggvisa* – Henrik Lindstrand and *Dusk* – Garth Stevenson

It can be used for any individual, acting class or company and lasts 10–12 minutes.

Participants are invited to lie down on the floor. Perhaps placing a book under their heads for support and wearing clothes for warmth. Participants are invited to guide their attention towards their abdominal area to watch their breath expand and contract. There is no correct rhythm, timing or pattern. If the mind is distracted to another object, bring it back towards the observation of the breath rolling in and rolling out. Can be done with or without gentle music. Once time is up, participants are invited to slowly turn onto their right-hand side, slowly making their way to seated to finish the exercise.

Notes

1 This idea of two central problems permeates Meisner literature, however, I thought it was best described in this article: https://www.immersology.com/meisner-for-the-immersive-actor/.
2 The 'pinch and ouch' principle is a simple analogy to describe the transactional nature of receiving behavioural information from your partner and then sending it back. For example, if I were to pinch an actor, they would instinctively respond with an 'ouch'. There is no thought or decision; it's an impulsive response to what's received.

References

Bartow, A., (2008). *Handbook of Acting Techniques.* London: Nick Hern Books.

Esper, W. and DiMarco, D., (2008). *The Actor's Art and Craft: William Esper Teaches the Meisner Technique.* New York: Anchor.

Henriksen, D., Heywood, W., and Gruber, N. (2022). *Meditate to Create: Mindfulness and Creativity in an Arts and Design Learning Context. Creativity Studies.* Vilnius, Lithuania: Vilnius Gediminas Technical University.

Henriksen, D., Richardson, C., and Shack, K. (2020). Mindfulness and creativity: Implications for thinking and learning, *Thinking Skills and Creativity*, 37, 100689. https://doi.org/10.1016/j.tsc.2020.100689
Maharishi, M.Y. (2001). *Science of Being and Art of Living*. New York: Plume.
Meisner, S. and Longwell, D., (1987). *Sanford Meisner on* Acting. New York: Vintage.
Shonin, E., Van Gordon, W., and Griffiths, M. D. (2014). *The Emerging Role of Buddhism in Clinical Psychology: Toward Effective Integration. Psychology of Religion and Spirituality*. Washington, DC: American Psychological Association.
Stanislavski, K. and Benedetti, J., (2009). *An Actor's Work on a Role*. Oxford: Routledge.
Williams, M. n.d. Mindfulness, NHS choices. Available at: https://www.nhs.uk/mental-health/self-help/tips-and-support/mindfulness/ (Accessed: 17.04.24).
Williams, M. and Penman, D., (2011). *Mindfulness: A Practical Guide to Finding Peace in a Frantic World*. London: Hachette.

5

THE ACT OF BEING PRESENT

Psychological Flexibility and the Art of the Actor

Benjamin Askew

ACT for Acting

For the past four years, I have been developing a project called ACT for Acting: an attempt to reexamine the processes of acting and actor training through the prism of a contemporary model of behavioural psychology called ACT. As first conceived by the US psychologist Steven C Hayes, ACT (pronounced as the word "act") stands for Acceptance and Commitment Therapy. When, as in my work, ACT principles are employed by non-clinicians in non-therapeutic settings, it stands for Acceptance and Commitment *Training*. There is no therapy involved in my work, but ACT has come to inform all aspects of my teaching practice, from giving feedback to the methods I encourage for interpreting character. Crucially for the purposes of this chapter, it informs my understanding of what it means for an actor to 'be present' and to achieve the forms of 'concentration and attention' described by Stanislavsky in *An Actor's Work* (Stanislavsky, 2017, 90–124). In short, for me, such notions have become interchangeable with the ACT concept of psychological flexibility:

> Psychological flexibility is the ability to be in the present moment with full awareness and openness to our experience, and to take action guided by our values. Put more simply, it's the ability to 'be present, open up, and do what matters'.
>
> *(Harris, 2009, 12)*

More formally, psychological flexibility involves the confluence of six interrelated psychological processes: present moment awareness; experiential acceptance

DOI: 10.4324/9781003517856-6

(the willingness to acknowledge and make space for emotions and other experiences); cognitive defusion (the ability to step back and 'disentangle' from one's thoughts); self-as-context (the development of an open and flexible sense of self); values clarification (taking a conscious and proactive stance in choosing what to prioritise in one's life); and committed action (setting and pursuing meaningful goals in alignment with one's chosen values).

Mindfulness is a crucial element of psychological flexibility. One of the key distinctions between ACT and mindfulness practice taken more broadly is the emphasis ACT places on valued living: 'taking action, on an ongoing basis, that is guided by and aligned with core values. Indeed, we teach mindfulness skills in ACT with the express purpose of facilitating valued action' (Harris, 2009, 8–9).

Within ACT, then, psychological flexibility is nurtured through evidence-based psychoeducation and practical skills-training, including the use of mindfulness meditation. In bringing this work to actors, I introduce various exercises in mindful attention. Some of these, such as exploring mindfulness of the breath, would be familiar as part of any mindfulness training programme. Others are more specific to ACT and use mindfulness as the starting point for exploring processes such as cognitive defusion, values clarification, or self-as-context.

Of at least equal importance to the exploration of such exercises, however, is adopting an attitude, and cultivating what I shall call a narrative context, that supports and promotes psychological flexibility as an ongoing stance within the rehearsal room. Unless we situate our use of mindfulness and other experiential exercises within a congruent narrative context, I suggest, we risk limiting or undermining their effectiveness.

For this reason, my intention in this chapter is not to discuss mindfulness exercises directly, but rather to examine the narrative contexts we cultivate in our classrooms and rehearsal rooms: to ask whether the stories we tell actors about what they *should* experience in their work might support or undermine their development of psychological flexibility. My argument is that by introducing students to the concept of psychological flexibility, and by using tools such as the ACT Matrix (discussed below) to frame our work, we can create a narrative context in which:

- There is a simple, shared language for discussing and understanding the challenges of the acting process.
- Mindfulness exercises are more likely to be effective.
- Behaviours and interactions that undermine (or reduce the workability of) actors' efforts to be present in their work are more likely to be noticed, acknowledged and disrupted without recourse to unnecessary judgement and criticism.

Meeting the Matrix

The ACT Matrix is a tool that I have found particularly useful in my own explorations of psychological flexibility and one that I now use frequently with students. As can be seen in Figure 5.1, the ACT Matrix is a simple diagram consisting of two lines:

The horizontal line highlights the fact that, as we go about our lives, we spend some of our time moving ***towards*** things that we want and some of our time moving ***away*** from things that we don't want. More formally, it distinguishes between behaviour under appetitive control (towards) and behaviour under aversive control (away). Such towards and away moves can be observed in most living creatures, from simple organisms to human beings.

The vertical line highlights the fact that, as human beings, we experience the 'external' world through our five senses, and we also have experiences that happen 'inside' our minds. I see the cup of coffee next to me: I can touch it, smell it, pick it up, take a sip, etc. This is all 'five-senses experiencing'. I can also think about my cup of coffee, form opinions about it, worry about my caffeine intake and so on. This is 'mental experiencing'.

> The key to psychological flexibility is noticing the difference between five-senses and mental experiencing and between moving towards who or what is important and away from unwanted inner experience.
>
> *(Polk et al., 2016, 2)*

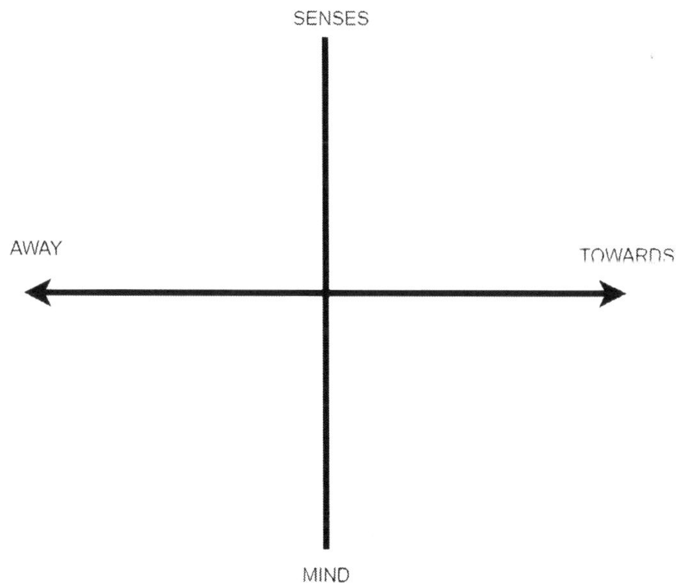

FIGURE 5.1 The ACT Matrix. All the figures in this chapter are created by the author based on the original ACT Matrix design by Kevin Polk.

There are clear and explicit connections between this process of 'noticing the difference' and mindfulness practice. Both psychological flexibility and mindfulness more broadly involve being actively engaged in our five-senses experiencing whilst continuing to accept and acknowledge our mental experiencing. Becoming overly involved in our mental experiencing is a lack of mindful attention and can be the catalyst for inflexible behaviours such as experiential avoidance and acting on autopilot. Within ACT, it doesn't matter whether our 'noticing' processes are evoked through formal mindfulness practice or through the use of tools such as the ACT Matrix: both are valid, each has its own strengths, and such techniques can support and inform one another as part of a multifaceted approach to developing psychological flexibility.

In using the Matrix, we can begin the process of noticing by filling out the four quadrants of the diagram:

Starting in the lower right, I think about my connection to the things in life I want to move towards. I can say who is important to me – my children, my partner, etc. – and what is important to me – acting, perhaps. Ultimately, this can lead to a consideration of values or 'chosen life directions' (Harris, 2009, 189). Values might include things like creativity, compassion, or kindness.

Shifting attention to the lower left, I consider aversive thoughts and feelings that I'd rather move away from and that can seem to get in the way of living in accordance with my values: feelings such as fear and anxiety, for example, and thoughts such as 'I'm not good enough'.

In the upper left, I name observable behaviours that I might notice myself doing when I try to move away from (to avoid, relieve or escape from) such aversive mental content. When fear shows up, I might run away, for example.

In the upper right, I name observable behaviours that I might notice myself doing when I try to move towards the things that are important to me. If my children are important to me, a simple towards move might be to play with them.

Having written something in all four quadrants of the diagram, I can draw a circle in the middle and write 'noticing' inside it (see Figure 5.2). The idea here is that, as this is my Matrix, I am the person best able to occupy this space to notice what is important to me, what aversive thoughts and feelings are showing up for me, what I'm doing to move away from the aversive stuff and what I'm doing to move towards the important stuff. I might further be able to notice which of my behaviours are working for me and which ones aren't. If I take the opportunity to notice all of that – to be mindfully aware of my experiences and behaviours – then this can be an important first step towards responding more flexibly to the contexts in which I find myself, cultivating my ability to open up, be present and do what matters as I go about my life.

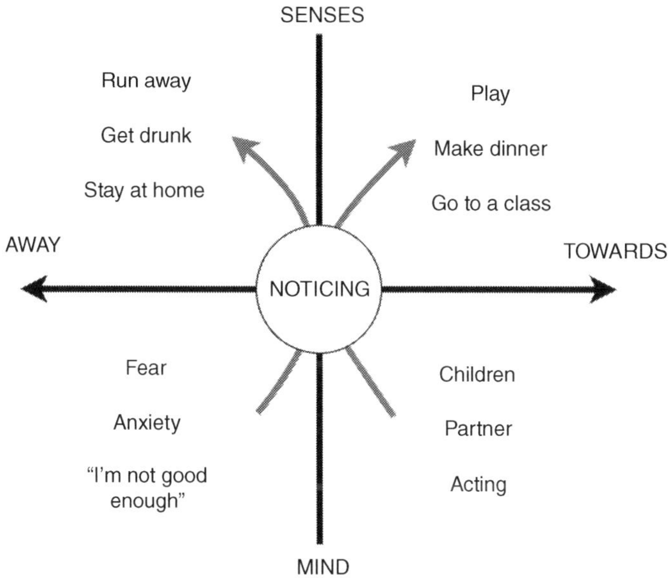

FIGURE 5.2 Filling in the four quadrants of the Matrix.

Getting Stuck

Unfortunately, human beings – including actors, and even acting teachers – don't always behave in ways that are psychologically flexible. Instead, we tend to get stuck: to lose our sense of mindful connection to the present moment and to persist in behaviours that aren't working for us. The Matrix is a valuable tool for mapping out and making sense of what is going on when this happens, whether in everyday life or in the specific circumstances we encounter in our classrooms and rehearsal studios.

A basic principle of ACT is that the human mind (the human capacity for language and cognition) is a double-edged sword. On the one hand, our abilities to think, plan, and problem-solve, to reflect on the past and imagine possible futures, are our greatest evolutionary advantages; allowing us, not only to survive, but to communicate and collaborate, develop science and technology, create art and culture, open drama schools, interpret plays, and do many of the things that make life meaningful for us. On the other hand, these same abilities play a leading role in the human capacity for suffering. We get tangled up in our aversive thoughts and feelings, reliving past mistakes and anticipating future catastrophes. When this happens, we can find ourselves feeling trapped in patterns of behaviour that simply do not work for us; exhausting ourselves in futile attempts to control, avoid, or escape from the contents of our own minds.

To see how this might play out in an acting context (and why the Matrix might be a useful tool to employ when it does), let's imagine that I'm a drama school student about to get up for an exercise. I have a sense that my aim is to get better at acting. I'll know I've done that if I gain the approval of my teacher or if I feel good after the exercise. I also have some uncomfortable thoughts and feelings emerging. I'm feeling anxious. My mind is saying things like: "I'm not good enough", "people will judge me", "I'm going to fail" etc. If we were using the Matrix to map this out, we might have something like Figure 5.3:

From an ACT point of view – made explicit by the Matrix – there are a couple of things to notice here. The first is that none of what I've put in the lower right constitutes a value. Values are 'statements about what we want to do with our life: what we want to stand for, and how we want to behave on an ongoing basis' (Harris, 2009, 189). I will find these poorly defined goals, emotional expectations, and hopes for external validation very difficult to move towards in the moment of doing my exercise. The more I focus on them, the more likely I am to lead my attention back to the lower left: "I'm not getting better", "I'm not impressing them", "This doesn't feel good", etc. The second thing is that ACT does not view the content of the lower left as being problematic. At least, not in itself. The human mind will always try to warn us about potential dangers and suggest strategies for avoiding or solving these perceived problems. Sometimes it will tell us helpful stories. Sometimes,

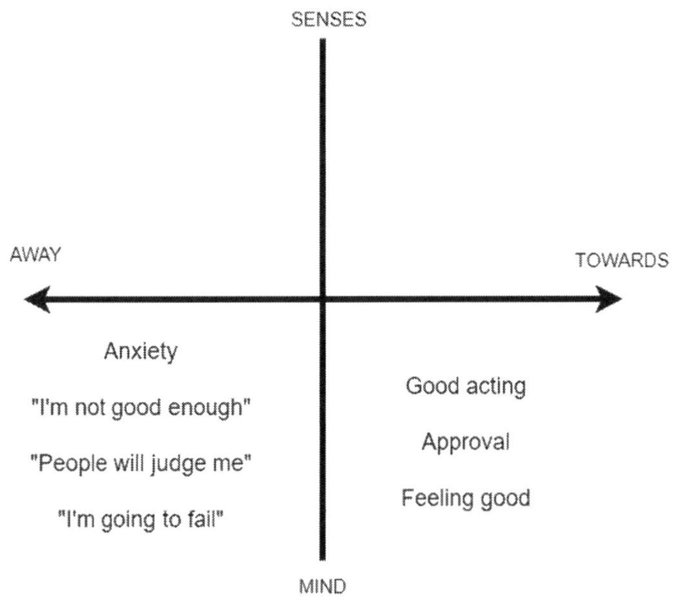

FIGURE 5.3 The Matrix used to map out the actor's experiences.

unhelpful ones. But it will keep telling us the stories whether we want it to or not. That's its job. Moreover, a key principle within ACT is that 'you hurt where you care' (Hayes, 2019, 23). If I care about acting, then my mind constantly warning me about everything that could possibly go wrong in relation to acting is more or less guaranteed. What matters from an ACT perspective is not that these thoughts and feelings are there but how I respond to them. If I can acknowledge and make space for them, accept them as part of my present experience, and recognise that such thoughts and feelings do not have to control my behaviour, then their existence is entirely compatible with a process of opening, being present and doing what matters.

What gets me stuck in this instance is that I have a natural human tendency to believe and identify with my thoughts – 'I am what I think and feel' (Louma et al., 2017, 97) – a process known in ACT as cognitive fusion: 'in a state of cognitive fusion, we're inseparable from our thoughts, we're welded to them, bonded to them' (Harris, 2009, 19). Moreover, as a product of contemporary Western society, I have been saturated in a culture in which I am forever being told that I should be feeling happy and having positive thoughts all the time. Uncomfortable thoughts and feelings are therefore 'problems' that need to be 'fixed'; signs that there is something 'wrong with me' or even that I am 'broken' in some way (Harris, 2008, 9–10). If I'm experiencing uncomfortable thoughts and feelings as I prepare for my exercise, then this is a *bad thing* and *something must be done about it*.

This being the case, I have two main strategies available to me. The first is to control the problem directly at the level of my mental experiencing: to delete or suppress my uncomfortable thoughts and feelings, or to fight with them until they go away. This time-honoured strategy makes intuitive sense because it often works when dealing with things we don't like in the physical world of sensuous experiences. If I don't like my coffee cup, I can throw it away, or smash it, and the chances are that the coffee cup won't bother me again. When dealing with cognitions rather than crockery, however, things are rarely so simple. ACT research suggests that such strategies are not only ineffective but actively counterproductive. If I try to control my experiences in this way as I prepare for my exercise, I am likely to get more tangled up in them and there's a good chance that I will end up *adding* to the content in the lower left quadrant of the Matrix. ACT practitioners often compare this experience to that of someone falling into quicksand: the harder you struggle, the faster you sink (Harris, 2008, 86).

Let us imagine, then, that the time for my acting exercise is looming and I'm back where I was in Figure 5.3, except that the lower left quadrant of my Matrix is a little busier now because I'm feeling anxious and stressed about my failure to control my anxiety and stress. Still fused with my uncomfortable thoughts and feelings, I need a different strategy, I need an away move: an observable behaviour that can allow me to avoid, relieve or escape from my aversive mental content. In this scenario, the most obvious away move is to avoid getting up for my exercise altogether. If I take this option, my hypothetical Matrix looks like Diagram A in Figure 5.4.

If the story ended there, it wouldn't be too much of an issue. I had a bad day, and I didn't get up for an exercise: hardly ideal but hardly the end of the world. If I'm back on course the next day, this brief excursion into the realms of what ACT practitioners call 'experiential avoidance' may well turn out to be perfectly workable for me in the grander scheme of things. The trouble is that experiential avoidance tends to beget experiential avoidance.

When I make the decision to avoid getting up for my exercise, this away move probably works to an extent: my anxiety levels may go down a bit. However, the same aversive thoughts and feelings are likely to be popping up again very shortly. In addition, perhaps I now feel guilty and ashamed for avoiding the exercise. My inner critic starts having a field day: 'See, I said you weren't good enough and now you've just proved it. You're failing. Everyone thinks you're pathetic.' If this happens, and if I get tangled up in these thoughts, I'm going to need another away move. Perhaps next week I'll skip the class altogether. Thus, I set in motion what is known as a 'stuck loop' (Polk et al., 2016, 49), as shown in Diagram B within Figure 5.4.

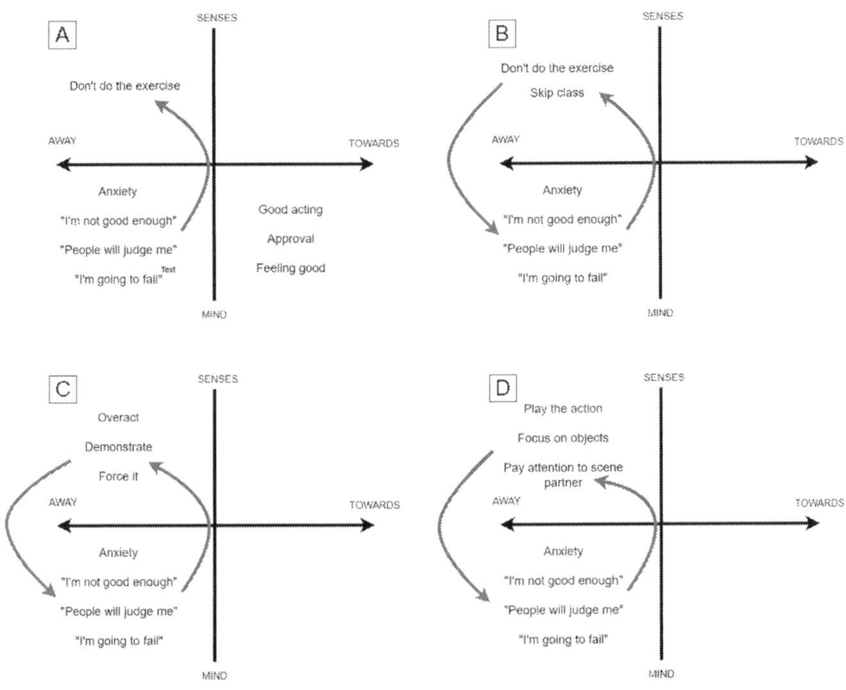

FIGURE 5.4 Four diagrams illustrating experiential avoidance within the Matrix.

Such spiralling avoidance may not be unheard of in drama school environments. We might, however, want to imagine a different version of this scenario in which my avoidance strategies are not quite so obvious. So, I'm back at Figure 5.3 and I'm about to get up for my exercise. In this version of events, I do, in fact, go through with it, but I still need some away moves. Perhaps I struggle against my feelings and try to suppress them by 'throwing energy' at the exercise: 'overacting', 'demonstrating' and 'forcing' my performance. This has the potential to set an avoidant cycle in motion even within the exercise, as each attempt at avoidance makes me feel worse about what I'm doing, and I double-down on my away moves in response. (See Diagram C within Figure 5.4.)

I end the exercise feeling upset and frustrated. Now it's time to receive some feedback. The first things I hear confirm just how right I was to buy into my difficult thoughts: 'You're too self-conscious', 'I don't believe you', 'You're blocking yourself', 'You need to find a way of controlling your nerves', 'You need to stop caring about what other people think'. That all goes straight into the lower left. Then I hear some potentially wonderful acting advice: 'Play the action', 'Focus on the objects you're working with', 'Pay attention to your scene partner'. This all sounds very sensible. 'Great!' I say to myself, 'So, *that's* how I get rid of my difficult thoughts and feelings!' (See Diagram D within Figure 5.4.)

What could have been towards moves have instead been coopted as part of my 'control agenda' (Harris, 2009, 81–82). Framed in this way, even activities such as meditation can become strategies for experiential avoidance. In a recent study, researchers examined the effects of meditation practice in two groups of people: one group meditated to manage and get rid of difficult feelings and the other group meditated with a focus on acceptance and making space for whatever feelings showed up. The results suggested that meditation was far more effective for the second group: it increased their mindful awareness, and – and this is the confounding element – they experienced lower levels of anxiety and stress. 'Participants using meditation with control-based intentions reported greater worry, depression, negative affect, and lower mindfulness relative to their acceptance-guided counterparts' (Tifft et al., 2022, 1407). In other words, meditation *did* work as a way of decreasing the presence and impact of difficult emotions but *not* if that was the aim.

What this suggests is that working from a narrative in which difficult thoughts and feelings are normalised, validated and accepted as part of a natural human response to pursuing something important to us (i.e. the kind of narrative promoted by ACT and using the Matrix) is going to be far more effective – and result in lower levels of distress – than allowing a narrative to emerge in which uncomfortable thoughts and feelings are 'problems' to be feared, managed and eliminated. To illustrate how easily practitioners can feed into narratives of rigidity and avoidance, I will turn to some examples taken from Stanislavsky's chapter on concentration and attention.

Sticky Stanislavsky

From the outset of their discussion, Stanislavsky's characters of Tortsov (the great teacher) and Kostya (our narrator) frame the whole issue of concentration as one of *avoiding distraction* and of finding the tools to *solve the problems* of performing in front of an audience: 'whichever way you look at it, the audience is the obstacle' (Stanislavsky, 2017, 94). If we were using the Matrix to map out this discussion, we might produce something like this:

Looking at Figure 5.5, we might notice that we have only populated the left side of the Matrix. This might encourage us to fill out the right side as well. If we did that, we would already be taking steps towards a more flexible view of the situation. We might also notice that we have been fusing together different aspects of our experience: 'the audience is making me do bad acting!' From a Matrix perspective there are three different elements here: the physical presence of an audience (context), my aversive thoughts and feelings within that context (lower left), and my observable behaviours (which, if their function is to move away from my difficult thoughts and feelings, can be sorted into the upper left). Noticing the difference between these elements is essential if we are to open up possibilities for a more flexible response. If we don't create that space between them, our options are very limited. We could get rid of the audience, but then, as Kostya notes, it would be 'boring playing without one' (94). That leaves us with only one strategy: to manage or get rid of the difficult thoughts and feelings.

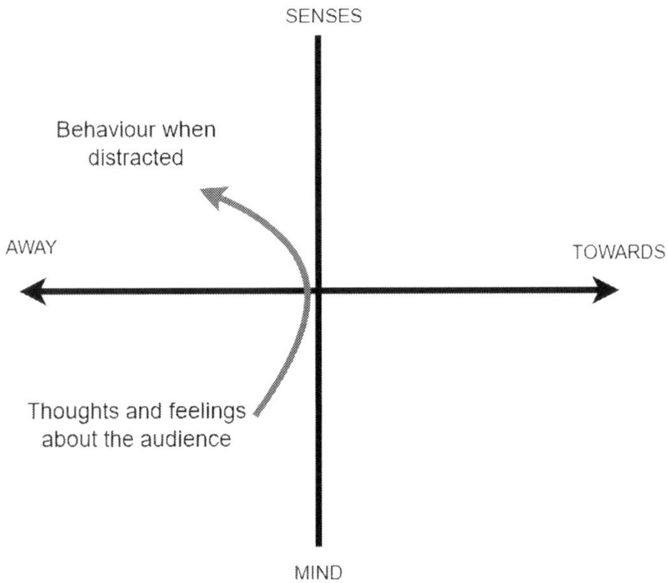

FIGURE 5.5 Matrix showing the audience as obstacle.

In the passages that follow, the issue of whether we're supposed to be making towards moves or away moves becomes, to my mind, increasingly confused. 'The secret is very simple', says Tortsov, 'to divert your attention from the auditorium you must become engrossed in what is happening onstage' (95). If we connected values to the idea of becoming engrossed in what is happening on stage, this could take us to the right side of the Matrix. By making 'diverting attention from the auditorium' the success criterium, however, we bring it back over to the left. This pattern continues as Tortsov describes and develops a sequence of exercises, which starts with focusing on single objects and then expands to explore 'circles of attention' (98–107).

When the students find themselves struggling to maintain their circles of attention – when the 'black hole' of the auditorium 'overwhelm[s their] powers of concentration', leaving them in a state of 'despair' and 'helplessness' (105) – Tortsov advises them to bring their attention back to a focal point: a single object within the circle of attention. This advice is perfectly compatible with the notion of psychological flexibility. What makes it rigid is that Tortsov frames this refocusing, not as a way of reconnecting with values – or of grounding oneself in the present moment with openness and acceptance – but as a way of avoiding 'disaster' (105). Finding a focal point becomes a defensive manoeuvre within an almost military narrative in which actors seem to be at war, both with the audience and their own minds: it is way of 'retreating', of 'clutching hold in moments of danger', of 'shutting things out' amidst 'panic and confusion', and of giving yourself 'complete control' (106–107). The actor's thought process in finding themselves distracted is given voice by Tortsov: 'Stop! Your concentration's gone! Latch onto your lifesaver!' (106). The behaviour of finding a focal point starts to look like Figure 5.6.

If my lifesaver lets me down – if my difficult thoughts and feelings remain – then I'll need another away move and another and another. We can contrast this with the refocusing process we might encounter as part of an ACT-based mindfulness exercise:

> From time to time your mind will succeed in distracting you: it will hook you in with a good story and you'll lose track of your breathing. This is normal and natural, and it will happen repeatedly. The moment you realise this has happened, take a moment to note what hooked you, and then gently refocus on your breathing.
>
> *(Harris, 2009, 46)*

As well as the difference in tone, the difference in process is significant. In this narrative, instances of being distracted (and any thoughts and feelings involved in that process) are normalised and validated rather than being catastrophised. Instead of trying to control and get rid of thoughts and experiences that distract us, we are encouraged to accept and acknowledge them, to allow them

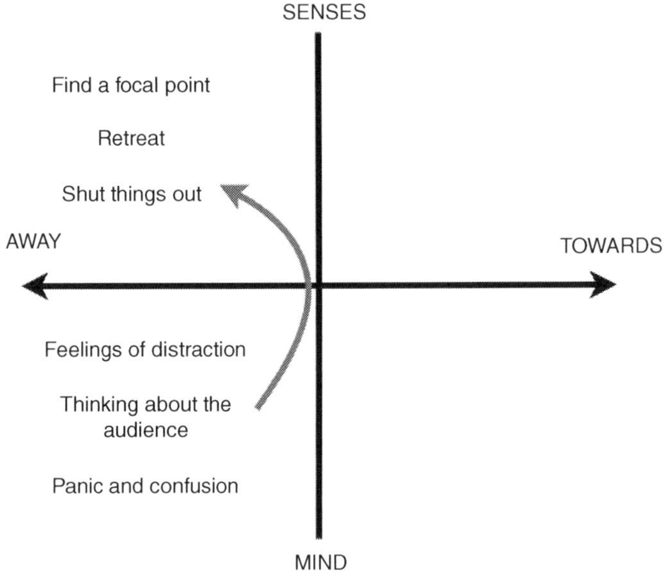

FIGURE 5.6 Matrix showing 'focus' as a form of avoidance.

to be as they are, and, from that position, to make a conscious choice to refocus our attention on what is important to us. Such a process seems to me to be more workable, more empowering, and more likely to illicit a response of opening, being present, and doing what matters in the moment.

Towards Moves

I have highlighted a few examples in which, whilst apparently calling for mindful attention and committed action from his actors, Stanislavsky seems, unwittingly, to be introducing and reinforcing narratives that promote experiential avoidance. I have suggested that by introducing the basic principles of ACT we might help our students to notice and disrupt such stories, encouraging in their place narratives that normalise and validate uncomfortable thoughts and feelings promoting the principle of acceptance. We can then build upon these narratives with mindfulness techniques, with ACT exercises in cognitive defusion and experiential acceptance, and, indeed, with acting exercises such as Stanislavsky's (assuming that these are framed flexibly).

Promoting experiential acceptance, however, is only half of the story (and only half of the Matrix). If we want to start making towards moves, then we need to know what we're moving towards. In ACT terms, these are values. Values are 'personally important ways of living that can never be obtained as an object, but rather are instantiated moment by moment' (Louma et al., 2017, 428). They are not goals, rules, the emotions we'd like to feel or the approval we hope to receive from others. They are 'leading principles that can guide us and motivate us as we move through life' (Harris, 2009, 189).

In Stanislavsky's discussion of concentration and attention, I think the closest we get to an explication of values is towards the end of the chapter, when Tortsov advises his students to develop a love of 'the supreme artist, Nature' (Stanislavsky, 2017, 120). That this is given more as an instruction than an invitation is still somewhat rigid. Nevertheless, giving one's attention to Nature is presented, not as a means to an end, but as an end in itself: as an endeavour that is meaningful and life-enhancing. It speaks to values such as curiosity and appreciation. It speaks, I think, to the values implicit in the very notion of psychological flexibility: values such as openness, awareness and engagement.

From an ACT standpoint, we cannot impose values on our students. We cannot simply bark our own values at them in the manner of Tortsov's assistant, Rakhmanov: 'An actor must be resourceful. Resourceful, got it?!' (101). We can, however, talk to them about values. We can give them the support to explore and clarify what really matters to them as they navigate their lives in art. We can make clear that, when they get up to do an exercise or to perform with an audience, the only thing we're inviting them to do is to commit to living, right here and now, in accordance with the values that they have chosen for themselves. By using ACT tools and techniques to promote the pursuit of valued living, and by coupling this with the principles of experiential acceptance, we create a space in which mindful attention can flourish: a narrative context in which actors feel empowered to open up, do what matters, and relish being present in their work.

References

Harris, R. (2008), *The Happiness Trap*. London: Constable and Robinson.

Harris, R. (2009), *ACT Made Simple*. Oakland, CA: New Harbinger Publications.

Hayes, S.C., (2019), *A Liberated Mind: The Essential Guide to ACT*. London: Vermilion.

Louma, J.B., Hayes, S.C. and Walser, R.D. (2017), *Learning ACT*. Oakland, CA: Context Press.

Polk, K., Schoendorff, B., Webster, M. and Olaz, F. (2016), *The Essential Guide to the ACT Matrix*. Oakland, CA: Context Press.

Stanislavsky, K. (2017), *An Actor's Work*, edited and translated by J. Benedetti. Abingdon: Routledge Classics.

Tifft, E.D., Underwood, S.B., Roberts, M.Z. and Forsyth, J.P. (2022), 'Using meditation in a control vs. acceptance context: a preliminary evaluation of relations with anxiety, depression, and indices of well-being'. *Journal of Clinical Psychology*, Volume 78, Issue 7, 1407–1421.

6

THE ACTOR'S DUAL MINDFULNESS

A Journey to Cognitive Empathy

Evi Stamatiou

Introduction: Stanislavsky as mindful practice

Stanislavsky's system has always been mindful. It was inspired by spiritual practices such as Yoga from the East and Christian Orthodoxy from the West, inviting self-awareness within meditation and prayer practices, respectively. It also drew on psychology, which studies human behaviour, including feelings and thoughts. The cognitive turn of psychology in the late 1950s that prompted '*multilayered computational theories of the mind*' [italics in original for emphasis] (Csaba, 387) inspired Stanislavsky scholars to investigate his system through scientific lenses. Among other scholars who have brought cognitive theories and neuroscience to the study of acting, Rhonda Blair highlighted that meditation illuminates the actor's understanding of how their body works with character, emotion and other aspects of the Stanislavsky system.[1] This suggests that, in ways both similar and distinct, mindfulness and Stanislavskian practice develop the actor to have a better understanding, and therefore agency, of their acting, including their behaviours on stage.

This chapter illuminates how such human development through acting goes beyond the stage to inform the actor's life. It is important to evidence the usefulness of acting in the current historical moment in the UK when drama is no longer a compulsory subject in secondary education, and higher education drama departments are increasingly shrinking, merging and closing. This chapter illustrates how acting benefits people by prompting the soft skill of cognitive empathy or social cognition. To make it clear to the reader how this works, the chapter investigates the cognitive mechanism behind the actor's dual mindfulness.

Mindfulness means 'paying attention to what is going on inside and outside ourselves, moment by moment' (NHS, n.d.). This echoes the characterisation

DOI: 10.4324/9781003517856-7

process because the actor engages their imagination, which triggers thoughts and emotions, manifested in their bodies through character behaviours. Mindfulness involves 'reconnecting with our bodies and the sensations they experience' by 'paying attention to the sights, sounds, smells and tastes of the present moment' (NHS, n.d.). This resonates with how Stanislavsky's sense and emotion memory have exploited the five senses. Mindfulness is also considered a mental well-being practice. Current concerns about the well-being of the youth, such as our undergraduate acting students, draw on mindfulness's potential to help individuals 'enjoy' life more by identifying negative emotions or behavioural patterns before they escalate (NHS, n.d.). This implies that the individual grows to know themselves better with mindfulness and gradually becomes better for themselves and others. As an actor and actor trainer, I believe that acting can similarly achieve that, and drawing and learning from mindfulness can support such an exploration.

Background: Mindfulness illuminating the actor's dual consciousness

To bring mindfulness to an actor training context, Dawn Ingleson identified key similarities between practising mindfulness and acting. Mindfulness requires '*[p]aying full attention* to all our experiences, including our body, thoughts, moods and emotions and to the small changes within them' [emphasis in original] which resonates with the actor's needs to be '[i]nfinitely alert in [their] attention'; in other words, 'engrossed in what is happening onstage' (Ingleson, 168). Mindfulness also requires 'listening and hearing (not shutting out anything) and accepting what is there', which reminds us of the acting expectation to '[o]bserve and listen to what's going on around you – be affected and be able to affect others onstage' (Ingleson, 168). Drawing on such 'parallels', Ingleson argues that mindfulness has helped undergraduate acting students to 'focus on being grounded in [their] body and the world around [them], going about their everyday business in life and on stage' (Ingleson, 161). The idea is that the same practice can reinforce the actor's focus on themselves and around them, both in their life when they are not performing and when they are in character.

Acting is a complex human process, especially when the actor portrays, represents or lives a character's life, and the words 'portrays', 'represents' or 'lives' reflect different psychological perspectives on the actor's process. If mindfulness works as 'an awareness of our thoughts and feelings as they happen moment to moment' (NHS, n.d.), how does mindfulness work during characterisation? To what extent is the actor aware of their **own** beliefs, thoughts and emotions on stage as they happen from moment to moment? How are these affected when in character? For example, where is the character when the actor senses a sudden upset stomach while on stage and hopes they won't vomit? The experience of the character's thoughts and feelings might involve extra effort, such as an ongoing mental process through techniques like subtext and inner monologue, to manifest such feelings and thoughts through the actor's physical score. Is the actor's attention in constant competition between their own beliefs, thoughts and emotions and the character's beliefs, thoughts and emotions? And how is it different if the upset stomach does not appear in front of an audience but while reading the play around the table, learning lines at home or rehearsing with a company?

Mindfulness can work for the actor in different ways during rehearsal and performance for text-based work, or during other acting processes that do not involve characterisation, such as warm-ups. Drawing on emotion psychology to test how the real emotions of actors resonate with the represented emotions of the characters, Elly Konijn's empirical study evidenced discrepancies in the psychological experience during rehearsing and performing a scripted character.[2] To create a hypothesis that could be investigated through questionnaires, Konijn highlighted that:

> [e]motions at the level of the actor-craftsman hardly ever come into view in traditional views on acting, except for, incidentally, stage fright or concentration. Usually, the character-emotions are related to the so-called private emotions of the actor, referring to questions like 'is Meryl Streep feeling as sad as Sophie is supposed to be?
>
> *(Konijn 2002, 65)*

Having explored the different legacies of Western acting concerning how the actor relates to the character, broadly discussed as Stanislavsky, Meyerhold/Brecht and Grotowski approaches, Konijn found that all three consider that during a performance the actor operates within 'a double consciousness' as a craftsman and a private person. As a craftsman, they are concerned with four main 'acting tasks' (Konijn 2002, 63): 'to imagine the character's life, including their emotions; to credibly portray the imagined life and emotions; to perform the character's physical score or their behaviours, and; to be spontaneous' (Konijn 2002, 64). As a private person, they are concerned with their 'competency, their image, aesthetics and "sensation seeking drives", and also the reactions of spectators and the generally difficult task of performance' (Konijn 2002, 67). Even though Konijn's study has some limitations,[3] it offers insights into how the emotional body state during acting can be studied.

To investigate whether the actor's emotions resonate with the character's emotions, Konijn sent a questionnaire to hundreds of actors in the US and the Netherlands. The results illuminate which emotions or thought processes are at the centre of the actor's focus in text-based performance or to what extent the actor is mindful of their own life and/or the life of the character. The study found that '[i]n studying the acting process, rehearsals need to be distinguished from live performances' (Konijn 2002, 78). During rehearsals, by 'looking for similarities between him/herself and the character, an actor can gain insight into real life emotions which may help him/her create an inner model of the intended character-emotions' (Konijn 2002, 78). On the contrary, during the performance, 'the demands of the actual context of acting – in front of an audience – will prevent the actor from losing himself in character-emotions' (Konijn 2002, 78). These findings suggest that an actor's dual consciousness affects their focus in different ways during rehearsal and performance. This indicates a complex process of mindfulness for the intensified focus on the experienced feelings and emotions moment to moment and the awareness of the body moment to moment, for both the private person and the craftsman as the character.

Mindfulness is more likely to be experienced as a split between the two consciousnesses of the actor during the early stages of rehearsal when the actor looks at their own life experience to create the imagined experience of the character, as indicated by an author but in need of being fully embodied through a private human. During the performance, the character is more likely to have become an automated script, and the mindful actor is more focused on the consciousness of the private human who might be experiencing anything from stage fright to satisfaction from an audience cheering. However differently distributed during rehearsal and performance, the actor's awareness is still divided between the two consciousnesses of their private life and the life of the character. Using the NHS definition of mindfulness: 'paying attention to what is going on inside and outside ourselves, moment by moment' to the process of the actor's dual consciousness, which is complex as Konijn's study illustrated, suggests that, in characterisation, the actor experiences and practices dual mindfulness in intricate ways.

Konijn's findings do not contradict Ingleson's. Ingleson practised mindfulness with her students as a warm-up, and primarily with a focus on their well-being generally in life but also directly for the stage, for example in tackling stage fright. The bringing of the two studies together creates a hypothesis that mindfulness within a warm-up process prepares the actor to tackle the dual mindfulness required during rehearsal and performance. This hypothesis resonates with the parts of Stanislavsky's work that incorporate what reminds us of core mindfulness practice. Stanislavsky's affinity with mindfulness is explicit in his use of muscle relaxation exercises, which he drew from Yoga. There is extensive literature about Stanislavsky and Yoga,[4] particularly concerning how Yoga-based principles informed the System through practices such as: relaxation of muscles; communication and prana; emission of rays and reception of rays; beaming of aura; sending of prana; attention, visualisations.[5] The fact that Stanislavsky started using them systematically as warm-up for the role indicates that, perhaps, these were tested and later adopted as part of the system because they addressed the problem with the actor's dual consciousness.

Sharon Carnicke writes that it was not until 1937, a year before his death, that Stanislavsky introduced Yoga-inspired exercises as *preparation* for rehearsal and performance.[6] He surprised a group of students by asking them

> first to focus on their breathing and to relax their bodies. Next, they study the details in the hall's old-fashioned chandeliers and then on the elaborately painted ceilings in order to practice their powers of observation and concentration.
>
> *(Carnicke 2023, 39)*

Because before that day, all the time was supposed to be used rehearsing a play, the students asked for a justification for his choice. He responded that such a preparation 'when performed properly, … becomes a necessary step in performance', '"[like tuning an instrument"' (Vinogradskal, 504, in Carnicke 2023, 39). From an actor's perspective, the key difference was that they weren't in character. They were invited to discover ways that would make mindful practice useful for the rehearsal in character that followed shortly after. Stanislavsky observed that the students 'achieved an astonishing "depth of their acting" as a result of the preparation' (Carnicke 2023). Even though unclear how and why the preparation worked, Stanislavsky's statement suggests that mindful preparation resolved the problem of superficial acting which is central in his work.[7]

Mindful preparation for characterisation seems to be one of the last techniques that he believed could solve the problem of 'superficial acting'. The core of the technique was to invite each actor to develop and manage 'an "internal monitor" that we can imaginatively send through our bodies, looking for areas of tension' (SS II, 188 in Carnicke 2023, 192), which can be also described as a body scan. Stanislavsky discussed muscular tension. However, the monitor metaphor implies that the actor can scout and identify acting problems such as areas of tension before they affect their performance in a similar way that mindfulness is expected to identify well-being concerns before they escalate by simply noticing them. Stanislavsky's Yoga-inspired exercises help with that in a way that was not as clear in his key works *An Actor Prepares* and *Building a Role*, in which most problems are tackled through improvisations involving characters and narratives. For example, Stanislavsky writes that '[c]learing the mind and preparing for the role consists in the following: not getting to your dressing room at the last moment as most people do, but (if it's a major role) preparing for your first entrance two hours before the show begins' (Carnicke 2023, 299). He continues suggesting muscle relaxation without a specific exercise and even as he starts describing an observation and concentration exercise, he invites actors to '[d]evise a physical task' (Carnicke 2023, 300) which puts the imagination in an overpowering position compared to body awareness, but still considers the body-mind holistically. In his later writing, Stanislavsky acknowledges that the actor's preparation involves discovering ways to improve their agency over their body state, such as in his above discussion about the 'internal monitor'.

Self-awareness is more prominent in exercises appropriated by Stanislavsky training as preparation, such as The Repose of the Cat exercise, which aims at relaxation in the sense of making your 'every motion 'count' (Ramacharaka, 175; 169 in Carnicke 2023, 191). Such Yoga-inspired exercises develop an actor 'who automatically relaxes, concentrates, and observes, making it easier for [them] to attend to [their] role and its interactive dynamics while performing' (Carnicke 2023, 190). Here, Carnicke acknowledges as a challenge that the actor's focus is constantly pulled away from their character in a way that resonates with Konijn's research about how the actor's dual consciousness works from an emotion psychology perspective. Carnicke has described the actor's dual consciousness as the actor's 'first self' and 'second self', which can even be distinguished through the study of screen performance.[8] So perhaps, and even though unclear of how it works, some of the mindful exercises addressed the challenges surrounding the actor's two selves. As Carnicke highlights, '[c]arefully chosen exercises can help actors overcome their specific difficulties' and they can be used to 'warm up daily and whenever you need to ready yourself for an audition, class or rehearsal' (Carnicke 2023, 190).[9] Mindfulness is embedded in the mechanism behind these exercises that tackle challenges related to the actor's dual consciousness.

Identifying mindfulness as integral to the characterisation process begs for further research. Among the many avenues that can be explored, it is intriguing to consider the potential to develop compassion and cognitive empathy, or social cognition, for the role (or the self-in-role). If mindfulness prompts self-knowledge through attentiveness to oneself and acting embeds a similar attentiveness to oneself, then acting can prompt self-knowledge. Because acting involves dual mindfulness that attends to both the self and the role (or the self-in-role) during rehearsal and performance, part of the acting process is the juxtaposition of the knowledge of the self with the knowledge of the role (or the self-in-role). To explore whether this can lead to the understanding of the role, or the prompting of cognitive empathy for the role, the following section focuses on the cognitive mechanism of approaching the role as a social construct.

Cognitive empathy through exploring the role as a social construct

A role is an imagined human as described in the text and performed by the actor. To imagine the role, the actor breaks it down into several components, including their social circumstances, for example, their financial situation, and their social identities, e.g., age and gender. As a simulation of a human with social characteristics, the role can be described as a social construct. The student's engagement with the role as a social construct involves and requires their critical approach to the role. The critical engagement with learning materials has been implied in Stanislavsky's writings and has been a priority in education more broadly. Stanislavsky's main goal 'to cultivate in students, abilities and qualities which help them to free their creative individuality – an individuality imprisoned by prejudices and clichés' (Zakhava in Malaev-Babel 2011, 23) resonates with bell hooks' suggestion that a self-liberating learning process starts with a 'historical moment when one begins to think critically about the self and identity in relation to one's political circumstance' (1994, 47). When the student engages with the role as a social construct, their prejudices are involved but also a critical process of juxtaposing their own social circumstances to the social circumstances of the character, developing an understanding of the role as a social construct.[10]

Such social understanding of the student can be taken beyond their acting. Because Stanislavsky was busy directing plays in rehearsal rooms and on stage,[11] such potential was left to other pedagogues that he influenced. The investigation of how Stanislavsky's training can work as a social development pedagogy in the actor training studio can only happen outside of the stresses involved in directing and mounting productions. A training studio that focused on the holistic development of the actor was run by Yevgeny Vakhtangov, Stanislavsky's colleague at the Moscow Art Theatre. Stanislavsky's statement that 'Vakhtangov teaches the "system" better than me' and Strasberg's advice to his students that 'Vakhtangov is there, in his books waiting to answer your questions' (in Manolikakis 1996, 13), confirm that Vakhtangov was influenced by Stanislavsky and contributed invaluably to post-Stanislavsky studio work.

The actor's attentiveness and agency concerning their feelings, in a way that resonates with mindfulness, have been clearer in Vakhtangov's writings. Vakhangov writes about the actor's preparation as the process of discovering their feelings through associating themselves with characters with the aim of self-control over feelings.[12] In *An Actor's Work: a student's diary*, Stanislavsky, in the guise of the fictional persona of tutor Tortsov, explains to student-actor Vanya:

> Bring all the Elements, the psychological inner drives, the Throughaction, to the point where they become normal, human – not convention-bound and actorish – activity. Then you will come to know the truth of your own mind and nature. You will come to know the truth of the character. You cannot but believe the truth. And where there is truth and belief the state of "I am being" arises of itself.
>
> *(Stanislavsky 2008, 330)*

Within his primal understanding of human psychology and the subconscious, Stanislavsky suggests that when the actor prepares a role, they develop self-knowledge and understand the truth of the character. When the actor understands the character through believing the character's truth, which means taking their perspective, they become (like) the character. This journey towards understanding the character's behaviours in given circumstances does not happen in a vacuum but through juxtaposing these behaviours to the actor's behaviours in similar lived circumstances.

Considering that empathy in sum involves 'knowing the experience of another person with cognitive, affective and behavioural components' (Goubert et al. 2005, 285), Stanislavsky's suggestion above implies that the acting process inevitably prompts the actor's empathy for the character. The acting process involves knowing the truth of the character, and even though the character is not real but imagined, it is important to investigate how empathy does not result in 'empathic distress' but in compassion, which is 'a feeling of warmth and concern for the other' (Preckel et al. 2018, 1). If the empathy that the actor develops for the character is more socio-cognitive than socio-affective, in other words more cognitive than emotional, any emotional harm is avoided. Socio-cognition means 'taking another person's perspective (also referred to as ToM [Theory of the Mind], mentalizing, or cognitive empathy)' (Preckel et al. 2018). In contrast to popular understandings of empathy as an emotional state, socio-cognition 'yields abstract, propositional knowledge about the other's mental state' within a process of 'inferring and reasoning about the beliefs, thoughts and emotions of others' (Preckel et al. 2018, 1–2). Socio-cognition, and therefore cognitive empathy, is primarily a critical process. To argue that the mindfulness of self and character in acting can facilitate cognitive empathy beyond acting, the next section employs the theory of Interacting Cognitive Subsystems (henceforth ICS).

ICS and the actor's cognitive empathy

Firstly, because ICS can 'explain all aspects of information processing' (Teasdale and Barnard 1995, 344), it can contribute to the theoretical understanding of acting from a cognitive theory perspective. Secondly, drawing on how 'the mere broad understanding of ICS allowed clinicians to focus on specific processes or aspects of ICS that pertain to a particular clinical phenomenon' (Cowdrey et al. 2017, 380), ICS helps us concentrate on how the actor processes the information from a text alongside the information from their lives to create a performance. Thirdly, it is timely to consider that 'ICS provides a theoretical rationale for the use of novel interventions, such as mindfulness-based interventions', and has foregrounded the 'interest and evidence in support of mindfulness-based interventions for a range of psychological and health problems' (Cowdrey et al. 2017, 380). Because such interest in mindfulness and its effects on actor training has recently engaged Stanislavsky scholars and practitioners around the *Stanislavsky and Mindfulness* symposium and beyond, the practitioner pedagogue can use ICS as a critical lens to investigate how characterisation processes during acting have the potential to influence the future behaviour of the actor during and outside of performances. Lastly, as 'a general framework of how the mind works and therefore a number of the predictions have been systematically tested in the general population', ICS has successfully explained 'a wide range of empirical phenomena in language, understanding, short term and working memory, visual attention, cognition and emotion' (Cowdrey et al. 2017), all of which relate to the actor's process.

The idea that the actor's double attentiveness to self and role during acting has the potential to influence their behaviour outside of performance is based on information processing. According to ICS, 'information is encoded as nine different mental codes, each by their respective subsystem: acoustic, visual, body-state, object, morphonolexical (speech forms), propositional, implicational, articulatory and limb' (Cowdrey et al. 2017). Each subsystem holds a different 'image record' for every memory, which 'can be drawn upon at times of remembering but also when trying to comprehend a specific situation or predict a future outcome' (Cowdrey et al. 2017). When information is processed upon recalling the image, records from the nine subsystems work together to produce behaviour which is based largely on previous experiences. When the actor starts imagining the role, they start processing information based on their previous experience. For example, suppose they are studying the role of a single mother. In that case, their visual subsystem will encode the words 'single mother' and process them through the propositional subsystem, which encodes information as facts like the mother is the sole carer of her child/children, and the implicational subsystem, which might prompt a general affinity for the role or stereotypical assumptions, based and depending on previous experience with single mothers or lack thereof.

Because 'within ICS, frequently co-occurring patterns of implicational code are thought of as "schematic mental models" of experience' (Cowdrey et al. 2017, 383), the actor, in imagining the role of a single mother, might draw on schematic mental models such as 'the fighter single mother' which is comprised of propositional code such as 'I am mentally strong and physically capable', an alert body-state and a good mood. The overall meaning of the three different propositional codes that comprise the schematic mental model of the single mother is different qualitatively from the sum of its parts and will be encoded by the implicational subsystem as a more general positive feel, and even admiration, for the single mother.

As the actor reads through the play, she gains more information about the specific role of the single mother, for example, Phyllis in Paula Vogel's *Mother Play*. The actor's propositional subsystem encodes new propositional code about the single mother such as 'self-medicating with alcohol' and moving her children constantly from one inappropriate accommodation to the next, all of which will inform new schematic mental models that will have a greater general awareness of the mental health and housing challenges associated with single motherhood. In a nutshell:

> The exchange of information *between* propositional and implicational subsystems is integral for the formation and maintenance of schematic mental models and functions as a control loop; schematic mental models generate specific propositions and propositions are processed and fed back to the implicational subsystem and used to modify the schematic mental model.
>
> *(Cowdrey et al. 2017)*

The transformation of the schematic mental model of the single mother (because preparing the role is integrated into the brain function of the actor) will be carried forward into other areas of their life. Therefore, the schematic mental model of the single mother affects the general feelings and attitude of the individual towards situations involving single motherhood, and their cognitive empathy, or social cognition, towards single mothers will be improved.

The use of ICS to argue that preparing a role promotes cognitive empathy prompts further questions: how is the process, and therefore the affect, different to reading or watching the play? How is the process, and therefore the affect, different as the actor articulates and embodies the imagined schematic models of single motherhood which involve all subsystems in different ways? How can these subsystems be isolated for further study? How can survey research be employed for testing and analysing the hypothesis from this chapter with participants? How can such benefits of acting be used for human development beyond actors?

Conclusion

This chapter used the Interacting Cognitive Subsystems theory to argue that Stanislavsky training facilitates the development of cognitive empathy, or social cognition, in actors. It was prompted through a desire to look more closely at how mindfulness works in the context of the actor's dual consciousness. It theorised the role as a social construct that interacts with the actor's experience despite not being real. It invites Stanislavsky practitioners to consider how a studio that trains an actor to prepare for a role, also prepares the actor for life through developing qualities and skills that support life-long well-being for themselves and others around them. The next steps include involving empirical research tools and participants to investigate how acting facilitates human development and evidence its impact to affect society positively.[13]

Acknowledgements

The author would like to thank Rhonda Blair and the International Network for Cognition, Theatre, and Performance (INCTP) at the American Society for Theatre Research (ASTR) for their useful advice in the development of this chapter and the projects involved.

Notes

1 See Blair 2010, 48.
2 See Konijn 2002, 74.
3 See Blair 2010, 49.
4 See Tcherkasski 2016; White et al. 2014.
5 See Tcherkasski 2016.
6 See Carnicke 2023.
7 See Stanislavsky 1989 298.
8 See Carnicke 2012.
9 For descriptions of exercises, see Carnicke 2023, and Tcherkasski 2016.
10 My essay 'Pierre Bourdieu and actor training: Towards decolonising and decentering actor training pedagogies' draws on sociology to explain how the acting process is inevitably a process of exploring the actor's biases. My monograph *Bourdieu in the Studio: Towards decolonising and decentering actor training through 'Ludic Activism'* offers a creative intervention for facilitating a conscious exploration of such biases.
11 Demidov in Malaev-Babel 2011, 8.
12 See Vakhtangov in Malaev-Babel 2011, 105.
13 This is an ambitious scope which has brought together an interdisciplinary team from Performing Arts, Media, Nursing and Psychology. For more information see Stamatiou & Sanni 2024, Stamatiou et al. 2025, and Stamatiou et al. 2026.

References

Blair, R. (2010). *The actor, image, and action: acting and cognitive neuroscience.* London and New York: Routledge.

Carnicke, S.M. (2012). The screen actor's 'first self' and 'second self': John Wayne and Coquelin's Acting Theory. In A. Taylor (ed.), *Theorizing film acting.* (pp. 184–200). New York: Routledge.

Carnicke, S. M. (2023). *Dynamic acting through active analysis: Konstantin Stanislavsky, Maria Knebel, and their legacy.* London and New York: Methuen Drama.

Cowdrey, F.A., Lomax, C., Gregory, J. D., and Barnard, P. J. (2017). Could a unified theory of cognition and emotion further the transdiagnostic perspective? A critical analysis using interacting cognitive subsystems as a case example, *Psychopathology Review*, a4(3), 377–399. https://doi.org/10.5127/pr.044714

Goubert, L., Craig, K.D., Vervoort, T., Morley, S., Sullivan, M.J.L., Williams, D.C.A. C., Cano, A., and Crombez, G. (2005). Facing others in pain: The effects of empathy, *Pain*, 118(3), 285–288. https://doi.org/10.1016/j.pain.2005.10.025

Hooks, B. (1994). *Teaching to transgress: Education as the practice of freedom.* New York: Routledge.

Konijn, E. (2002). The Actor's Emotions Reconsidered: A psychological task-based perspective. In P.B. Zarrilli (ed.), *Acting (re)considered: A theoretical and practical guide* (2nd ed, pp. 62–81). London and New York: Routledge.

Malaev-Babel, A. (ed.) (2011). *The Vakhtangov sourcebook.* London and New York: Routledge.

Manolikakis, A. (1996). Σημείωμα του μεταφραστή (Translator's note). In A. Manolikakis (Trans.), *Βαχτάνγκοφ: Μαθήματα σκηνοθεσίας και υποκριτικής (The art of stage: For the director and actor).* Athens: Medousa.

NHS. (n.d.). *Mindfulness.* NHS.UK. Available at https://www.nhs.uk/mental-health/self-help/tips-and-support/mindfulness/. (Accessed 02.02.24)

Preckel, K., Kanske, P., and Singer, T. (2018). On the interaction of social affect and cognition: Empathy, compassion and theory of mind. *Current Opinion in Behavioral Sciences*, 19, 1–6. https://doi.org/10.1016/j.cobeha.2017.07.010

Stamatiou, E., Cox, G., Sanni, T., Balla, G. and Thoma, V. (forthcoming 2026). Ethnoacting in VR: An equivalent to role-playing in healthcare education. In Tizzard-Kleister K. and Firth T. *Using applied drama in nursing and healthcare education: A handbook for educators*. Routledge.
Stamatiou, E., and Sanni, T. (2024) A smart act to follow [British Science Association], *British Science Festival*. https://britishsciencefestival.org/event/a-smart-act-to-follow/
Stamatiou, E. Sanni, T. and Thoma, V. (forthcoming 2025) Ethnoacting in VR for Resilience in Screen Actors: A Vakhtangov-inspired intervention. In Stamatiou E. and Carnicke S. *Stanislavsky and Screen Actor Training*. Routledge.
Stanislavsky, K. (1989). *An actor prepares*. New York: Routledge.
Stanislavsky, K. (2008). *An actor's work: A student's diary* (J. Benedetti, Trans.). Routledge.
Tcherkasski, S. (2016). *Stanislavsky and yoga*. Abingdon: Routledge.
Teasdale, J. D., and Barnard, P. J. (1995). *Affect, cognition and change: Re-modelling depressive thought* (repr. in paperback). New York: Lawrence Erlbaum Associates.
White, R. A. (ed.) (2014). *The Routledge companion to Stanislavsky*. London: Routledge.

7

SUPPORTING MINDFUL ACTING AND WELLBEING IN ACTOR TRAINING

Elisa Lewis and Edward McGurn

The acting profession is frequently perceived as a desirable and glamorous career, attracting significant public attention.[1,2] However, behind-the-scenes research indicates that professional actors experience poorer mental health than the general population, with high levels of depression and anxiety reported.[3,4] Occupational factors which contribute to increased risks of mental ill-health include unstable employment, irregular and intermittent working schedules and low and fluctuating pay.[5,6] Supportive relationships which are protective against mental ill-health may also be disrupted owing to both time spent away from home on tour and anti-social working hours.[7]

In view of the challenges faced by those in the profession, attention has also turned to actors in training. There is evidence to suggest that student actors may be more vulnerable to mental ill-health than those training in other creative arts.[8] It has been proposed that the skills needed to maintain mental well-being and resilience should be developed during training before actors enter the profession.[9] One potential risk to mental health, which is specific to acting training and the profession, is the requirement to authentically portray a wide variety of characters, including characters who experience extreme emotions and traumatic events. This may entail entering the lifeworld of the character by drawing on personal or vicarious memories.[10] It has been demonstrated that vicarious memories can impact upon emotional wellbeing to the same extent as personally experienced memories.[11] As such, actors who portray intense traumatic roles could be at risk of emotional distress, particularly as they may dwell in these roles for extended periods of time. As stated by McDonald et al. in a study exploring student actor wellbeing during rehearsals for *King Lear*, 'audience members confront these cruelties only once, yet

DOI: 10.4324/9781003517856-8

actors embody them on a nightly basis' (McDonald et al. 2019, 69). The cumulative impact of repeated exposure to traumatic events may well compound the potential for distress.

Mindfulness is one possible response to supporting actors in training and preparing them for the profession and its associated challenges. Rooted in ancient Buddhist teachings, mindfulness as a clinical practice was introduced in the late 1970s by Jon Kabat-Zinn, who developed the Mindfulness-Based Stress Reduction programme.[12] Mindful practice is associated with numerous benefits to mental health and wellbeing, including lower levels of anxiety,[13] depression[14] and psychological distress,[15] as well as enhanced emotional regulation,[16] empathy[17] and self-esteem.[18] The core tenets of mindfulness whereby one cultivates 'focused attention and awareness in the present moment without judgement and with acceptance' (MacDonald and Baxter 2017, 398) are also directly applicable to those working within the performing arts. Mindful practice enables actors to be fully aware of their breath, mind and body, and to attune to their environment and to those around them. It also supports actors in being present in the moment and enhances creativity.[19]

Ingleson (2022) highlights the striking similarities between the disciplines of mindfulness and theatre practice; both require an attitude of curiosity and openness, being in the moment and an acceptance of things as they are now. Acting students who engaged in mindfulness warm-ups and meditation as part of weekly classes reflected that the practices supported them in their training through enhanced relaxation, focus and preparedness. It also aided their technique, including controlling the breath, being creative and getting into character.[20] Another study involving music conservatoire students found that, following an eight-week mindfulness course, the participants reported increased focus, lower self-criticism and enhanced body awareness.[21] They also described how mindfulness encouraged them to be more creative in their music practice and reduced pre-stage anxiety.

Mindful practice, therefore, seems a promising approach to supporting trainee actors' wellbeing and equipping them with skills that they can take forward into the profession. In the following section, Edward (Ed) McGurn gives an account of the sessions he delivered to second-year Acting and Performing students at London South Bank University during March and April 2024. Participants were guided through a series of meditation and breathwork exercises designed to reduce stress and enhance resilience, while visualisation exercises supported them in disengaging from character and temporarily leaving behind the challenges of the rehearsal room. Here, Ed describes the approach that he took, its theoretical foundations and its links with Stanislavskian practice. This is followed by reflections from three of the participants on their experiences and how this relates to actor training.

Enhancing Actor Training through the Alpha State

In almost any industry, particularly in the creative fields, periods of inspired invention can arise out of, or directly accompany, periods of deep relaxation. In actor training, much time is spent on relaxation, muscular release and creative visualisation. During these times, we hope that students can surrender deeply enough to these exercises that they might enter into the alpha state, whereby there is increased alpha wave activity in the brain. Moving into the alpha state through deep breathing techniques produces increased levels of calm and improvements to an individual's overall levels of mental and physical wellbeing. The alpha state is best described as the space between sleeping and waking, a rare moment of our waking day when we are not yet trying to consciously control every aspect of our lives. In this state, our levels of creativity and intuition are much higher. Many great discoveries have been attributed to the alpha state. One notable example is how Albert Einstein had his major breakthrough in understanding the mechanics of the Theory of Relativity and the creation of the E=MC^2 formula while sunbathing. In this highly relaxed state, he found the clarity to explain the phenomenon.[22]

For this reason and more, I wanted to support actors in training by offering techniques and approaches that gave them the opportunity to enter into the alpha state. The alpha state is an interchangeable term for allowing the subconscious mind to take the driving seat when an actor is performing, a state extensively described in Stanislavski's writings. Kostya, the fictional student of Stanislavski in *An Actor Prepares*, is quoted as saying, 'I am overjoyed, I am walking on air. Now I know completely, in practice, the meaning of the words: "Through the actor's conscious psychotechnique to nature's subconscious creative power!!". For me, this now means: spend years and years of your life developing that psychotechnique and you will create the soil for inspiration. Then it will come to you of its own accord' (Stanislavski 2010, 42).

With my participants, I decided to take them through a series of sessions of Nadine George Voice Work® (NGVW).[23] There were several reasons for this. My first experience with meditation and mindfulness was through Zen Buddhism, a form of meditation practised with the eyes open. Given that we hope actors can have flashes of inspiration while connecting with their scene partners in a rehearsal, I knew that I wanted to focus on a technique that required the balance of both a meditative state and an outward focus. NGVW is unique in its approach to voice work in that one of the main aspects of the work is a vocal–ocular connection. The vocal aspect involves voicing an 'AW' sound that originates from a connection made through deep diaphragmatic breathing and then to a series of 'sung sounds' that build the voice from this place of deep connection. The 'AW' breath is achieved by drawing the corners of the mouth together so that the lips propel forward. When a student is learning the technique, they are encouraged to exaggerate this mouth position as best they can (see Figure 7.1).

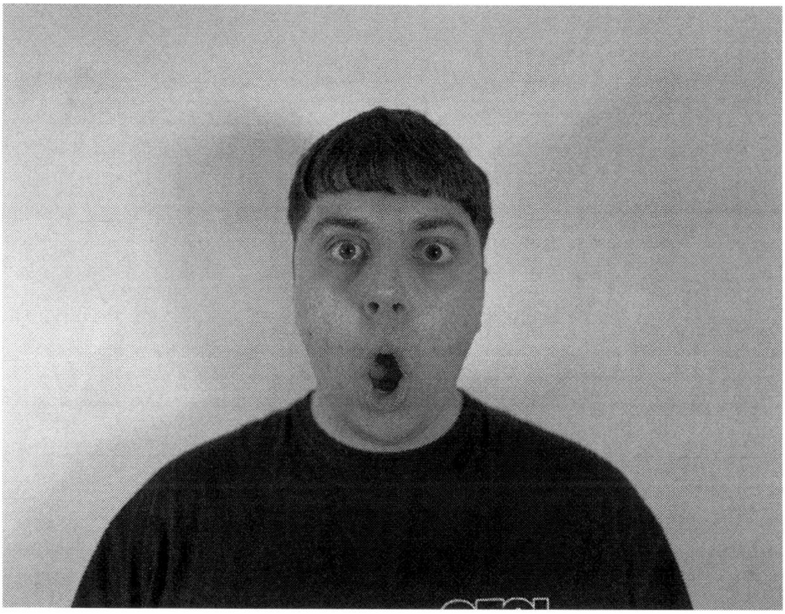

FIGURE 7.1 A student workshop participant practicing the 'AW' breath with lips forward and with 'dramatic focus in the eyes'. Photo by Nico Heugh Simone.

After the initial period of breathing, lying on the floor with the eyes closed, the 'AW' breath and the sung sounds are continually practised with what is referred to as 'dramatic focus in the eyes'. As the lips propel forward, the eyes follow this motion, widening and stretching and engaging the muscle directly behind the eyeball (superior oblique). Participants will feel a pulling on this muscle. Another description for the sensation might be that of the eyes 'driving forward'.

A common description of mindfulness is that 'It is natural for the mind to wander; with mindfulness, you return your attention to the breath' (Kabat-Zinn 1994, 3). The exaggerated form of NGVW, which is probably most comparable to the deliberate eye movements found in the traditional Indian art form of Kathakali, requires calm, focused attention in order to synchronise the balance between the eye widening, ensuring this is sufficient to feel the pull of the muscle behind the eye and also the forward position of the lips. Participants in the work are also required to keep their forehead and eyebrows free of tension, meaning that there should be no frowning or raising of the eyebrows taking tension into the forehead. This is a very delicate balance to strike as the pulling of the muscles behind the eyes does make the eyebrows and forehead want to move. It is a fine balance to achieve the correct amount of muscular engagement of the eyes, while ensuring this does not spark sympathetic motion in the eyebrows and forehead. With each new breath the student becomes aware of taking, they know that they must remain in a place of calm, centredness and release to achieve this delicate physiological balance.

The student is then engaged in what is referred to as the 'walking section' of the work. This is where all the participants keep the breath work going while walking through the room on various diagonals. The student keeps the coordination of the out-breath, eye gaze and forward position of the lips while walking in the room. They must also be mindful to stay hip-width as they walk, keep the knees soft and find the horizon each time they change position in the room, all while ensuring that they do not collide with any other participants. Again, mindful attention is paramount here, and this section of NGVW is where the practice can be best identified as a 'dynamic meditation'. The participants must remain calm and centred and remember to keep all the physiological details of the work going, but also keep moving forward. Moving forward not just kinetically, but forward into the new experiences and insights that can open for them when they are working with a sense of 'flow' and not having their work dominated by tension both physically and mentally. If a student is ever seen to be jutting their head forward or disconnecting the head in any way from an anatomically desirable connection to the spine, this is pointed out and corrected while in the walk. In everyday life, we continually disconnect our body as we navigate our day. This prolonged period of anatomical harmony between the connection of the head and the spine houses students in their 'back brain'.[24] This part of the brain not only controls physical actions and reactions instinctively but is also the main physiological hub of the subconscious and the gateway to accessing intellectual and emotional processes. The front part of the brain deals with conscious control and direction of our actions.

In the end, with NGVW, we have a process that not only helps participants to access the alpha state by way of deep breathing, increasing their levels of calm and improvements to their mental and physical wellbeing, but also, by harmonizing the head and neck relationship while in a waking state, allows the subconscious mind to inspire the actor's choices when working. The walking section is possibly best compared to the moment when we are looking for something such as a lost key and are extremely focused on finding it (front brain conscious control). Then, as soon as we stop concentrating so hard, relinquish control and drop the tension of the search, we move into the area of our back brain, and, in many cases, the lost object appears. With the walking, if a student is concerned that they will bump into people, this is what will generally happen. If they can surrender to what Clive Barker refers to in his actor training manual *Theatre Games* as their 'kinaesthetic sense' (Barker 1977, 48), they will find that they never collide with anyone, no matter how cramped the walking space might be. This is an approach to actor training that stresses the importance of actors developing a deep instinctual understanding of their own bodies and their positions in space, as well as a sensitivity to the body's internal sense of movement and balance that allows them to move with precision and fluidity. By focusing on the 'kinaesthetic sense', actors can better connect with their back brain, which Barker refers to as 'the seat of the actor's subconscious creativity' (Barker 1977, 46). Barker's work encourages a deeper connection between physicality and subconscious creativity. Interestingly, Stanislavski is noted as saying 'In total opposition to some teachers, it is my view that students, beginners, who, like you, are taking their first steps on stage, should, within the limits of the possible, be led immediately towards the subconscious. This should be done in the earliest stages when working on the elements, on mental states, on all the exercises and improvisations' (Stanislavski 1936, 306).

It is widely acknowledged that the final working form of Stanislavski was the process of 'Active Analysis'; a process that prioritises action over intellectual analysis. With NGVW we have a process that supports overall physical and mental wellbeing, while also taking us directly to the crystallisation of Stanislavski's life work, the conscious liberation of the actor's subconscious mind via the methods we use to train them. 'Try to give free play to the creative subconscious! Remove the things which hinder it, and make the things which help it stronger. And so, the basic task of our psychotechnique is to bring the actor to the state in which his creative subconscious can burgeon' (Stanislavski 1936, 303).

Student Experiences

Three participants in Ed's sessions – Aaliyah, Lucie and Rebecca – spoke about their experiences.

All three participants highlighted the importance and relevance of mindfulness to acting and to the profession. Aaliyah states that 'being an actor is quite a vulnerable kind of job' in which actors need to be present, aware and attentive in their craft. For this reason, she says mindful practices 'are probably more useful in our field of work than others'. She describes how they help actors 'to be aware of their surroundings (…) and to have a curiosity'. Lucie echoes this. During the sessions she recounts being 'present in the space' and overcoming a habitual tendency to 'overthink so much', which takes her away from the present moment. She recalls waiting for her turn to speak in the group, which would typically be a source of stress:

> I just felt at peace. This is weird because usually I would be thinking about 5000 different things I could say, but at that point I was like I'll see whatever comes to me instead of trying to pre-empt what I'm going to say.

Mindfulness also supports the wellbeing of the actor, a topic which the participants felt was often overlooked. As Rebecca says, 'People forget about the mental bit with acting, because your body is your instrument. But don't forget about your wellbeing.'

The participants describe how the sessions with Ed helped to reduce fear and the propensity for self-doubt, thus allowing for more spontaneous decision-making. Aliyah speaks to this when she says:

> It felt like a release of fear, because a lot of the time I would be scared to make those decisions within my own acting (…) It instilled this thing of go for it. Just let all of that insecurity go. It did feel like a purging of that little voice in your head that says 'don't! don't do that!'

Rebecca describes 'a nice energy in the room with every session, because everyone just let go, no judgements', and with the letting go of judgement she felt 'safe and secure, you can go for it, do what you need to do, do the best you can'. Aaliyah articulates the freedom and spontaneity engendered by practising mindfulness and states that 'most of the time the best acting happens when you're not doing it, when it's spontaneous. A practice like that, I feel would be very, very helpful in honing the organic-ness of performance in audition.'

During the sessions, the participants were encouraged to meditate with their eyes open. Aaliyah felt that this was more beneficial to an actor than closed-eyes meditation: 'I think when we close our eyes, we can block everything out and just go inward, which I don't think is the most amazing practice for acting.' Rebecca echoes this in saying that 'if I close my eyes meditating, I *will* just fall asleep, but with the eyes open you're present, which I guess is what they're trying to do, because you need to be present when you're acting'. For Lucie, the walking exercise brought about an enhanced, relaxed awareness that increased her confidence and helped with decision-making:

> Usually there's a constant back of your mind of, I'm gonna bump into someone, but that didn't happen. I made the choice to go that way, and I'm going to trust the people around me to see where I'm going, and they are going to make sure that they do not hit me, and they trust that I won't hit them.

Aaliyah agreed 'I do not recall at any point being like I hope I'm not going to bump into somebody (…) you were making the choices, which again, is so important in acting.' She expands further on a sense of more instinctual and confident decision-making:

> Being more self-assured with the decisions you're making you could become more mindful and confident within your thought patterns. Just being like I'm gonna do this, having one thought instead of having three, four. It's nice, simple.

The participants considered that the practice introduced in Ed's sessions was more dynamic than previous meditative work they had experienced. Speaking about the 'AW' breath, Aaliyah says 'it takes a lot of energy, and the fact that you're doing that is releasing tension, that's something I don't think I do in my mindfulness practices, creating tension to create relaxation'. Both Aaliyah and Lucie describe the practice as 'very cathartic'. Lucie says that 'it was a catharsis, it was really nice to just feel and let loose (...) you just act on impulse'.

Following the sessions with Ed, Aaliyah says that she felt 'very relaxed afterwards, in body and in mind, I left every session feeling very rejuvenated' while Lucie felt 'very light, very calm after exiting the space. I felt like a different person exiting than I did coming, I didn't realise I was carrying so much tension.' Similarly, Rebecca shares that:

> It was relaxing, but also afterwards you felt more alert, more energized, like a cup of coffee or something! More clarity, for someone like me who really, really struggles to focus, I felt focused afterwards.

For Aaliyah, there was also a sense of enhanced clarity of thinking: 'your head would feel so clear that you would have a thought, and it would just pass, cos usually I'm very much thinking all the time'. She saw benefits to her mental wellbeing too, stating that the sessions 'definitely [helped] with anxiety, definitely relieved stress'. She describes leaving the sessions with feelings of 'just go with the flow, don't worry about everything you need to do in your entire life right now, which usually I have a tendency of doing. So, massively for me it did relieve anxiety.'

As well as experiencing greater psychological wellbeing, the participants also spoke about the physical benefits of the practice and a reduction of bodily aches and pains. Lucie recalls that 'in the first session, I came in and I had a headache, so I thought I don't know how much I'm gonna be able to apply myself, but at the end of the session I was like, oh my God, the headache is practically gone!' She attributes this to the exercises undertaken during the session and says that 'afterwards there was a moment of stillness, I just felt peaceful. It got all the tension out of my body.' Aaliyah also spoke about a reduction of tension following the sessions: 'I hold all of my tension in my head, shoulders up. I would leave and I would feel very relaxed. I think it's because you're releasing all the tension from your lips and your eyes, so you're literally releasing tension through your face.' Rebecca came into one of the sessions 'with a massive headache' which was 'gone afterwards'. She goes on to say that after the sessions she 'just felt lighter afterwards, and that would obviously affect acting as well. If you're feeling lighter mentally, no headache, you're just more free to do what you need to do.'

Going forwards, the participants all said that they would benefit from integrating mindful meditation into their acting practice. Lucie had already implemented it before a performance and found that it 'massively helped' her to stay present and in the moment:

> Because usually that's the time when I'm going, where are my lines? And constantly going over them. But no, I know my lines, I trust that I know them, so I'm just gonna focus on the breath, not focus on everything else and what other people do, just stop and take a moment to prepare mentally. And it really did help in the performance.

Rebecca echoes this when she says that 'auditions can be *so* daunting, especially when everyone else is there. So, if you're doing that, the meditation, you're not focused on them anymore, you're focused on your breath. It does help.' Aaliyah encapsulates the holistic support that mindfulness provides to both actor and craft:

> To be able to go into a space where you can relax yourself and create your own bubble, but still be aware and present in the space is very helpful for what we do specifically. There's not a lot of practices specifically honed for actors like that to actually improve the mental wellbeing. There's a lot of improving skill, improving technique, but not a lot on our brains.

The participants all recounted a heightened sense of wellbeing following the sessions and felt equipped with skills that they can use to support both their technical development as actors and their wellbeing in the future.

Concluding Thoughts

The integration of Nadine George Voice Work® (NGVW) into actor training offers a powerful means to enhance both the creative and the personal wellbeing of actors. By guiding students into the alpha state—a meditative space where creativity and intuition naturally thrive—NGVW fosters a profound connection between the mind and body. This approach aligns closely with Stanislavski's teachings, which emphasise the conscious cultivation of an actor's subconscious creativity.

The unique vocal–ocular connection practised in NGVW helps actors to maintain a balance between relaxation and focused attention. This balance allows them to enter a state where spontaneous and organic performance becomes possible; a key goal in Stanislavski's psychotechnique. The student experiences discussed earlier further reinforce the benefits of this practice. Participants reported a greater sense of presence, reduced anxiety and improved clarity of thought, both during and after the sessions. This indicates that NGVW not only hones the actor's technical abilities but also supports their mental and emotional wellbeing—an often-overlooked aspect of actor training.

By integrating this mindful approach into their regular practice, actors can better manage the pressures of their profession, enhancing both their performances and their overall wellbeing. NGVW serves as a crucial tool in realising Stanislavski's vision of empowering the actor's subconscious mind, thereby unlocking their full creative potential.

Notes

1 Dumas, Doherty, and Organisciak 2020.
2 Kogan 2002.
3 Maxwell, Seton, and Szabo 2015.
4 Van den Eynde, Fisher, and Sonn 2016.
5 Clements 2022.
6 Robb, Due, and Venning 2018.
7 Van den Eynde, Fisher, and Sonn 2016.
8 Siddins, Daniel, and Johnstone 2016.
9 See note 8 above.
10 Arias 2019.
11 Pillemer, Steiner, Kuwabara, Thomsen, and Svob 2015.
12 Kabat-Zinn 2004.
13 Vøllestad, Siversten, and Nielsen 2011.
14 Cash and Whittingham 2010.
15 Coffey and Hartman 2008.
16 McDonald, Sherman, Petocz, Kangas, Grant and Kasparian 2016).
17 Dekeyser, Raes, Leijssen, Leysen and Dewulf 2008.
18 Randal, Pratt, and Bucci 2015.
19 Ingleson 2022.
20 Ingleson 2022.
21 Czajkowski, Greasley and Allis 2022.
22 The anecdote about Albert Einstein having a breakthrough in understanding the mechanics of the Theory of Relativity while sunbathing is often cited in discussions about the alpha state. Although it remains anecdotal, the story underscores the idea that deep relaxation can lead to moments of profound insight. For more on the relationship between relaxation, the alpha state and creativity, see *The Creative Brain* by Nancy C. Andreasen (2006) and *The Eureka Factor* by John Kounios and Mark Beeman (2015), both of which explore how these mental states contribute to problem-solving and innovation.
23 Nadine George Voice Work® (NGVW) is the main vocal practice taught at the Royal Conservatoire of Scotland. It is a daily practice for first-year students in the BA Acting course. Each session typically lasts three hours, particularly when working with text. This intensive schedule allows students to deeply integrate the physical and mental techniques of NGVW into their routine, fostering a strong foundation in the mindful practices that support both their craft and overall wellbeing. While NGVW can be effectively practiced on a weekly basis, the daily commitment at the Conservatoire emphasises its importance in the development of a responsive and instinctive actor, ensuring that the techniques become second nature by the time students progress to more advanced stages of their training.
24 The connection between the "back brain" and creativity, as well as its relevance to Nadine George Voice Work® (NGVW), is supported by studies in neuroscience that explore the role of the cerebellum in creative processes. The cerebellum, often associated with motor control, has been increasingly recognised for its contributions to cognitive functions, including creative thinking. This part of the brain, which

operates largely on a subconscious level, plays a critical role in coordinating physical actions and facilitating spontaneous, creative impulses. In NGVW, the alignment and engagement of the body, particularly through the relationship between the head and neck, are designed to optimise this connection, allowing actors to access deeper levels of creativity and instinctual response during their work.

References

Andreasen, N. C. (2006). *The creative brain: The science of genius*. Penguin.

Arias, G.L. (2019). *In the Wings: Actors & Mental Health a Critical Review of the Literature* (Master's Thesis).

Barker, C. (1977). *Theatre Games: A New Approach to Drama Training*. London: Eyre Methuen.

Cash, M., and Whittingham, K. (2010). What facets of mindfulness contribute to psychological well-being and depressive, anxious, and stress-related symptomatology?, *Mindfulness*, 1177–182.

Clements, L. (2022). Equity global scoping review of factors related to poor mental health and wellbeing within the performing arts sectors. Equity. https://www.equity.org.uk/news/2022/may/equity-global-study-finds-those-working-in-the-performing-arts-are-more-likely-to-experience-poor-mental-health/ (Accessed 21 November 2024)

Coffey, K. A., & Hartman, M. (2008). Mechanisms of action in the inverse relationship between mindfulness and psychological distress. *Complementary Health Practice Review*, 13(2), 79–91.

Czajkowski, A. M. L., Greasley, A. E., and Allis, M. (2022). Mindfulness for musicians: A mixed methods study investigating the effects of 8-week mindfulness courses on music students at a leading conservatoire, *Musicae Scientiae*, 26(2), 259–279.

Dekeyser, M., Raes, F., Leijssen, M., Leysen, S., & Dewulf, D. (2008). Mindfulness skills and interpersonal behaviour, *Personality and Individual Differences*, 44(5), 1235–1245.

Dumas, D., Doherty, M., and Organisciak, P. (2020). The psychology of professional and student actors: Creativity, personality, and motivation, *PLoS One*, 15(10), e0240728.

Ingleson, D. (2022). Stanislavski training and mindfulness–being in the moment, *Stanislavski Studies*, 10(2), 161–176.

Kabat-Zinn, J. (1994). *Wherever you go, there you are: Mindfulness meditation in everyday life*. New York: Hyperion.

Kabat-Zinn, J. (2004). *Full catastrophe living: How to cope with stress, pain and illness using mindfulness meditation*. London: Piaktus.

Kogan, N. (2002). Careers in the performing arts: A psychological perspective. *Communication Research Journal*, 14(1), 1–16.

Kounios, J., and Beeman, M. (2015). *The eureka factor: Aha moments, creative insight, and the brain*. Random House.

MacDonald, H. Z., and Baxter, E. E. (2017). Mediators of the relationship between dispositional mindfulness and psychological well-being in female college students, *Mindfulness*, 8, 398–407.

Maxwell, I., Seton, M., and Szabo, M. (2015, January). The Australian actors' wellbeing study: A preliminary report. In *About performance*. (No. 13, pp. 69–113). Sydney: Centre for Performance Studies.

McDonald, H.M., Sherman, K.A., Petocz, P., Kangas, M., Grant, K.A., and Kasparian, N. A. (2016). Mindfulness and the experience of psychological distress: the mediating effects of emotion regulation and attachment anxiety, *Mindfulness*, 7, 799–808.

McDonald, J., Alderdice, S., and Cutcliffe, K. (2019). The clown and the king: undergraduate actor training and wellbeing, *Theatre, Dance and Performance Training*, 10(1), 68–84.

Pillemer, D. B., Steiner, K. L., Kuwabara, K. J., Thomsen, D.K., and Svob, C. (2015). Vicarious memories, *Consciousness and Cognition*, 36, 233–245.

Randal, C., Pratt, D., & Bucci, S. (2015). Mindfulness and self-esteem: A systematic review, *Mindfulness*, 6, 1366–1378.

Robb, A.E., Due, C., and Venning, A. (2018). Exploring psychological wellbeing in a sample of Australian actors, *Australian Psychologist*, 53(1), 77–86.

Siddins, E.M., Daniel, R., and Johnstone, R. (2016). Building visual artists' resilience capabilities: Current educator strategies and methods, *Journal of Arts and Humanities*, 5(7), 24–37.

Stanislavski, C. (1936). *An Actor Prepares*. (E.R. Hapgood, Trans.). London: Geoffrey Bles.

Stanislavski, K. (2010). *An Actor's Work*. London: Routledge.

Van den Eynde, J., Fisher, A., and Sonn, C. (2016). *Working in the Australian Entertainment Industry*. Melbourne: Victoria University.

Vøllestad, J., Siversten, B., & Nielsen, G. H. (2011). Mindfulness-based stress reduction for patients with anxiety disorders: Evaluation in a randomized controlled trial, *Behaviour research and therapy*, 49(4), 281–288.

8

ACTOR TRAINING AND SELF-RELIANCE – THE AUTHENTIC VOICE AND KINDNESS

Dawn Ingleson

Introduction

In this chapter, we are '... seeing what happens when you begin to pay attention and act with kindness and compassion towards yourself and others, ...' (Kabat-Zinn in Williams and Penman, xi). I will outline why I think mindfulness is advantageous if not essential and perhaps inevitable, to explore in depth when working with Stanislavskian techniques. I will underline the similarities between what is being asked of us when we practice both Stanislavskian acting and mindfulness. I will also investigate and present the findings of teaching mindfulness with my first-year undergraduates at London South Bank University (LSBU) where I held the position of Course Leader for *Acting and Performance*. The constraints of this chapter are clear as I need more words than we have space for in a collection, and I feel like I am writing only an introduction to this exploration. However, starting points are necessary.

A Starting Point

The Coffee Cup Exercise is something that we have possibly taught or learned at some point in our training, an exercise in which you concentrate on experiencing a real coffee and then use the memory of it in performance. I was reminded of it this morning, having a cup of coffee as part of my mindfulness practice (and my breakfast), recognising experientially, once again, that actor training and mindfulness practice are the same learning in so many ways.

The 'Coffee Cup Exercise' was a favourite of Lee Strasberg's and, as we know, his Method Actor training comes from the English translation of the first half of Stanislavsky's System. As Sharon Marie Carnicke states in *Stanislavsky*

DOI: 10.4324/9781003517856-9

in Focus (2nd Edition), in the United States, practitioners, 'privileged the psychological techniques of Stanislavsky's System … The Method, as it became known in New York, defined itself primarily through this one aspect of the multivariant, holistic System' (Carnicke, 2009, 9). The Coffee Cup Exercise (outlined at the end of the chapter) is a way for actors to explore sensory/sense memory, a sibling or variant of emotion memory.[1] Drinking a cup of coffee mindfully is also a variant, this time of the 'Raisin Meditation' (a practice of slowing down and noticing everything about the raisin you are eating, using all your senses), included in Jon Kabat-Zinn's Mindfulness-Based Stress Reduction (MBSR) programme.[2] I studied the 8-week MBSR course in 2018, with weekly sessions and homework, including mindful practice in everyday experiences like walking, eating, drinking etc.

So, while having my coffee this morning, I was both practising mindfulness and participating in a classic acting preparation exercise in my awareness of what I was experiencing in the present moment, focusing, through all my senses, on an object. My personal experience underpins the rationale behind my practice-as-research with my students.

Scholars have been discussing Stanislavsky's use of Eastern techniques and yoga for years now, although it was at first veiled by the other more prominently placed ideas that were explored more fully in both the United States and the USSR. Stanislavsky was introduced to yoga and meditation by practitioners who worked with him (e.g. Demidov and Sulerzhitsky, his colleagues at the Moscow Art Theatre [MAT]) and books he had read (e.g. *Hatha Yoga* and *Raja Yoga* by William Walker Atkinson [or Yogi Ramacharaka as Stanislavsky knew him; for further information on his influences see Hitendra Kanji Solanki's chapter in this book]). He taught yoga and breathing exercises to his acting students. His interest in these techniques included how they could help actor to be fully focused and at the same time be relaxed in body and mind. This, in turn, was crucial to being open and present to hear, feel and experience what is on stage (or set) at any given moment. A relaxed (or released) body (and mind) help prevent any kind of stage fright as the concept of the 'negative' self-consciousness is accepted in a non-judgemental way and, with mindfulness, becomes a more 'positive' self-awareness: *The art of being present*. This encompasses the idea of the actor's dual-consciousness or double-consciousness[3] and meta-awareness, as Zarilli explains: 'The actor … is able to stay on task or in action while making adjustments as necessary to others, the activity, the audience, etc. in the moment' (Zarilli, 2009, 83). Although the term mindfulness was not used during this period, Stanislavsky leaned into mindfulness through yoga and meditation.

It has been shown now through evidence-based research that 'mindfulness training has the ability to improve our mental habits of attention at both the conscious and non-conscious levels' (Vago, n.d., TEDx Talk). Mindfulness also invites us to focus on the present helping us to engage in our lives, training and performance in a more able way. 'Thou shalt always live the given moment with all thy being' (Stanislavski, 2010 in Senelick, 248). Among others, the University of Huddersfield (UK), through their Mindfulness and Performance Project (MAP),[4] Centre for Psychophysical Performance Research and *Journal of Performance and Mindfulness* have researched the relationship between performing arts and mindfulness since at least 2016.

I came to mindfulness relatively late – but I now know it as a practice, a training, a way of being, of life, an attitude? Simply put, it is making a choice to be aware of the present moment, of whatever is arising in that moment, in a non-judgemental way. Mindfulness strips everything away, only *you*, your breath and whatever is there is present. On stage or in rehearsal, a mindful actor is in the present moment, aware of all their senses and experiencing each moment as it arrives, a simple, 'I am being' (Stanislavski, 2010, 69, 330). In this *being*, a lot is going on, and if we can understand or *notice* a bit more about what is happening in this moment, *the present*, we can be more truthful or believable and communicative actors. We can reach the creative state more easily and organically through the unconscious mind via intuition, inspiration or flow, and we can also look after ourselves better in rehearsal, in performance and in life. Mindfulness gives us an overview, a way through, and we can all access it as there is no right or wrong way to 'do it.' Zarilli states, when discussing actor training and the synthesising of two learned disciplines, 'a shift is necessary in order to apply what has been learned from the traditional training to a new form of artistic practice.' He gives an example of one traditionally trained actor's journey retraining to become a contemporary actor, saying that it 'necessarily involved an attempt to learn how to bring what he had absorbed from his traditional training to the unique problems of contemporary acting. But this is neither easy nor obvious' (Zarilli, 2009, 82). Mindfulness is a contemporary Westernised practice and is, as exemplified above, easily synthesised into modern acting techniques with no need to transpose or change any approach. However, it also talks to global perspectives on the mind and body and the Eastern (Asian, including Japanese and Chinese) concepts of the heart and mind being synonymous, as Zarilli discusses further on 'Asian Perspectives on mind, body, and emotion' (Zarilli, 2009, 76) in his exploration of Psychophysical Acting.

Mindfulness can allow us to be more aware of our habits; it can enable us to break these habits or release ourselves from them. It shifts us into a 'being mode' rather than a 'doing mode' (Williams and Penham, 2011, 34). It can release us from the grip of our autopilot. Autopilot is obviously a habit we have formed over our evolution, and is something that we clearly need sometimes when we are in doing mode (driving a manual car and changing gears automatically etc.); however, it is useful to engage in our awareness to override this option to us at times, to stop trying to solve any issues arising, but to just be with them as they float past in mental thoughts. All these aspects of what mindfulness asks us to do consciously, feed into our sub-conscious and opens us to being able to accept and receive what is there, in the present moment ('the transient now' [Stanislavsky in Merlin, 2001, 99]). We can then really see, hear, feel and be affected by our scene partners in etudes, rehearsal and performance.

Here, Today, Now

The biggest difference between when Stanislavsky was originating his actor training and modern-day actor training encompasses the ideas of distractibility and social interaction. These aspects of modern life have completely transformed into ways of being that Stanislavsky and his contemporaries possibly could not have even imagined. He knew that science in the future was going to reveal ideas about the brain, the mind, and even the spirit, and that cognitive science and neuroscience were going to develop much better knowledge of how the 'bodymind' (Zarilli, 2009, 4) work together. In her abundance of reflections on Stanislavsky, Merlin, over twenty years ago, was propounding that 'the compartmentalisation of thought, feeling and will becomes increasingly problematic with further investigations into the "bodymind" or brain-body interdependence of neuronal activity. I certainly foresee some evolutions in the forthcoming years of Stanislavski's "system" in this area too, as indeed I intuit will be the case with "soul" and "spirit"' (Merlin and Мерлин, 2012, 54). Stanislavsky knew instinctively that the body and mind work together and that is what the actor had to engage with to make believable truthful performance. However, I am not sure many of us would have foreseen the intrusion in our lives, on our focus and communion that social media and the smartphone has had. Social media and the internet have obviously helped us to communicate further and with more people than we could have done so easily in the past. It has many positives, as we know because most of us in the West use a smartphone as part of our everyday life. In fact, in their 6th annual report, published in October 2023, the Global System for Mobile Association (GSMA) – an association that was set up to ensure that all mobile phone systems were able to communicate seamlessly across the world – revealed that, 'smart phone owners are now the global majority' (Shanahan and Bahia, 2023, 4), basically 4.3 billion people – over half of the global population. There is still a coverage and usage gap, and 3.4 billion people remain unconnected, most of them female and from rural areas, especially in Sub-Saharan Africa and South Asia.[5] However, the impact on our lives is huge. For the digital native, this world is the only one they have known and the pressures of using the myriad platforms are real and pressing. We are asked to multi-task, feeding our need for dopamine, and reducing our attention span as much of what we watch and read online is short and pithy. Bad behaviour due to anonymity is prevalent, trolling is a thing, and we have figured out how to bully each other in cyber space. Yet, we can experience fear of missing out (FOMO) by the swipe of a screen, peer pressure constantly making demands of us, and the whole phenomenon is comparable to an addiction. The explosion of opportunities to communicate has simultaneously, and ironically, led to a rise in social isolation (simply google it!). This, alongside aspects of our lives like Covid-19, identity crises, culture wars, the #MeToo movement and the murder of George Floyd has created both a different kind of interaction with others and a different relationship with ourselves. It is in this moment that I suggest that Stanislavsky's System can be foregrounded efficiently and kindly with mindfulness.

Kindly with Mindfulness

I led mindfulness practice in one first-year module of the Acting and Performance undergraduate course at London South Bank University (LSBU).[6] It was a process-based module, focusing on what we were doing in class, not creating any polished performance at the end of semester, although there were mini projects throughout resulting in short performances from a set of etudes etc. It was about focus, responding to your scene partner/s or creating a connection with your audience, exploring different techniques and being present for yourself and each other. Some of the work was individual, some with a partner, a small group or the ensemble. It was about communication and communion, and it was my role to provide a space that was 'safe', but only in so far as within that space, we could take risks and be brave. In fact, it was not a safe space as such, but an empathetic and compassionate space that gave everyone the confidence to trust and be trustworthy. This allowed it to be a creative space because, as Merlin states, 'a creative atmosphere is safe. It's trusting and nurturing. At the same time, it's bold. It's dangerous and daring. It's playful – yet serious. It's sincere – yet mischievous. To exist in it is joyous' (Merlin, 2007, 50). It was a class where we could ask ourselves to go further than we thought we could (and students often did, with great pleasure and increased self-awareness), with the knowledge that our classmates were there for and with us, supporting each other with humour and kindness. We did not judge in this space, or at least we did not pre-judge; we critiqued both our own work and the work of each other via feedback as part of the class by discussing what we saw as audience, what we felt as performer, what we would be interested in seeing more of, and what we perhaps didn't fully follow. We practiced critiquing our own work privately and used a well-known reflective cycle[7] to evaluate what we were doing, how we experienced the learning/tasks, and how we could use those exercises in the context of our other modules, especially our plays in production.

There is nothing unusual about this. Similar modules take place at any institution undertaking undergraduate actor training. However, the mindfulness before each class seemed to be more of a settling force than what had preceded it. We used to 'Check-in', going round the circle of students before the warm-up, asking everyone to actively listen, but with no response or habitual mirroring (nodding etc.) as each student would say how they were feeling physically, mentally and about the work. This felt important, especially after the pandemic and the enforced separation it led to. It seemed to be the right thing to do to try to articulate how we were on that specific day/moment so that we all knew and could respond to it. Then the idea was to leave that at the door and to get on with the work renewed with the knowledge that everyone was clear 'where we were coming from'. I am unsure that this helped anyone, ultimately, to leave their outside life at the door, as we had already 'checked it in'. So, I changed to 'checking in' with ourselves via mindfulness and a focus on 'choosing kindness' above everything else in the room. In this space, and with this attitude, it seems we can leave our outside lives at the door, or at least they would not interfere with what is happening within the classroom/rehearsal. Indeed, more awareness is present. Students evidenced this, stating, for example, 'I've felt a lot more productive and aware of people's emotions', another student adding how mindfulness affects their approach, 'before lessons, to clear my head and bring a positive ready to learn head space, but also that I am focused and have left any dramas or worries then and there'.

The yearly cohorts were diverse groups. It was part of my role as their guide and teacher to help them to find their authentic voice. To do this, they must know themselves and use their university career to develop their self-knowledge so they can draw on their lived experiences and feel empowered to do so knowing that others will listen.

Mindfulness helped with this process as the starting point of each session was to notice our inner self and what 'is happening right now'. We needed to take time to find our real selves, beyond the habits and conditioning that have created the 'you' you know so well. When my colleague, Hitendra Kanji Solanki, and I worked with my students on prolonged mindfulness practice, we discussed moving from conceptual thought to non-conceptual experience. The beginner's mind, being aware to all your senses. The breath allowing us to ground into *this present moment*. We opened to see/observe/notice our mind as it really was. As actors, we were getting to know ourselves more in each moment, we noticed the habitual patterns in the mind, the automatic pilot that we use. With kindness, we began organically to lengthen our attention span and increase our ability to be patient and concentrate. This is the safe – and brave – space that we can cultivate as training actors. In mindfulness, we talk about thoughts passing like clouds, emotions can too as we develop compassion for ourselves.

What the Students Say

I worked with all first-year students each week for a whole academic year (2023–24). 16 out of a year group of 33 were available to continue studying mindfulness for a further 3 weeks, in a more intensive practice after the end of the spring/summer semester. These were the students I surveyed. (Students both had opportunities to reflect on their practice in the sessions verbally and

FIGURE 8.1 Students feedback after an intensive mindfulness session. Photo by Dawn Ingleson.

afterwards in writing, see Figure 8.1 above.) The survey was checked by the university Ethics Committee and the questionnaires were carefully anonymised. Having written about my practice-as-research for a *Stanislavski Studies* journal article in 2022,[8] I wanted to find out, in more detail, if and how prolonged mindfulness practice could help the acting students become more 'mindful actors'. This included a self-reliance and an ability to tune into their authentic self to begin to play other characters with more awareness and presence.

58% of this cohort had heard of mindfulness before coming to university, and 42% had practiced it. When asked about anxiety, the entire sample were affected to some extent or other: 71% replied they did experience anxiety and 29% said they did 'sometimes'. To alleviate anxiety and too much stress, 33% of students were in therapy or took medication, and a third used 'distractions' to stop negative thoughts. The rest employed a mixture of calming affirmations, the use of quiet spaces, listening to music or 'doing something else' like walking or watching TV. Some students mentioned aspects of what seems like mindfulness, e.g., 'not fight against the feeling, when I respect it and let it pass, it feels a lot less world-ending' and breath work. In answer to the question – *Are you diagnosed with any form of mental ill-health that affects your levels of anxiety?* 43% of the cohort said they were and 14% said they suspected they should be. Everyone suggested that they spent too much time on their mobile phone. The most time being 'more than 9 hours' a day by 21%, 7–8 hours (21%), 6–7 hours (7%), 5–6 hours (21%) and 3–4 hours (29%). Nobody thought they should be on their phone for more than 5–6 hours and the biggest group (37%) thought they should only be on it for 1–2 hours per day to have a healthy relationship with it. As a cohort, they spent much less time exploring other interests, even though as a group they mentioned a wide range of activities (ranging from individual pursuits such as writing, reading, playing an instrument and baking to activities with others, including socialising, spending time with family and being a member of a dance or music society/group).

Regular mindfulness practice throughout their training has been a positive experience for all, increasing everyone's concentration and ability to focus, apart from one student, who was unsure but stated that they were more aware of their concentration span. Another said they needed to do it more for *more of* an affect; however they said that they felt kinder towards themselves because of it. Everyone, with the exception of two students who did not respond, said that they had become better listeners after practicing mindfulness and most had noticed an increase in their confidence levels: Two students did not answer about confidence, a third said it was 'not applicable' and a fourth said they 'were not quite sure about this one'. All, with the exception of one respondent who said, 'maybe', said they wanted to carry on with mindfulness, 70% saying 'definitely' rather than just answering 'yes'.

The students noticed new things about themselves and recognised that they had a different relationship with their classmates. 'A stronger sense of community', one stated. They described having 'more focus and awareness of their surroundings', being 'more productive as a group/cast and aware of people's emotions', 'more attentive to what ideas and opinions one might have', 'listening more', 'centred, present to the task in hand', 'more comfortable' and 'closer to the other students'. 'We all feel ready to work.' One student reported that they could 'be vulnerable openly and allow myself to feel how the character feels in truth without a mental block'.

When asked '*Does mindfulness affect your acting and, if so, how?*' the students described finding a 'stronger sense of meaning within a character or dialogue', being, 'more in the moment', 'a sense of calmness – can separate myself from my character', 'helps to find a truth to my characters, being able to approach their feelings with clarity and brings me closer to achieving an impulse to be more alive and aware on stage'. Students mentioned 'being more connected to others' and 'more at ease with creative risk taking'; one student declared that they have 'more confidence in playing with choices I have been told that I seem more natural and calm'. Each student had gained something positive from the work, which filtered into the acting process and seemed to give them more of a grounded experience starting with themselves and a more compassionate view of their own self-worth. I noticed that mindfulness was allowing them to take more risks in rehearsal, knowing that the cast was behind them and, in turn, it gave them more moments of finding the 'creative state' in performance.

Rather than concluding, as we are still all on our journeys, I have listed a small selection of exercises that I used. However, I paid attention each day to myself and my students being curious about the world (of the play or in general), and taking a moment to step aside, 'watching the world as it unfolds, while allowing it to be *just as it is* for a moment … without preconceptions … In this way, [we] are saved from closing down [our] creative options' (Williams and Penham, 2011, 40), which is what Stanislavsky asks us to continue to develop at all times.

What We Did in Class

Each class began with phones off and away and mindfulness. There are many practices to choose from and they can last anything from a 3-minute breathing space which you can take with you anywhere (I use mine most often travelling on the underground), a 20-minute sitting practice to a 45-minute body scan and beyond, including movement meditation and in everyday moments – including queuing and washing up.

Exercise 1 3-minute breathing space

Narrate the students through the exercise starting with something like:

Ring chimes x3

1 Ask the students to sit erect and dignified as a signal to themselves that they are about to take some action to look after themselves.
Feet on the ground, inviting an awareness of our inner experience – perhaps closing our eyes and noticing our experience from the inside – noticing thoughts. Not struggling to find them but noticing if they are there right now. If not, noticing that our mind is blank. Either is fine.
Tuning in *as best we can* to emotions and mood, with an open heart, noticing what is there and acknowledging the presence of feelings or the relative absence of them. Perhaps scanning through the body noticing any tension or temperature, any areas that are relaxed.
2 Move our attention to the breath – we can place our hand on our tummy and picking up the movement of the breath, bringing our full attention to the breath moving in and out, a wave-like motion. When we notice that the mind has wandered (as it will), simply bring it back, picking up the next wave of breath.
3 Gently expand our attention to the rest of the body – move up the body from our feet to our legs, trunk, shoulders, arms. Notice how our arms are hanging from our shoulders here and now in this moment. Bring awareness to our head and face – our jaw, eyebrows. Gently noticing our whole-body experience. Now notice any sounds around us; notice the space that we are in, the world surrounding us as we breathe. Open to our environment, we can open our eyes and gently take our practice into the rest of the day as best we can.

Ring chimes x 3

Exercise 2 Circles of Attention

Mindfulness *'Circles of attention'* **Anchor points of awareness**

Body grounded to the earth.

Breath grounded within the body.

The attention grounded to the breath.

Stanislavsky's *'Circles of Attention'* & **Objects of attention**

Small – imagine a pool of light that just illuminates your immediate surroundings – Stanislavsky uses a 'little lamp' (Stanislavsky & Benedetti, 92) in *An Actor's Work* on a small table to hold a tight focus.

Medium – adding more objects to the bigger circle of focus which may cover most of the playing area for example.

Large – expanding the circle to the full size of the room/theatre with all its objects.

You define your circles as you perform, including the objects of attention that you need. You can return to your breath for focus/awareness/attention within your body and you can return to the smallest circle of attention on stage if you need to re-focus your concentration.

Bella Merlin has already synthesised mindfulness to attention through Stanislavsky's circles in *The Complete Stanislavsky Toolkit*. You will find the full version of this exercise on pages 280–281.

Exercise 3 Chakras and Grasp (Merlin, 2007, 314–316)

Again, I refer the reader to the relaxation exercises in Merlin's *Toolkit*. We would start with an exploration of our Chakras (Merlin, 2007, 269) and explore solo and partner work with non-verbal communication.

This is a version of *Grasp* with a scene partner adapted from a workshop with Bella Merlin. It also draws on practice learned from Robert and Elen Bowman (Living Pictures Productions):

Check that students know where the solar plexus is. Remind them throughout to force nothing, censor nothing, dare to be simple. What are you feeling here, today, now? What is there in your partner's eyes?

Check that people are being physically relaxed throughout – face, jaw, arms etc.

After this exercise you can move to performing the scene with a focus on eye contact, responding and being alive in the moment to each other.

1 At the start, you are working as yourselves, not in character. Let go of the need to be interesting or entertaining. Decide who is A and B and always keep eye contact with each other. Don't speak verbally, let your eyes communicate. Touch palms, use the same hand as your partner, maintain eye contact. This might make you feel vulnerable, or laugh; this is fine. Imagine that there is a golden ball of energy/yellow light in your solar plexus that is gently rotating and massaging you from the inside. Imagine a coiled spring of energy between your solar plexus and your partner's or a golden beam of light.

Now A will lead B in the space.

Maintaining eye contact, pause, lower your hands, shake out, move to the other hand, swap leaders.

Again, lower, shake, swap hands. Now let the change of leaders happen organically. Come to moments of pause when you change the leadership.

2 Now work with your hands about 10 cm apart. Imagine that the energy that connects you comes from your solar plexus. Now that the hands are gone, the connection between you is perhaps stronger than before.

3 Let your arms drop but maintain that sense of connection.

4 Imagine that you are a vessel of clear water into which drops of your character are dropping and percolating one at a time. See what you get from them today.

30% character, 70% you

50% character, 50% you

70% character, 30% you – now add the last drops, so you are fully in character.

Still working with your partner:

Think about a happy time with this person

A less happy time (specific imagery/memory)

What you like most about this person

What you like least

Something that you would like to tell this person (something specific)

Something you hope they never find out (something specific).

Exercise 4 Imaginary Coffee (or any drink) for Sense Memory/Mindfulness

(a variation of the Mindfulness 'Chocolate' (Williams & Penman, 55) or 'Raisin' meditations (73)).

1 Sit comfortably with a real cup of coffee.
2 Look at it in detail, notice all its physical qualities.
3 Pick it up, feel its weight and notice how you hold it.
4 Feel the heat of the cup and the drink.
5 Smell it. How does it smell?
6 Taste it. How does it taste?
7 Experience the drink slowly and notice everything you can about this moment.
8 Now put it down and repeat 'the exercise' with an imaginary coffee cup.

This exercise helps you to develop belief in the imaginary as well as a mindful enhancement of the 'joys of daily life' (Williams and Penham, 2011, 54). To conjure a believable and useful world of the play, this exercise, when set up mindfully, can be a reminder not to 'pretend' but to engage in the moment of action in a believable way.

Notes

1 See chapter 9, Stanislavski, (2010), *An Actor's Work*. Oxon: Routledge.
2 Outlined in detail in Kabat-Zinn, J. (2008), *Full Catastrophe Living*. London: Piatkus Books.
3 See page 47 in Zazzali, P. & Питер Заззали (2014) Examination of the Actor's Double-Consciousness Through Stanislavski's Conceptualization of 'Artistic Truth', *Stanislavski Studies*, 2:2, 47–65, DOI:10.1080/20567790.2014.11419723.
4 The Mindfulness and Performance Project Team were Deborah Middleton and Franc Chamberlain (both University of Huddersfield) and Daniel Plá (University of Santa Maria, Brazil).
5 See https://www.gsma.com/r/somic/ for further details.
6 See my article that prefaced this collection for further information: Ingleson, D. (2022). Stanislavski training and mindfulness – being in the moment. *Stanislavski Studies*, *10*(2), 161–176. https://doi.org/10.1080/20567790.2022.2094103.
7 See Gibbs' Reflective Cycle | The University of Edinburgh.
8 For further details, see note 6.

References

Carnicke, S.M. (2009) *Stanislavsky in Focus (2nd Edition) An Acting Master for the Twenty-First Century.* Oxon: Routledge. https://www.gsma.com (Accessed 29.08.24).

Merlin, B. (2001), *Beyond Stanislavsky. The Psycho-Physical Approach to Actor Training.* London: Nick Hern Books.

Merlin, B. (2007), *The Complete Stanislavsky Toolkit.* London: Nick Hern Books.

Merlin, B. and Мерлин, Б. (2012). 'Where's the spirit gone?' The complexities of translation and the nuances of terminology in *An Actor's Work* and an actor's work, *Stanislavski Studies*, 1(1), 43–86.

Shanahan, M. and Bahia, K., (2023), *The State of Mobile Internet Connectivity 2023*, GSMA. https://www.gsma.com/r/wp-content/uploads/2023/10/The-State-of-Mobile-Internet-Connectivity-Report-2023.pdf (Accessed 18.09.24).

Stanislavski, K. (2010), *An Actor's Work.* Oxon: Routledge.

Vago, D., n.d., Self-transformation through mindfulness, TEDxNashville https://www.youtube.com/watch?v=1nP5oedmzkM (Accessed 19.09.24).

Williams M. & Penham, D., (2011), *Mindfulness: A Practical Guide to Finding Peace in a Frantic World*, London: Piatkus.

Zarilli, P., (2009), *Psychophysical Acting – An Intercultural Approach After Stanislavski.* Oxon: Routledge.

9

THE IMPORTANCE OF MINDFULNESS IN THE ACTOR'S PREPARATION FOR THE ROLE IN STANISLAVSKY'S SYSTEM

Inga Romantsova

In the realm of acting, the pursuit of authenticity, and a profound connection with character and the audience is of utmost importance. Actors often explore a variety of techniques and practices to achieve these goals. One technique that has gained prominence in recent years is mindfulness, which involves a state of self-awareness and being present in the moment. This chapter will examine the significance of mindfulness in an actor's preparation for a role using Stanislavsky's techniques. Konstantin Sergeevich Stanislavsky believed that, in cultivating authentic performances, actors must develop creative intuition, depth of knowledge, and an active imagination through self-awareness.

My exploration of the significance of self-awareness and mindfulness in an actor's preparation for a role draws inspiration from John Kabat Zinn's definition of mindfulness, purposefully paying attention in the present moment without judgement. This definition aligns with Stanislavsky's concept of *public solitude* in *Zapisnye knizhki* (Stanislavsky, 2003, 1912–1938),[1] Stanislavsky's *Notebooks*[2] reveal how he viewed public solitude on stage to free the actor from the debilitating effect of a large audience. An actor must immerse himself in the powerful experience of public solitude to unlock the true essence of stage artistry. Only then is an actor able to feel the freedom to express themselves authentically on stage, letting go of all inhibitions and self-consciousness, embrace the transformative practice and watch as the performances reach new levels of character emotion. To experience on stage, to truly embody a character, actors must first immerse themselves in a profound sense of isolation; by focusing inward and avoiding external distractions, actors can tap into

DOI: 10.4324/9781003517856-10

their deepest emotions and circle of attention, or *solitude in public* (*publichnoe odinochestvo*).

> What could be more distracting for an actor, than the huge black hole of the portal…it's not so difficult to distract yourself from it; the secret turns out to be quite simple; in order to distract yourself from the audience, you need to get carried away by what's on the stage…
>
> (*Stanislavsky, 1985, 112, trans. I.R.*)

Purposefully paying attention in the present moment without judgement.

However, what we naturally do in life may not always be easy to replicate on stage.

> Remember now, all, even the simplest, most elementary actions which we know perfectly well in life fall apart when someone makes an entrance onstage, in the glare of the footlights, in front of a packed house. That is why we must learn to walk, move, sit, lie down all over again…you must learn to look and see, listen and hear onstage, too.
>
> (*Stanislavsky, trans. Benedetti, 2008, 122*)

This concept is tied to how actors focus their attention on stage. Normally, our attention is driven by what is around us. But on stage, actors need to focus deliberately and mindfully on their character's situation, tasks, and actions.

> Actors can train their attention through various exercises, learning to concentrate on different levels. They can make their focus broad, like imagining themselves in the whole universe, or very narrow, like concentrating on the chair they are sitting on.[3]
>
> (*Stanislavsky, 1986, 63–64*)

Stanislavskian belief is that an actor with good technique can selectively focus within this circle of attention. They will be aware of their surroundings but not distracted by them, almost feeling alone even in front of an audience. In this public solitude, actors can portray their characters more believably and authentically.

It is within this space that true artistry is born, where actors can fully connect with their character on a profound level. The power of solitude in public and self-reflection underscores the significant impact it can have on the art of acting and on the relationship with the audience.

Stanislavsky's invention of the first/small circle of attention acts as a tool for actors to prevent themselves from being distracted by 'the black hole' or from feeling 'the magnet of the audience' (Machková and Rais, 2023, 69–86). An actor develops a state of pure awareness involving entering the theatrical realm with a beginner's mind, experiencing everything as if it were happening, organically, and for the first time, the actor must understand the organic elements of their own nature:

> To explore and understand your organic elements, as well as the habits that have become ingrained in your life. It is important to work on oneself not only on stage, but also in everyday life. I suggest taking some time to reflect on yourself when you are alone or at night when everything is quiet and peaceful. Perhaps it is best to embrace tea, surrounded by nature while on vacation, or at any other time when we can be truly authentic. It is important to connect with the organic elements of our soul, much like a tuning fork finds the right tone in music. By staying true to our nature and being honest with ourselves, we can have a more genuine and fulfilling creative experience as artists.
>
> *(Stanislavsky, 1986, 62)*

Mindfulness served as a foundation for Stanislavsky's training exercises. These principles were deeply rooted in yoga. The extent of influence of yoga in Stanislavsky's work initially surprises many actors, teachers, and students. It certainly was news to me, as a graduate of St. Petersburg National Academy of Theatrical Arts during Soviet times, that nearly 40 percent of the fundamental exercises in modern Stanislavsky-based acting training programs can be traced back to yoga.

Sergei Tcherkasski's research in *Stanislavsky and Yoga* (2012) delves into the principles of yoga embedded in Stanislavsky's System. Tcherkasski explores concepts like muscle relaxation, communication through *prana* (vital life force), attention and concentration, and the use of mental images for affective memory, interacting with real and imaginary individuals, and establishing a shared atmosphere with the audience. The goal is to impact viewers on a profound level, transcending personal identities and fostering a sense of communal connection with a strong emphasis on the subconscious. However, it is worth noting that the terms yoga or subconscious were omitted from Stanislavsky's later writings due to censorship, and certain words and terms like spirit, and subconsciousness disappear during Stanislavsky's time due to the Communist Party-political constraints in the Soviet Union in 1930.

> It had involved Stanislavsky in one final ideological battle with the authorities. On receiving the proofs, he noted that the word 'unconscious' had been systematically struck out. He was obliged to write to the Central Committee of the Communist Party to have the word restored. He also decided, wisely no doubt, to styling the book's final paragraphs in which he had spoken once more of the Unconscious.
>
> *(Benedetti, 1999, 375)*

Benedetti's research also reveals that editors of *An Actor Prepares*, for example, removed certain words from Stanislavsky's notes such as 'spirit'. Self-imposed censorship also demonstrated how Stanislavsky adapted his teachings to prevailing societal norms.

Despite the challenges, he incorporated yoga exercises into his teachings across various acting studios and classes. Yoga's influence can be observed throughout his career, from the early stages at the Moscow Art Theatre to his later years at the Opera Studio. Stanislavsky's interest in yoga is well-documented and offers a fascinating insight into the intersection of acting and ancient wisdom.

One of the most popular exercises recommended by Stanislavsky involves mindfully paying attention to everyday tasks using both real and imaginative objects. This exercise trains muscle memory and affective (emotional) memory and helps actors bring life to inanimate objects on stage. By observing minuscule details in the performance of these tasks, actors develop a deep connection to their characters, the scene, and stage partners during the creative process and self-awareness on stage.

Another exercise for self-awareness is the use of silent etudes, and this might be described as a meditative state, in which an actor achieves stillness and concentrates on the silence of their own heart. Playing etudes and characters without words helps actors convey the essence and energy of a scene through non-verbal communication. The organic creation of life on stage can awaken a similar spirit in the viewer, fostering a feeling of communion. Stanislavsky emphasises the importance of communication through ray energy, which involves sending and receiving energy streams from people and objects. This practice extends to talking to both real and imaginary people, communicating through eyes and body language, and creating a shared atmosphere with the audience.

The idea of being fully present in each moment is explored through Active Analysis and touches upon the concept of the supertask and throughline of action. Such ideas go beyond the objectives and tasks of a character; focusing on the artist's desire to communicate something profound and important through their work and connect with the audience on a subconscious level to create an atmosphere of shared experience. This is the artist's goal. However, Stanislavsky does not explicitly define the subconscious. Instead, he acknowledges its presence as a phenomenological fact, derived from observation, without engaging in theoretical speculation. Stanislavsky himself experienced the joy of inspired performances through the observation of great masters.

How did great performers effectively navigate the unique energy that exists between the audience and the actors? Stanislavsky's approach to integrating mindfulness into an actor's preparatory process, with the goal of tapping into subconscious processes, was designed to enhance authenticity and credibility in stage performances, thereby fostering a deeper connection with the audience. The primary focus for artists should be on cultivating a genuine creative mindset based on truth, nature, and beauty. By tapping into this state, our innate creative elements can surface from our innermost feelings, evoking instinctive, natural subconscious creativity, which is intrinsically valuable in art. The second concern of the artist is the connection with the audience, through creative tasks that captivate natural creative will.

> To act without an audience is like singing in a place with no resonance.
>
> To perform for a receptive audience is like singing in a room with perfect acoustics. The audience provides the spiritual acoustics for us, reflecting the living human emotions they receive from us.
>
> *(Stanislavsky, 1986, 63)*

The challenge lies in managing emotional connections with both our stage partners and the audience. With the former, our connection is direct and conscious, while with the latter, it is indirect and unconscious. An important aspect to highlight here is the role of the subconscious relationship with the audience; it is vital to ask how an actor can participate in a communal relationship with the audience. This represents one of the major advancements in Stanislavsky's theory of acting – that the spirit of theatre, the spirit of performance, is a communal spirit. This realisation elevates acting beyond mere performances in a theatre building. He recognised that this state of mind is not common among artists, and he dedicated his life to helping them find techniques and tools that could elicit this heightened creative force deliberately. These techniques include evoking plausible emotions, employing the power of imagination, creating specific circumstances, focusing on the task at hand, engaging in rich communication with partners, and awakening the artist's civic and human consciousness. The goal is to tap into the artist's true passions and provide a genuine source of inspiration to activate the subconscious processes in an actor's preparation for a role.

This subconscious process, in my opinion, aims to create a communal effect; the actor establishes a connection with the audience, breaking down the imaginary barrier between them and encouraging emotional engagement. It also highlights the challenge of navigating the complex dynamics between the actors and the audience; actors must be aware of their dual-mind participation in a communal relationship with the spectators. Be aware of themselves, their character objectives and how it influences the audience. Once more, this impact on the audience places a significant emphasis on the role of the subconscious mind, recognising that the spirit of theatre extends beyond the confines of a physical theatre and becomes a shared experience. Despite this, Stanislavsky abstains from defining the concept of the subconscious. Instead, he avoids any attempts to theorise about this crucial element, opting to simply acknowledge its existence as mentioned previously, a phenomenological fact, as an observation.

Drawing inspiration from observing masterful performances, Stanislavsky experienced the joy of inspired play. He perfectly remembered Pushkin's definition of inspiration as 'the disposition of the soul to the liveliest perception of the impressions of life' (Senelick, 1981, 59). He knew that such a disposition of the soul rarely occurs in an artist, and he spent his life helping to find 'tools' and devices that evoke this higher creative force 'by order'. Specialists are also endeavouring to scientifically comprehend Stanislavsky's practical insights,[4] particularly his distinct differentiation between the inspiration, 'subconscious' and 'superconscious' aspects of an artist. It might be suggested that these terms represent profound connection in the creative process, with the superconscious delving into uncharted territories of discovery and invention while the subconscious deals with automated responses and expressions of familiar emotions. Stanislavsky's efforts aimed to harness the energy of the superconscious, which fuels innovative artistic concepts that challenge conventional consciousness.

Performing with inspiration means performing mindfully with the beginners' mind,[5] here and now. Mindfulness, which both cultivates and allows for inspiration's natural occurrences such as subconsciousness, is discussed by many academics. According to Bella Merlin's book, *The Complete Stanislavsky Toolkit*, being present in the moment can facilitate inspiration and improve subconscious communication between performers and the audience.[6] It seeks to engage the psychophysical body and stimulate active imagination.

In his book, *Psychophysical Acting – An Intercultural Approach After Stanislavski*, Phillip Zarrilli's exploration of the psychophysical actor further elucidates the significance of mindful breath as a vital force in acting. Zarrilli's concept of the psychophysical body highlights the role of vital energy, particularly in the form of breath, in animating an actor's performance.

> Acting should not be viewed as embodying a representation of a role or character, but rather as a dynamic, lived experience in which the actor is responsive to the demands of the particular moment within a specific (theatrical) environment.
>
> *(Zarrilli, 2007 638)*

Stanislavsky's focus on breath during rehearsals at the Opera-Studio exemplifies the vitalising nature of this essential life force. The utilisation of energy and subconscious exchange behaving as a catalyst for heightened awareness aligns with Zarrilli's notion that feelings manifest outwardly in expressions simultaneously.

> According to this alternative paradigm or meta-theory, it may be more useful to consider acting in terms of its dynamic energetics than in terms of representation. Acting according to an inactive paradigm is not in the first instance about meaning or representation; rather, it implies an energetic

> theatre is a theatre not of meaning but of forces, intensities, present affects. Meaning and representation may present themselves to the viewer or critic of a performance, but they are the result of the actor's immediate energetic engagement in the act of performance and the spectator's experience of that performance.
>
> *(Zarrilli, 2007, 647)*

To summarise, Stanislavsky's emphasis on the energy that animates and activates actors underscores the profound effect of breath and vitality in the performance process. The mindful integration of breath as a potent force in mindful acting practice illuminates the interconnectedness of physical and psychological dynamics in the art of performance.

The mindfulness in an actor's preparation for the role is a process which involves tuning into the silence within one's own heart, allowing oneself to relax and access a state of deep connection with one's true organic nature, to tap into a unique inner power that goes beyond mere cognitive comprehension. However, reaching this potential is often impeded by entrenched habits and stereotypes prevalent in the acting industry. Furthermore, the discourse on an actor's preparation emphasises exploring subconsciousness.

Mindfulness has gained popularity among modern actors, and many have integrated mindfulness practices, such as meditation, focusing on the breath, and active imagination/visualisation, into their contemporary preparations for roles and routines. These methods assist in alleviating anxiety, enhancing focus, and promoting emotional depth in performances on both stage and screen.

From the plausibility of feelings, the magic if, the proposed circumstances, and the awakened fantasy, from the ability to concentrate, determine the task and through action, the ability of rich communication and interaction with a partner, and from civil and human awakening, Stanislavsky's integration of yoga principles and mindfulness practices into the acting techniques offers valuable insights for modern actors. The following exercises and concepts discussed pave the way for authentic performances, creative intuition, and a profound connection with both the characters and the audience. By embracing mindfulness and self-awareness, actors can tap into their true potential and evoke powerful emotions on stage and embodying organic existence, tap into the subconscious creativity that is akin to the forces of nature. My personal experience as a professional actress, and my pedagogical attitude in actor training of the System, places a great importance on the spiritual and communal aspects of stage performances. It is a training of self-awareness; a wholehearted, meditative state, a professional tuning of an instrument, concentrating on the silence in the actor's heart. This mindful, organic state of being fosters unconscious creativity, often referred by Stanislavsky as the sorceress of nature.[7]

During training, my first-year students' tasks consist of playing silent etudes and animals/characters – where words are not required, but the essence of the scene, and the energy between actors and subtext must be very clear. The main outcome of this is that the *living spirit of the viewer* awakens under the influence of the organically created *life of the human spirit* on stage, and the viewer ascends from her personal identity by joining an experience of communal spirit.

Exercise 1 Attention and concentration

Typewriter

Develops concentration and trains the ability to think on stage.

A warm-up for a class of 16 people (10 minutes) to focus on attention and to train the ability to think on stage.

You can start with one word and then progress to whole phrases.

1 Organise the group in a semicircle. Distribute letters of the alphabet, so each person is a letter (in a small group everyone can get two or three letters).
2 The teacher says one word, example: "white"
The participant, who is the letter W, claps when it's his/her turn.
Then the student who was assigned the letter H, claps.
Those students who have the letters "I", "T", "E", clap in turn

Exercise 2 Public solitude

Reading the newspaper

Aimed at training the ability to think on stage by working with the small circle of attention.

Exploring concentration and attention, public solitude with dual consciousness.

A solo activity (5 minutes per student). Severity of time and difficulty of the article progressively grows.

You need a newspaper or magazine article or a chapter of a book.

1 Student reads an article in a newspaper on stage and describes what it is about OR
Teacher gives the student something to read, sitting on the stage, while the others make noise, sing, talk loudly and/or ask questions.
The student keeps reading, trying to answer the questions.

2 After finishing the exercise, the teacher and other students, who are observing the reader, ask the student what the article is about. The student must summarise what they have read.
3 The teacher and classmates ask specific questions about statistics, names, or objects etc., mentioned in the article. They can ask about questioning itself, e.g., "Who asked you this question?", "Do you remember what you have answered?" etc.

Exercise 3 Playing an animal as a silent etude

The organically created "life of the human spirit"

For 2–5 participants (10–25 minutes per lesson). You can practice through one term, creating the scene for a 5-minute performance.

To help, you can visit the zoo or farm for observation and practise. This helps with observation skills.

1 Mime the movement of animals, for example, Sparrow, crow, hedgehog, ram, raccoon, wolf, turtle.
2 Create a scenario with the chosen animals' interactions e.g., a tiger in sleeping position, waking up, moving towards the zoo worker, to grab his piece of meat for dinner.
   Obstacles are the tiger stops and concentrates on the surroundings, observes the audience etc.

Exercise 4 Silent etude

"Moving to a new apartment"

Building the logic of behaviour on stage and inner monologue for 2 people (20 minutes). Practise through the term to create a scene for assessment. Use a real set with real aspects of an apartment and a doll for the baby. The aim is to build the logic of the human spirit in silent behaviour.

1 The child is sleeping. Parents move to a new apartment.
2 The car has arrived, and the careful removal of items begins, silently, so as not to wake the child. Almost all things are taken out, and the parents say goodbye to the old apartment.

Exercise 5 Saw the log

Working without an object *Invincible object as precise as real object.*

These exercises, for two players, are called PFD (*pamyat' phyzicheskih deistvii* – memory of physical actions). Repeating an exercise a few times, remembering nuances and muscle tension. (About 10–15 minutes) This trains concentration and attention, partnership and public solitude.

1 Two participants pick up a heavy log and saw it in two with a two-handled saw. The actors must concentrate on the object and their activity, but they also must pay attention to each other.
2 Pick up the log (which can be real or imaginary): practice by themselves.

   Observe the heaviness and muscle tension.
   Feel it, weigh it.
   Make a note of a small detail on the log.
   Start to saw it – notice each move of the saw.

3 Repeat from the start
   Do it without object if you had previously done it with one. (The goal is to perform the exercise without a real object as precisely and accurately as possible.)

Notes

1 K. Stanislavsky (1986), *Zapisnye Knizhki*. I have translated a section from *Notebooks in 2 volumes*. 1988–1911 and 1912–1938 published by Vserosijskoe Teatralnoje Obshestvo, Moscow. *Zapisnye knizhki (Notebooks)* is a collection of notes written by Stanislavsky during his work on the System, and during various rehearsals, edited from MAT archives by Prokofiev B.N., and previously not translated.
2 Stanislavsky wrote about the concept of 'public solitude' in his *Notebooks* directly related to another element of the System – stage attention. Unlike attention in everyday, stage attention is arbitrary, i.e. the actor, through an effort of will, mindfully concentrates and maintains attention on the proposed circumstances, task, action with which she/he is directly engaged on stage. Attention is quite amenable to training; in acting schools, there is appropriate training, above all, on 'circles of attention.' The circle of attention can be infinitely wide (position yourself in the universe, country, city), narrower (a house, a room, a chair on which I am sitting) or extremely narrow (inner monologue and inner thoughts and vision).
3 K. Stanislavsky (1985), in *An Actor Prepares part 1* (*Rabota aktera nad soboj v tvorcheskom processe perezhevanja. Dnevnik uchenika*), there is a whole chapter related to scenic attention and how to train it. In this chapter, I have used my own translations; they might differ from Jean Benedetti's, which I highly value and refer to later.

4 See R. Blair (2008) *The Actor, Image and Action – Acting and Cognitive Neuroscience* and R. J. Kemp (2023) *The Secret of Action: A Cognitive Exploration of Eyewitness Accounts of Stanislavsky's Active Analysis.* Both authors provide the connection between the cognitive neuroscience with theory grounded in phenomenological experience to better understand how Stanislavsky's Active Analysis stimulates these responses.

5 My interpretation of the beginners' mind on stage is an idea that suggests approaching acting, as if you're experiencing it for the first time. This openness allows you to find new insights and perspectives in the moment as a character. It's about staying curious, which can get lost as you become more familiar with a character or a play. Essentially, it's about maintaining a sense of wonder and freshness in your performance.

6 B. Merlin (2014, 214–216).

7 K. Stanislavsky (1954–1961). *Collected Works: in 8 Volumes.* Stanislavsky throughout his work on the System talks about the "sorceress of nature" to explain the magical and mysterious power of intuition and subconscious creativity in acting. The meaning is that these inner forces can be used to create a believable and compelling performance.

References

Benedetti, J. (1999). *Stanislavski: His Life and Art: A Biography.* London: Methuen.

Benedetti, J. ed., trans., (2008). *Konstantin Stanislavsky, An Actor's Work. A Student's Diary.* London: Routledge.

Blair, R. (2008) *The Actor, Image and Action – Acting and Cognitive Neuroscience.* Oxon: Routledge.

Kemp, R. (2023). The secret of action: A cognitive exploration of eyewitness accounts of Stanislavsky's Active Analysis. *Stanislavski Studies*, 11(2), 189–201.

Machková, M. and Rais, M. (2023) On the hidden potential of public solitude, *Stanislavski Studies*, 12(1), pp. 69–86.

Merlin, B. (2014). *The Complete Stanislavsky Toolkit.* Rev. ed., Nick Hern Books.

Senelick, L., ed. (1981). *Russian Dramatic Theory from Pushkin to the Symbolists* 1st ed. Austin: University of Texas Press.

Stanislavsky, K. (1954–1961). Collected works: in 8 volumes/Ch.ed. M.N. Kedrov. Preparation text and notes N.D. Volkova and V.R. Kanatchikova; entry article by N. Volkov. Moscow: Art.

Stanislavsky, K. (1985). *Rabota aktera nad soboj v tvorcheskom processe perezhevanja. Dnevnik uchenika.* Moskva: Isskustvo.

Stanislavsky, K. (1986). *Zapisnye knizhki.* Moskva: Isskustvo.

Stanislavsky, K. (2003). *Inner Motive Forces.* London. Penguin.

Tcherkasski, S. (2012). *Stanislavsky and Yoga.* London: Routledge.

Zarrilli, P. (2007). An enactive approach to understanding acting. *Theatre Journal*, 59, pp. 635–647.

10

COMMUNION, MINDFULNESS AND THE IMAGINATIVE ACTOR

Georgina Sowerby

Necessary Metaphors

For some readers, it will not be possible to see the word *communion* without summoning images or even personal memories of the Catholic Eucharist, where, in a most profound sense, something stands in for something else.[1] Certainly that is the case for me; I grew up attending church every Sunday, not Catholic but 'high' Episcopalian.[2] The strange-tasting sugar paper melting on the tongue, the sip of sweet wine, the metallic tang of the silver cup on my lips, having to hold very still whilst someone else fed me, the queuing, the candles, diffracted light streaming through stained glass, red, gold, incense … And also the strange act of repetition, of singing things in unison: *O Lamb of God, who takes away the sins of the world, have mercy on us; grant us peace.*[3] The mystery…

We were an odd mix of people, an unlikely community of what seemed like mostly old ladies and me—all 'standing up and sitting down at the same time', as my late stepfather once described it. It was beautiful, tedious, and resonant—a sort of theatre where the drama plays the same way each time and the outcome is inevitable. But occasionally the air thickened, time slowed, I became more aware of my senses, my focus deepened, and I was struck by a concept or image that had floated over me previously. Perhaps this was my first significant experience of mindfulness.[4]

As actors, of course, we are not dealing with bread and wine standing in for the body and blood of Christ, but rather characters and dialogue standing in for the bigger ideas underpinning and driving the drama. It is this *standing in for things* that gives the material we work with its own agency and authenticity.

DOI: 10.4324/9781003517856-11

And, as Lakoff and Johnson argue in *Metaphors We Live By*, that's because we *need* it to.

> The objectivist philosophy fails to account for the way we understand our experience, our thoughts, and our language'. [...] Among other elements necessary to describe the human experience, they suggest that 'an adequate account requires ... viewing categories as experiential gestalts defined via prototype instead of viewing them as rigidly fixed and defined via set theory.
>
> *(Lakoff and Johnson, 2003, 210)*

Mindful Communions

These experiential 'gestalts' could be used to describe actors' energetic communications with each other (or with character, object, memory, idea, audience, or our own potent inner material); communications that momentarily become *real things* with their own needs, energy, and form.[5] These shifting emergences, or experiences happening between us that are created afresh each time, could be called *communions*. They are reflected in Stanislavsky's chapter on Communion/Communication, as the (imagined) teacher Tortsov asks his (fictional) pupil:

> Did you feel that, apart from the verbal, conscious argument and intellectual exchange of ideas, a current was streaming into and out of your eyes?
>
> That was invisible communication, the emitting and receiving that, like an underwater stream, flows continuously under our words, in silences, and forms the invisible link between objects which creates an inner connection.
>
> *(Stanislavski, 2010, 248)*

Curiously, something similar is suggested in Buddhist monk Thich Nhat Hanh's classic text, *The Miracle of Mindfulness*:

> It is autumn here and the golden leaves falling one by one are truly beautiful. Taking a ten-minute walk in the woods, watching my breath and maintaining mindfulness, I feel refreshed and restored. Like that, I can really enter into a communion with each leaf.
>
> *(Hanh, 2008, 16)*

And Tcherkasski, in *Stanislavsky and Yoga*, explores the deep inspiration and reverence Stanislavsky held for the Sanskrit concept of *Prana*[6]: 'it is the emission of *prana rays* that becomes for Stanislavsky the means of securing genuine communication for an actor.'

'All plasticity and its spirituality are connected with *prana*' (Tcherkasski, 2016, 87).

What is beautiful about all these descriptions is the suggestion that, when this mindful merging with the other (leaf, actor, audience, or hidden aspect of self) takes place, the weight is lifted off the lonely individual to 'perform'. Total control, deadly perfection, or even a performance of the 'correct' values acceptable to the group, are not on offer because this new state has its own way of operating, its existence depending more on the creativity and mindfulness of all involved than the ego's concerns. In mindful communion, there is potential for a co-created, spacious, *imaginative realm* to exist, which the actor and audience can expand into. (The thrilling feeling of making, then dwelling in, such a place, must surely be part of why actors fight so hard, against impossible odds, to act—if only to get back *there*.)

Communication/Communion

Communion, though, is a loaded word.[7] While it might suggest for some an act of profound intimacy, 'a close relationship with someone in which feelings and thoughts are exchanged', ('Communion', BBC), others may feel ambivalent about it, and some readers will associate the word itself with a very real sense of threat—the church for them being the embodiment of an unquestionable, even abusive, power. Since the dictionary definition also gives us 'a group of people who are united by the same, especially religious, beliefs' ('Communion', BBC), using the word can lead to suggestions that acting and actor-training is a form of mind control, or cult-membership, or, at the very least, of taking ourselves too seriously.

In *An Actor Prepares*, Hapgood uses the word 'Communion' to translate Stanislavsky's concept of '*obshchenie*' (Stanislavski, 1936, 198), which Benedetti, in the glossary of key terms for his translation, *An Actor's Work*, describes as 'the act of being in contact with an object or in communication with another person, verbally or non-verbally' (Stanislavski, 2010, 683).

Benedetti has changed the word *communion* to '*communication*'. Something is both gained and lost with this new word. Benedetti opens his translator's foreword, being careful to point out that his book is attempting 'to provide an accessible account of the system for actors in training without abstract theorising' (Benedetti, xv). And I can see that, after decades of mis-categorising Stanislavsky's work as purely psychological rather than profoundly practical (in both the physical and imaginative senses), finding a matter-of-fact word like *communication*, evoking our material, systematised, technological age, must have seemed appealing.[7]

But even since 2008, when Benedetti's translation was published, times—and trainee actors—have changed. I have observed in the learning space and rehearsal room a certain persistent wakefulness, developed in part in response to our increasingly online existence.[8] This has led not towards a hoped-for clarity but instead to a deep-rooted and fearful self-consciousness, which is extremely detrimental to the process of acting. Practitioner, theorist, and activist Augusto Boal's idea of the *cop in the head* speaks to the behaviours, fears, and impossible expectations of a generation of actors who have grown up with constant digital monitoring documenting their outward existence, inserting fear into the actor's psyche, and altering their relationship with their own interiority.[9]

Psychoanalyst and philosopher Julia Kristeva, in *This Incredible Need to Believe*, refers to the 'management via technology of the human species' (Kristeva, 2009, 29). And trainee actors developing personal identities can be co-opted into, and even shaped by, (sometimes well-meaning, sometimes cynical) social media trends masquerading as support. But as psychologist Lucy Foulkes points out in her article questioning the perception of a mental health crisis, 'we may be in the realm, not of psychiatric disorder, but rather in the tangled landscape of our rich and painful lives', which, of course, is where acting and drama have such profound roles to play (Foulkes, 2021).

The complex relationship between our online existence and creative inner life has meant a repositioning of the self in relation to the work. This can include a mistrustful perception of the work itself, a restriction by the individual of their expression, and even a collective doubt within the rehearsal room about the right to freedom of expression.[10]

Shadowy Monsters

The main anxiety appears to stem from the development of a very literal mindset, where things no longer *stand in for other things*. Instead, as one playwright-in-training told me, 'Words *mean* things.'[11] This excerpt from Wallace Stevens' poetic treatise on creativity, *The Man with the Blue Guitar*, speaks directly to the problem:

> They said, "You have a blue guitar,
> You do not play things as they are."
> The man replied, "Things as they are
> Are changed upon my blue guitar."
> And they said then, "But play, you must,
> A tune beyond us, yet ourselves,
> A tune upon the blue guitar
> Of things exactly as they are."
>
> (Stevens, 2010, 42)

Recently, in a preparatory rehearsal for a Shakespeare project, I asked students to bring in song lyrics they loved in order to explore their relationship with text, share their passions, and play with words without the weight of 'doing Shakespeare'. Instead, they started mumbling their words, losing eye contact, and shutting down any hint of expression. When I asked why, one trainee actor suggested, 'it's because it's personal'.[12] In other words, they felt the need to hide their private *feeling self* from potential judgement.

Because we as trainers and makers have been unable recently to separate the material we programme from historically abusive training and hierarchical rehearsal room practices and people,[13] or properly frame and defend the imaginative *place-in-between* scripts offer when we enter into mindful communion with them, students often stay in a literal realm, prioritising social approval over the beneficial power of metaphor contained within the story.[14] They are starting to conceive of the script itself as a frightening thing that might cause them direct harm, so even reading a play out loud is a dangerous event, potentially causing the actor-in-training to need a darkened room to lie down in to recover.[15] But a script is not itself traumatising: how many UK schoolchildren will tell you how boring they find *Macbeth*, for instance, when it is approached in a dry way and presented as exam fodder? Rather, when we start working with a script, it is the emotions, urges, and reactions we experience *within ourselves* that are disorienting or disturbing to us, surely exactly what the writer wanted us to feel, and certainly what we train to recognise, value, and understand. Anyway, as one student noted, 'characters are not our role models'.[16]

We may feel we are helping to protect students with our (futile) search for completely 'safe' texts, but by banishing the baddie, what are we telling them about their own inner shadowy monsters: their abject feelings, potent desires, confusing dreams, powerful imaginings? These things, which may have driven them to want to act in the first place, are part of the human condition and are certainly the stuff of theatre plays and film scripts. We all, including young people, have the right to experience the pleasure of feeling 'ugly' emotions.

> A human being, every human being, is complicated—layers upon layers of ideas, feelings, perceptions, recollections, reactions, desires and dreams. By placing us into boxes they are denying us our own truth. By placing others into boxes we are denying them their own truth. And so it goes.
>
> *(Shafak, 2020, 35)*

Instead, we appear to be in the process of trying to sanitise our rituals. The removal of the 'body and blood' from our artistic communion, from the imaginative space of the play, simply leaves the congregant with tasteless sugar paper and a sip of cheap wine out of a tin cup. For the actor and audience, the job of communion has become more than *sitting and standing at the same time*. It is now more urgent, shadowy, and visceral, involving the resurrection of a sacred act: ingesting our broken body politic and drinking in the abject together.

Transmuting Suffering

Kristeva, when talking of Christianity's 'discovery' that 'depression is an indispensable and decisive stage of thought', states that 'suffering is the flip side of creative exaltation (in the artist, for example)' (Kristeva, 2009, 84). Later she goes on to say, 'I don't accept suffering; I try to transmute it' (Kristeva, 2009, 86).

This theme of *transmutation*—the act of changing something completely, in this case by staying with it rather than running from it—is further developed by Buddhist nun Pema Chödron: 'If we feel distress, embarrassment, or anger, we think we've really blown it. Yet feeling emotional upheaval is not a spiritual faux pas; it's the place where the warrior learns compassion. It's where we learn to stop struggling with ourselves. It's only when we can dwell in these places that scare us that equanimity becomes unshakeable' (Chödron, 2001, 120).

As actors, we can learn to use mindfulness to make space for, sit with, or dwell momentarily within these 'ugly', exposing, or even vulnerable places; only then can we begin to transmute them. In our *mindful communion* and willingness to be surprised, they become no longer frightening wounds that must be covered up, hidden, and avoided, but instead, deep, sacred resources, pools of human understanding, lending maturity, depth, and detail to our expression. These pools inform the deeper 'why' of acting: why do we act? We do it because it is needed: actors remind us that we are only and incredibly human.

In the case of the student song lyrics, I reassured them that the audience cannot know what you're *really* thinking, and even if you are extremely expressive, they cannot *actually* see inside your heart and mind. Instead, they use the very personal energy you exude to reflect on their *own* experience. And out of that exchange process, a new thing is born that does not belong solely to either the actor or the audience. This is part of the process of mindful communion—the need to *co-believe a shared imaginative realm into being* where new things can be created and experienced by all parties (See figure 10.1).

Collective Resonance

The action of searching for and dis-covering the underlying purpose of each project enables actors to become immersed in their story-world so that self-consciousness starts to slip away and they find themselves in a state of heightened receptivity.

In his book, *The Actor and the Character*, Mirodan describes this altered state as *reverie*: this 'feels like a reverie: a state of "suspension", in which the boundaries between my sense of self ("I") and the character ("it") are significantly blurred'. He continues, 'Psychoanalyst Wilfred Bion also uses the term "reverie" to describe the way a mother and baby are totally absorbed in each other...Contemplating (it) involves an element of kindness and tolerance and, above all, of identifying with or "loving" the character, or, if one wishes, of "containing" it' (Mirodan, 2019, 142).

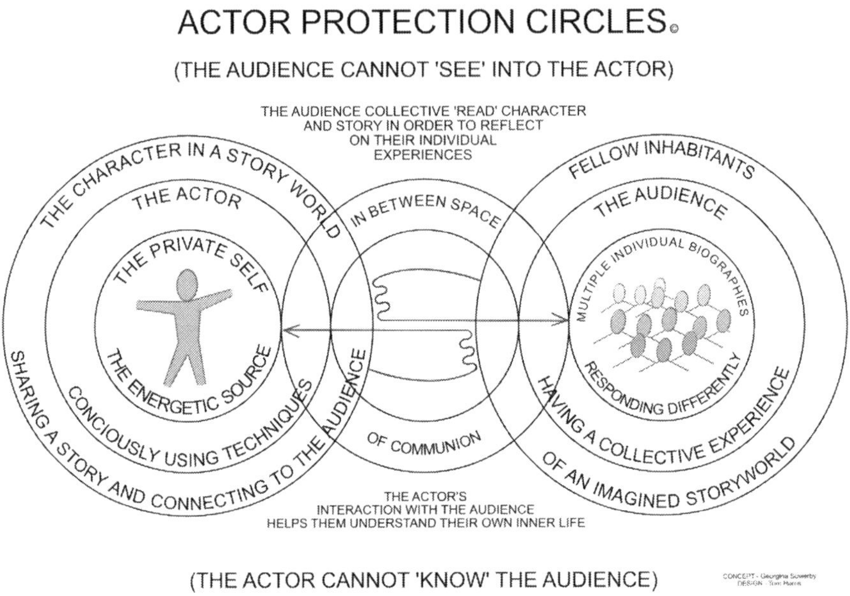

FIGURE 10.1 Acting protection circles.

This process is not just a matter of the actor embodying the text, storytelling, or even manifesting the 'actor-in-character' (Mirodan, 2019, 163). It isn't simply about the company connecting, and it is not exclusively down to the actor drawing on a personal experience from their unique perspective, though all these things are important elements contributing to the whole. Rather, by actively searching together for both a personal and collective, deep-rooted 'why', we enter into an altered state where the energy in the room becomes charged by this new-found, deeper purpose.[17] Anne Bogart describes this imaginative, mindful communion as *collective resonance*.

> Most actors recognise the moment on stage when their own volition recedes, and they start to follow a power that has come into play. And here the process of unfolding takes over. The actors' resonance can be contagious and transferred to the audience and vice versa. Audiences, in the heat of performance, suddenly feel that they no longer need to concentrate in order to follow the narrative. In that moment, they become part of the aesthetic experience and have joined with the flow of the performance. Something is *at work*: resonance. This now shared journey is what sociologist Helmut Rosa calls 'collective resonance'.
>
> *(Bogart, 2021, 15)*

Like Thich Nhat Hanh with the autumn leaves, a tolerance for ourselves and respectful curiosity in each other, starts to materialise: ideas open up, focus deepens, elements combine, and something borne of our merged imaginations comes into being. Bogart suggests it 'thickens the air between actors and their environments' (Bogart, 2021, 15).

And it is the search for the collective 'why', the underlying idea the metaphor of the play is standing in for, that allows actors to become mindful, releasing themselves more fully into the aesthetic experience. When this happens, the unfolding of *something else* becomes palpable.

Imaginative Alchemy

> Each phenomenon, including myself, appears clearly as itself, a separate entity, whilst taking its place in the codependent stream of everything else.
>
> *(Zaporah, 2014, 71)*

Here, Zaporah is describing her heightened awareness within improvisatory live performance, almost as if she has entered an alternative energetic field of the imagination. And Hanh, too, suggests a shifted perception of nature and the everyday:

> When reality is experienced in its nature of ultimate perfection, an almond tree which may be in your front yard reveals its nature in perfect wholeness … Because of a more open heart, a certain communion already exists between the artist and the tree. What counts is your own heart. If your heart is not clouded by false views, you will be able to enter into a natural communion with the tree. The almond tree will be ready to reveal itself to you in complete wholeness.
>
> *(Hanh, 2008, 58)*

In both cases, neither the realm of the imagination nor the almond tree can *reveal themselves to us* if we take everything literally and don't perceive it with the 'heart of an artist' (that is, through metaphor). The almond tree in our case is the script, the company, or the world of the project itself, and this material, just like the tree, has its own locked, potent, almost sacred quality. It requires things of us, and it is important we know *something is required of us*. Poet and playwright Kae Tempest calls this creative requirement Love:

> Creativity is the ability to feel wonder and the desire to respond to what we find startling. Or more simply, creativity is any act of Love.
>
> *(Tempest, 2020, 5)*

In all instances, the quality of attentiveness, respectfulness for 'the other' (both without and within ourselves), an open-minded willingness to engage, to experiment, and to be surprised, or even amazed, by what emerges *of its own accord*, are the essential components required. It is through this 'act of Love' that communion, mindfulness, and the actor's imagination intertwine. To experience *things revealing themselves in complete wholeness to us* is part of the pleasure of making work.

Dreaming Process

A return to the curious spaciousness that the trinity of communion, mindfulness, and imagination calls into being is an essential shift we need to make to respond to our wakeful, dis-eased, anxious, and creatively challenged selves and times.

Arnold Mindell, the founder of Processwork and expert in working with highly conflicted groups, describes in *Sitting in the Fire* the collective 'dreaming process' (or living, active metaphor)[18]: 'Whenever we come together, what indigenous people call the 'dreaming process' is present. In this altered state of consciousness, fantasies, intuitions and insights can be noticed right alongside today's problems' (Mindell, 2014, 186). Communion here is more ancient than the Catholic mass mentioned at the beginning of this chapter. This 'dreaming process' echoes Stanislavsky's understanding of *Prana*, Hanh's *Almond Tree*, and Mirodan's *Reverie*. It evokes *collective resonance*, the places *in-between*, and nature itself (including our own deep nature). What he describes seems to offer a way to meet the intense challenges and needs that we, as actors, teachers, directors, writers, and makers, face in our creative work now.

> To move from democracy to deep democracy, we need only to ask:
> Who is noticing something interesting?
> What does it feel like here?
> Who is dreaming something they can barely notice?
> Why does the spirit of the earth say now?
> What other spirits are present?
> What are you feeling?
> Who is comfortable? Who is uncomfortable?
> ...
> The future depends on enabling what is unknown to appear.
>
> *(Mindell, 2014, 187)*

These are frenzied and unsettled times, so it is incumbent on us to return to this work of slowing down, deepening our focus, and restoring our ancient ability to be in mindful communion with our own and the collective's imagination. Perhaps then we can hope to hear what the silenced states of consciousness have to say to us, see what the unknown has to show us, and even enable a transformed artistic future to come into being, both inside and between ourselves.

Exercises

NB: All these exercises are about mindfully 'preparing the ground' and feeding the imagination, thus enabling communion to happen. They work with both professional and amateur groups.

1 ***Project Purpose***. Begin your production or project by establishing the collective and personal 'why'. Give your group or company flip-chart sheets and colour pens. In groups of 4–5, they discuss their personal attitudes towards the themes of the course, play, or playwright. Everything gets written down, whether or not the group agrees with each other—you are laying down practices of tolerance. Allow 10 minutes for discussion and notes, then each group feeds back the most important points to the ensemble. Capture what they are saying—underlying attitudes will surface here, providing rich material to work with while airing old wounds and blocks that could otherwise unbalance the project.
2 ***Hopes and fears***. A solo exercise. Lay out two sets of post-it notes. E.g. pink for hope, green for fear. Give the group a few minutes to write down their hopes and fears for the project or for themselves as actors within the project, etc. At the end, they can choose to share what they've written. (NB: If someone doesn't want to share, that's fine, but ask everyone to stick up their hopes and fears on the wall at the end.) You don't have to comment but again, it can help surface internal material.
3 ***Move***. I use Bogart's *Viewpoints*, Zaporah's *Actiontheatre* exercises, and animal work to create the physical texture of the piece. These exercises are too complex to go into here, but they can be found in *The Viewpoints Book* and *Actiontheatre* listed in the References section. The important thing is that the whole company works with the body, on the floor, and with music ASAP. Too long 'at the table' can really kill off the natural energy that exists at the start of the project, which will feed the company when rehearsals get more challenging. I extend this principle into the first couple of weeks of rehearsal. If we read a scene, we immediately get up to improvise it, identifying lively content that is useful for the scene. This helps the actors to think of themselves as collaborative creatives, generating material.
4 ***Free-writes***. Use free-writing after big physical exercises (e.g., Bogart's *Viewpoints*) to capture the subconscious material bubbling up. As they get scrap paper and pens, explain the rules: 'Without chatting, please focus on the exercise you've just done. Put your pen to the page and keep writing without reading back or worrying about spelling. You can write anything in any language while focusing on the theme. This is for you, and you don't have

to share it. (If you can't think of any words, do a squiggly line, but just keep the pen moving.)' Now I share a topic or heading with the group (e.g., What do you see when you think of this play? What can you remember about the exercise you've just done?). Set a timer for 90 seconds to 2 minutes, and off they go. Keep the pen moving! At the end, I ask the group to share one word, sentence, or phrase from their writing.

5 ***Research Groups***. There's often fear around actors' research e.g., It will 'keep the actors in their heads'. However, if done well, research empowers practical acting choices and informs the project's collective 'why'. Here the company is giving the play/project its own agency. (Remember, it will need to have that for the company to go into Communion with it.) Groups of 4/5, depending on cast size, are given a topic to research e.g., The Playwright's Life and Work. Politics and Power. Family Life and Society. etc. They need enough time to be able to meet, research, and decide on a presentation style (e.g., one/two weeks). Research should be shared in an interactive, immersive, or otherwise performative style. (e.g., gameshow, religious ceremony etc.). They should NOT just stand up and read. They MAY include some performed script excerpts (but not the source play) or they can write an original script. They should be driven by the focus: what do the actors need to know to help them act this? Each presentation slot should be no longer than 20 minutes.

6 ***Boundaries***. Ask the actor to identify where they are similar and where they are different from the character. Make clear lists. The actor relaxes with the similarities and works into the 'difference'. This can be through gestural work, transformative animal work, character questions, actors' 'real-life' acquaintances, people-watching in cafés, etc. The important thing is that the actor builds a strong consciousness and a detailed process around *differentiation*, so they are able to identify at all times that they are not their character. They can be encouraged with the knowledge that, far from being 'fake', this is where the actor's interpretative skill and creative artistry lie. This process is personal but also creates the energy required for 'transmission' in performance.

7 ***Audiencing***. As a company, give the audience a task or role. Establish what the play asks of them. This liberates the actors from the need for acceptance from the audience, instead helping them view the audience as fellow creative collaborators—or collective resonators.

Notes

1 For further information, see this brief outline, designed for schools, that gives a breakdown of what happens during Catholic Mass/Eucharist (BBC, 2024).

2 Here, the Episcopal Church outlines their distinct beliefs and values, especially 'a legacy of inclusion' (The Episcopal Church, 2024).

3 These words accompany communion, sometimes spoken, sometimes sung (BBC 2024).

4 This guide, provided by Mind, explains mindfulness: 'noticing what's happening in the present moment without judgement' (Mind, 2024).
5 'Gestalt is based on the principle that everyone is a whole—made up of mind, body and soul—and draws on the philosophical idea that the whole is other than the sum of its parts' (BACP 2024).
6 *Prana* is a Sanskrit concept meaning 'breath' or 'vital force' (Oxford University Press, 2024).
7 'Over time gross misunderstandings grew about Stanislavski and his 'system', such as the overreliance on psychological approaches that led to the American conception of method acting.' See Jean Benedetti's Obituary (Early, 2012).
8 'Web inventor Sir Tim Berners-Lee reflects on how the web has changed our world' (Berners-Lee, 2019).
9 Practitioner and activist Augusto Boal believed the Global North internalised its own oppression (McLaverty-Robinson, 2017).
10 Angelina Jolie: 'I wouldn't be an actress today' (Pulver, 2023).
11 G. Sowerby (2019) Personal Notes, MA Dramatic Writing DCL, 13 March.
12 G. Sowerby (2024) Personal notes, *Comedy of Errors* Project, 17 July.
13 The Royal Court held events 'to confront the abuses of power that have been occurring in the theatre industry for years' (Royal Court, 2017).
14 Will Storr explores proven psychological benefits of working with metaphor (Storr, 2019).
15 Some students felt Behn's subject matter should not be used comedically and left the read-through to lie down. Sowerby (2022) Personal notes, *Supporting Behn Project Director*, 10 October.
16 Other students pushed to defend the material. G. Sowerby (2022) Personal notes, *Supporting Behn Project Director*, 10 October.
17 A company finding its driving 'why' is spoken about in more depth in this article exploring the concept of *Halting*, which is 'aimed at training actors' capacity to make ethical and aesthetic choices' (Tinius, 2017).
18 'Originally developed by Dr Arnold Mindell and colleagues in the 1980s.' 'Processwork is awareness based. Its methods allow us to perceive the creative nature of processes, even within apparently very disturbing and complex situations' (Processwork UK, 2024).

References

BACP (2024), *What is Gestalt Therapy?* Available at: https://www.bacp.co.uk/about-therapy/types-of-therapy/gestalt/ (Accessed: 18.08.24).

BBC (2024), *BBC Bitesize*. Available at: https://www.bbc.co.uk/bitesize/guides/zkwhcqt/revision/8 (Accessed: 18.08.24).

Berners-Lee, T. (2019), '30 years on, what's next for the web?', *World Wide Web Foundation*, 12 March. Available at: https://webfoundation.org/2019/03/web-birthday-30/ (Accessed: 18.08.24).

Bogart, A. (2021) *The Art of Resonance*. London: Methuen/Drama. Cambridge University Press (2024), *Communion*. Available at: https://dictionary.cambridge.org/dictionary/english/communion (Accessed: 18.08.24).

Chödron, P. (2001) *The Places That Scare You*. London: Thorsons, Harper Collins Publishers.

Early, M. (2012), Jean Benedetti Obituary, *The Guardian*, 20 April. Available at: https://www.theguardian.com/stage/2012/apr/20/jean-benedetti (Accessed: 18.08.24).

Foulkes, L. (2021) What we're getting wrong in the conversation about mental health, *The Guardian*, 29 March. Available at: https://www.theguardian.com/

commentisfree/2021/mar/29/conversation-mental-health-psychiatric-language-seriously-ill (Accessed: 18.08.24).
Hanh, T. N. (2008) *The Miracle of Mindfulness*, UK: Rider. Ebury Publishing, Random House Group.
Kristeva, J. (2009) *The Incredible Need to Believe*. New York: Columbia University Press.
Lakoff, G. and Johnson, M. (2003) *Metaphors We Live By*. Chicago and London: The University of Chicago Press.
McLaverty-Robinson, A. (2017) 'Augusto Boal: The Rainbow of Desire', *Ceasefire Magazine*, (August). Available at: https://ceasefiremagazine.co.uk/augusto-boal-rainbow-desire/ (Accessed: 18.08.24).
Mind (2024), *Mindfulness*. Available at: https://www.mind.org.uk/information-support/drugs-and-treatments/mindfulness/about-mindfulness/ (Accessed: 18.08.24).
Mindell, A. (2014) *Sitting in the Fire*. Florence and San Francisco: Deep Democracy Exchange.
Mirodan, V. (2019) *The Actor and the Character*. London: Routledge. Oxford University Press (2024), *Prana*. Available at: https://www.oxfordreference.com/display/10.1093/oi/authority.20110803100341947 (Accessed: 18.08.24).
Processwork UK (2024), *What is Processwork?* Available at: https://www.processworkuk.org/processwork/ (Accessed: 18.08.24).
Pulver A. (2023), 'Angelina Jolie:'I wouldn't be an actress today.' *The Guardian*, 6 December. Available at: https://www.theguardian.com/film/2023/dec/06/angelina-jolie-i-wouldnt-be-an-actress-today (Accessed: 18.08.24).
Royal Court (2017) *No Grey Area*. Available at: https://royalcourttheatre.com/whats-on/no-grey-area-your-stories-heard/ (Accessed: 18.08.24).
Shafak, E. (2020) *How to Stay Sane in an Age of Division*. London: Profile Books, Wellcome Collection.
Stanislavski, C. (1936/2013a) *An Actor Prepares*. Reynolds Hapgood, E. (trans.) London: Bloomsbury.
Stanislavski, K. (2010) *An Actor's Work*. Benedetti, J. (trans.) Oxon: Routledge.
Stevens, W. (2010) *Selected Poems*. London: Faber and Faber.
Storr, W. (2019) *The Science of Storytelling*. London: William Collins, Harper Collins Publishing.
Tcherkasski, S. (2016) *Stanislavsky and Yoga*, Oxon: Icarus Publishing Group and Routledge.
Tempest, K. (2020) *On Connection*. London: Faber and Faber.
The Episcopal Church (2024), *What We Believe*. Available at: https://www.episcopalchurch.org/what-we-believe (Accessed: 18.08.24).
Tinius, J. (2017) 'Art as ethical practice: anthropological observations on and beyond theatre', *World Art*, 7 (2), 227–251, https://doi.org/10.1080/21500894.2017.1308966
Zaporah, R. (2014) *Improvisation on the Edge (notes from on and off stage)*, Berkeley: North Atlantic Books.

Bibliography

Avatar, M. (2016) *Better Magic: A Toolkit for Inspiration*. London: Kiosk Publishing.
Bogart, A. and Landau, T. (2005) *The Viewpoints Book: A Practical Guide to Viewpoints and Composition*. New York: Theatre Communications Group.
Zaporah, R. (1995) *Action Theater: The Improvisation of Presence*, Berkeley: North Atlantic Books.

11

ACTING WITH (COM)PASSION: AN INTRODUCTION TO CBCT® (COGNITIVELY BASED COMPASSION TRAINING)

Exploring the Agency to Build Resilience and to Enhance and Expand Our Awareness and Connection to Self, Character and Community

Laura Smiley

COMPASSION: '*The warm-hearted concern that unfolds when we witness the suffering of others and feel motivated to relieve it.*' (Negi, 2023, 6)

SELF-COMPASSION: '*Self-compassion is a practice in which we learn to be a good friend to ourselves when we need it most – to become an inner ally rather than an inner enemy.*' (Neff and Germer, 2018, 9)

CBCT® (Cognitively Based Compassion Training) is meditation-based training that aims to develop empathy and compassion towards oneself and others, with the goal of expanding one's sense of connection and care of humanity in a larger capacity. Developed by Geshe Lobsang Tenzin Negi, Tibetan monk and scholar at Emory University, this secular contemplative practice combines traditional Tibetan meditation techniques with modern cognitive psychology. CBCT® involves progressive practices and protocols that aim to increase awareness of one's emotions and thoughts, cultivation of empathy and compassion, and the development of cognitive skills such as attentional stability and perspective-taking. Once the foundation of practice is established, the journey first delves into self-compassion as a catalyst to understanding how we can practice self-care and self-kindness to ground us in being present in the moment, to the moment, as it affects ourselves and others. It fosters resilience to more gracefully bounce back from adversity.

The body of this chapter introduces the foundation of CBCT® and offers two practices that would scaffold with the progression of protocols in eight modules. (See Appendix at the end of this chapter.) However, for the purposes here, the practices address the topics at hand, not necessarily corresponding to the order of protocols.

DOI: 10.4324/9781003517856-12

In Ubud, Bali, summer of 2017, I was in conversation with Yogini Linda Madani, my teacher, when the subject of compassion arose. In yogic practices, the goal is to accept yourself in all your humanness. 'Yoga is not about self-improvement, it's about self-acceptance.' Gurmukh Kaur Khalsa (*from my yoga journal – as shared from teacher*). But what of compassion for others? How come there are those who seem to have no compassion? We unpacked this and posited that we are all born into this world, to life, with a modicum of compassion. We are here, in this world for starts, born of a person. As infants, we innately search for care, security and love. Sometimes, along the way, things can happen that deprive us of or negate that feeling of being loved. Not feeling loved could bury one's desire to love and perhaps numb the desire to live life with compassion. So, our question was 'Can compassion be taught?' With this in my head, I rushed home and googled 'Can compassion be taught?' This led me to an article about veterans and post-traumatic stress disorder (PTSD) and how CBCT® had been effective in helping treat them. There was a link. I connected to it. That is how I discovered CBCT®. By the wee hours of the morning, I had signed up for an intensive, in three weeks – the first weekend of the 2017 fall semester.

I was inspired. I felt that this program would give me the tools and resources to help my students. This was in 2017, before the national awareness and focus on supporting our students' mental health soared to the forefront with urgency. But I had already experienced and witnessed the suffering my students were navigating: the anxiety, the depression, the self-doubt, the self-loathing. I knew this would help. I had no idea how much this work would open my heart as well – I mean, I was a yogini, I had accepted my imperfections! CBCT® changed my life. But that is a joyful story for another time.

The creation of CBCT® stemmed from an urgent plea from a student at Emory University over 20 years ago. In 2003, when the Emory community experienced the loss of several students to suicide, Geshe Lobsang was teaching a class in Tibetan Buddhism. The student, Molly Harrington, was convinced that the principles and practices taught in the class could lend itself to the creation of a technique that would benefit the many students who were struggling. He tasked himself to create a program – a series of protocols – that could give students a foundation of resilience to navigate the challenges and pressures of college life. These skills could be cultivated and strengthened to also support their lives beyond their university experiences. This program became CBCT® (Cognitively Based Compassion Training), a set of contemplative practices and exercises that help participants establish and cultivate safety, mindfulness, self-compassion, and compassion for others. CBCT®, as stated in the Preface (xiv) of Negi's 2023 guide, was created with the goal of contributing to greater human flourishing. Geshe Lobsang was inspired by the writings of the Dalai Lama on the indispensable need for compassion to live, indeed for humanity to survive. The Dalai Lama says that love and compassion are necessities, not luxuries and without them, humanity cannot survive.[1]

I attend the foundational intensive at Emory University in Atlanta, Georgia. There are about 40 people in the room with Geshe Lobsang and other CBCT® teachers. As we introduce ourselves, I realize that I am surrounded by doctors, nurses, psychiatrists, social workers, health care professionals and here I am, a yogini and theatre professor! I was a curiosity, but I knew why I was there – to learn techniques to cultivate resilience in my students.

At present, the student body as a whole is more acutely affected, and the population at large suffers from a greater degree of depression and anxiety, often in isolation. CBCT® is the most prominent program to teach the power of compassion, and yet public awareness of such opportunities and even other programs is just beginning to gain traction. Given the state of the world, still recovering from the isolation and tragedy of the pandemic, in the midst of war, poverty, inequity and divisive politics, imagine the possibilities that a program that teaches and nurtures compassion for ourselves and others can have to alleviate societal ills and live in a kinder and more caring world.

QUESTION: As humans, what do we all have in common? What connects us no matter what culture, religion, country, gender or politics?

ANSWER: We all strive for the same thing: the desire for happiness, security, acceptance, success, recognition, which can all be boiled down to one thing: LOVE. We are also all connected by the experience of suffering. In life, we all suffer, we fail, we make mistakes, we hurt, we experience loss.

A conscious practice to cultivate self-compassion gives us the tools to navigate our suffering with more grace. It gives us the agency to step back with awareness, the opportunity to shift our perspective, the courage to be vulnerable and to lean into emotions without spiraling. We can become aware of embers before they turn into forest fires. And have grace to forgive ourselves when we do spiral or when the embers burst into flames…we are only human after all 'To Err is Human, to Forgive Divine,' as penned by Alexander Pope, poet of the Enlightenment. But this practice, we can have the resilience to bounce back from adversity. As theatre artists, compassion gives us the agency to truly explore the characters we play with curiosity, truthfulness, and equanimity. As Kirsten Neff states, having compassion for yourself means that you honor and accept your humanness.[2] (*See Exercise 1: Revealing Self-compassion*)

What does it mean to be 'in the moment?' Tortsov says 'in our art you must live the part every moment that you are playing it, and every time' (Stanislavsky, 1946, 18). Uta Hagen further expands on its importance to the craft of acting. It is something that actors strive to experience, the ultimate moment of connection when we are one with the character, fully living the journey, truly being in body, mind and spirit.

But, perhaps, before we can explore being in the moment for our characters, we must learn to be in the moment for ourselves: in our personal lives and endeavors. Being in the moment is to be present. Present for yourself, present for others, present in the world, with an awareness of your emotions, how they inform your actions, and how these, in turn, affect others.

Contemplative practices can be challenging to harness at first and are best done by approaching the work with an open mind, an open heart, and curiosity. Ideally stillness is involved, to relax, yet maintain an active body. As the body is connected to the mind, this allows a flowing conduit of energy from head to toe which supports the thoughts and feelings we need to notice within our practice. But what if there is a time when stillness is not possible? 'There is no such thing as being good or bad at meditation. That's just not the point. Every time you get distracted, you start again, so noticing the distraction is actually proof of success,' says Jeff Warren, a meditation teacher with ADHD (Shilton, 2022, New York Times online). There are many solutions to work with the stillness. Start with a minute…then two. Walk in nature, aware of your surroundings. Or, given our obsession with our phones, whenever there's a ding, notice, or ring, take a breath before opening, looking, answering. The important thing is to commit to the practice until it becomes habit. It will take patience, and time. Give yourself grace if you are pulled away and bring yourself back around to it and start over. The goal is embodied understanding, so that practicing compassion becomes second nature. This can only happen by choosing to practice, and consciously practicing to choose compassion.

The importance of acting with (Com)Passion moves to the forefront in terms of developing the character's journey, as well as having the grace and warm-heartedness to collaborate creatively and freely with each other as a company in community. (Com)Passion: This word-design was created to highlight a double-meaning: I. As human beings we can strive to live our lives informed by compassion while living with passion. II. As theatre artists we can choose to create our characters with passion while also understanding them with compassion, e.g., Iago: He is a villain. He says, 'I am a villain.' But if an actor only focuses on that statement, that Iago is a villain, the connotation of 'villain' is that he is bad. And it is easy to judge someone who is bad. So, they judge Iago as bad. However, if the actor approaches Iago with compassion, with the curiosity to figure out why he is a villain, perhaps they can relate to his rejection for promotion by Othello. Or perhaps a rumor that he has been cuckolded. Having compassion inspires them to find his humanity. This allows them to walk in his shoes without judgement.

One of the benefits of CBCT® is the opportunity to increase emotional awareness, which is essential for when we need to connect with emotional truth to create believable characters. Torstov says, 'Everyone at every minute of his life must feel something. Only the dead have no sensations' (Stanislavsky, 1946, 22). In creating a moment of nurturance (*see Exercise 2 on recreating a nurturing moment*) we visualize a personal moment in our life in all its detail with a meta-awareness of how our senses and body responds. Stanislavsky says, 'An actor's imagination can draw to itself the life of another person, adapt it, discover mutual and exciting qualities and features' (Stanislavsky, 1971, 19). As an acting exercise, this can be used to visualize given circumstances and events experienced by our characters by stimulating our artistic imaginations to create connections that can generate a visceral response.

Acting is a demanding art that requires both cognitive and emotional skills to be present in the moment. Uta Hagen and Stanislavsky have devised various exercises and techniques to help actors become more present and authentic in their performances. However, we must remember that both Stanislavsky's and Hagen's discoveries were based on *their* understanding and observations of human drives and struggles as informed by the early- to late-twentieth-century world. Uta Hagen writes, 'Sticking slavishly to his doctrines is an injustice to Stanislavski himself. It is wrong to assume he would have stood still, clinging to the conclusions to which he came at the early part of the twentieth century' (Hagen, 1991, 46). So, too with Hagen, there are so many findings since her death that help us to understand ourselves as we relate to our present twenty-first-century world. The development of neuroscience, evolutionary biology, continued development of psychology and the recognition of compassion as a scientific study informs the continuing development of CBCT® in real time. CBCT® works to enhance awareness as a vehicle to greater compassion, which are important qualities for actors who need to understand the emotions and motivations of their characters and how that informs their actions.

I told Tim Harrison, CBCT® senior teacher and Associate Director for CBCT at Emory Center for Contemplative Science and Compassion-Based Ethics, that in five years, I would have a foundation class within the Bachelor of Fine Arts (BFA) curriculum at Slippery Rock University, PA where I teach. The BFA degree is more specialized than the traditional Bachelor of Arts (BA) liberal arts degree. It allows a theatre concentration in acting in a conservatory-style learning environment. For the last five years, there has indeed been an official class 'Wellness for the Actor' which commences as the first class at 9 a.m. on Monday morning of the Fall semester for all the new BFA actors. I work intensively with the freshman in their first year, leading them through the eight protocols of CBCT®, as well as boundary work and other resources to build self-awareness, compassion and resilience. I also observe them in Freshman Acting to tie-in their acting work to the CBCT® protocols we've been learning. In the spring I have them for Uta Hagen and within that class we continue to practice CBCT® as well as utilizing the practice to inform their work in this class.

A major take-away from CBCT® that I have witnessed in my students is how much better they know and accept themselves. Even more than that, however, they honor themselves by understanding that self-compassion is not a weakness but a strength, and that self-kindness is not selfish but a necessity. As vulnerable freshman, the realization that they are not alone – everyone has failed in class or bombed an audition.

As they embraced self-compassion, their acting choices have been braver and more deeply supported because the more you know about yourself and what makes you tick, the fuller your characters have the potential to be. There is a freedom in the sharing instead of fear. The fear of "Am I good enough?" is lessened in potency.

The Greater Good Science Center[3] reports that the early CBCT® studies suggests a clear link between cultivating compassion and improved resilience – our ability to bounce back emotionally from stressful experiences. The field of compassion science has since grown, and numerous studies also suggest that compassion training is linked to improved emotion regulation and wellbeing – decreasing rumination, activating pleasure circuits in the brain, increasing self-reported happiness, creating more optimistic and supportive communication styles, and serving as an antidote to burnout.

Incorporating CBCT® into acting training can benefit both the mental health and the performance of actors. By developing compassion, emotional awareness and cognitive skills, actors can become more present and authentic in their performances while also promoting their own wellbeing. Acting with (Com)Passion not only benefits the theatre artist but, more importantly, the humans that we are, by cultivating the resources to stay present in the moment while living one's truth with grace, compassion and resilience.

This is a sample of the research I've been exploring over the last few years to promote CBCT® and compassion work in general, with an eye toward molding the practices to both inform and support actor training. My goal is to gather all the research I have and create a guide using CBCT® formal and informal practices to complement actor training. This is the first step.

'We need a revolution of compassion based on warm heartedness that will contribute to a more compassionate world with a sense of oneness with humanity.' (Lama and Altz, 2020, 45)

For more information about CBCT® consult CBCT® | Cognitively-Based Compassion Training – Emory University

Dedicated to Samuel Carriba Fernandez my warm-hearted and generous mentor. You inspired and believed. Thank you. (In memoriam 11/26/22)

Exercise 1 Revealing Self-Compassion

Objective: *To become aware of how we treat ourselves*

Lasts 30–50 minutes + discussion; can adjust for class size/period as appropriate.

There are three questions to reflect and respond to. Allow 10–15mins for each. Follow up with share/discussion.

Have participants write down each question as you read it (or better yet prep on board or screen for easy viewing)

Take 10–15 minutes to reflect on question & pen discoveries.

1 Close your eyes and reflect on the following question:
Think about a time when you were feeling in a good way and a close friend is struggling in some way: a loss, a failure; a misfortune, a mistake, feeling of inadequacy. How do you typically respond to your friend? What do you say and do? How do you receive it? Non-verbal gestures? Physical posture? What do you say? How do you say it? What do you want to accomplish?
Reflect and respond.

2 Close your eyes again.
Think about the various times that You have struggled in some way: a loss, a failure; a misfortune, a mistake, feeling of inadequacy. How do you typically respond to yourself? What do you do? How do you receive it? Non-verbal gestures? Physical posture? What do you say to yourself? How do you say it? How do you view yourself?
Reflect and respond.

3 Finally, compare the way you treat your close friends in their struggles vs. how you treat yourself when you struggle. What are the differences?
Reflect and respond.

Open floor for share/discussion.

Often, when participants do this exercise, they are shocked at how badly they treat themselves in comparison to their friends. If they are in this position, support them by sharing that they are not alone. Recent data reveals that a vast majority of people are more compassionate to others than to themselves. This is a direct result of the pervading culture that does not encourage us to be kind to ourselves. We must intentionally practice shifting our perspective about ourselves to break this often lifetime habit.

Exercise 2 Moments of Nurturance

Objective: *To use as a resource to shift/diffuse mood/perspective by activating feelings of safety and comfort.*

Lasts *2–5 mins. connect to moment. 5–10 mins. to journal. 10–15 mins. Can adjust to class period.*

1 Make a list of three moments or circumstances in your life that help you feel more at ease, calm, protected, or centered. List moments that, when recalled, fill you with a sense of greater safety, comfort, or warmth.

Moments of nurturance can be many things. It does not have to be a major event. It can be a quiet moment or a lively event. Some might recall a time we received compassion and kindness from a loved one or perhaps a stranger. Moments might include those where we are with someone whom we trust or feel close to. Someone we trust, who protects us, is kind to us, cares for us, or helps us during stressful or difficult times. It can also be the unconditional love of a pet, a warm smile from a stranger, or support from a neighbor or teacher. It can be an imagined memory of how we were cared for as an infant, or of being encouraged by a famous role model, even if we've never met them.

1 Close your eyes. See if you can settle on just one moment. Recall as many details about it as you can.
  Take a few minutes, even 5 or 10 as needed, to really take the time to recreate this moment of nurturance.
2 Use your senses to explore: who are you with? Picture that person(s) in your mind's eye. What do you see in their face, their eyes, their expression? Do you remember any scents or smells? Touch? Taste? Where are you? What does it look like? What time of day was it? As you fully reconnect to this memory, notice what sensations you feel in your body.
3 Next, turn your attention to the present, the now. What feelings, emotions, sensations arise as you recreate this moment? What shift, if any, do you notice in your feelings from the start of this practice to now?
4 Then take a breath and a sigh of release. In your journal write down your experience of this practice.

A moment of nurturance is one strategy for regulating our bodies and minds. By simply recalling a time when we felt safe or comforted in the past, we can reconnect to those same feelings in the present.

In this way, we can move from feelings of distress or discomfort to feelings of groundedness and release. A shift.

With practice, these moments of nurturance can be more easily recalled, bringing us more in touch with those feelings of safety, calm, and contentment.

In your journal, reflect on how important such moments of comfort and safety for your wellbeing are.

Furthermore, how important are acts of kindness and compassion to create feelings of safety and security where your fellow human beings can thrive? As you connect to the values of kindness and compassion, how might you with your actions impact your life and your relationships? Those who are willing, can share this experience – not necessarily the moment they chose, but the effects of recreating it and the sensations it elicited, as well as thoughts about the above reflection.

Moments of nurturance can be used anytime to reset when you are feeling vulnerable or emotional. Its power can ground you and settle heightened feelings and emotions.

Notes

1 See Dalai Lama (1999). *The Art of Happiness.* 1st Edition. London: Hodder Paperbacks.
2 See K. Neff and C. Germer (2018). *The Mindful Self-Compassion Workbook.* New York: The Guilford Press for further thoughts.
3 See Gilbert, P. et al. (2011). Pace, T.W.W. et al. (2009) The Greater Good Science Center at UC Berkeley (2023) (qtd Negi).

References

Hagen, U. (1991). *A Challenge for the Actor.* New York: Scribner.
Lama, Dalai (1999). *The Art of Happiness.* London: Hodder Paperbacks.
Lama, Dalai and Altz, F., (2020). *Our Only Home: A Climate Appeal to the World.* Toronto, Ontario: Hanover Square Press.
Neff, K., Germer C. (2018). *The Mindful Self-Compassion Workbook.* New York: The Guilford Press.
Negi, L.T. (2023). *Training Compassion: The Official Guide to CBCT.* Atlanta: Emory University.
Shilton, A.C. 'How to Meditate When You Can't Sit Still.' *New York Times.* A.G. Sulzberger. (23 August 2022). (Accessed 21.05.24).
Stanislavsky, C. (1946), *An Actor Prepares.* New York: Theatre Arts, Inc.
Stanislavsky, C. (1971), *Creating a Role.* New York: Theatre Arts Books.

Appendix

CBCT® protocols: There are 8 modules that build upon each other. Listed below are the modules and the enduring capabilities that one works toward achieving (Negi, 2023, 237–239).

Module 1: Connecting to a Moment of Nurturance

1.1 Attuning to one's sensations and feelings
1.2 Accessing moments of nurturance to activate feelings of safety and comfort
1.3 Valuing being nurtured as a way to increase motivation to provide nurturance to others

Module 2: Developing Stable and Clear Attention

2.1 Enhancing the ability to sustain attention on our chosen task, object, or experience
2.2 Increasing the ability to notice unhelpful impulses, emotions, and distractions
2.3 Strengthening our ability to disengage and redirect the attention where we want it to be

Module 3: Enhancing Self-Awareness

3.1 Enhancing awareness of the patterns of thoughts and emotions in our inner life
3.2 Strengthening the ability to distinguish reality from our projections
3.3 Deepening the understanding that thoughts and emotions are fluid and changing, not fixed or solid
3.4 Increasing the gap between impulse and behavior, allowing greater choice and flexibility in our responses

Module 4: Cultivating Self-Compassion: Part 1

4.1 Sustaining awareness that we are not alone in having setbacks and limitations
4.2 Maintaining the broader perspective that, while we may have limitations and challenges, we also have strengths and opportunities
4.3 Applying a systems-thinking perspective to setbacks, understanding that there are many contributing factors to any outcome that are not all within our control

Module 5: Cultivating Self-Compassion: Part 2

5.1 Sustaining the awareness that we can grow and learn from our mistakes, failures, and setbacks
5.2 Using adversity as a way to clarify our core values and purpose

5.3 Enhancing sensitivity and compassion for others who share our experiences of vulnerability
5.4 Strengthening self-agency and fostering confidence in our ability to alleviate our distress

Module 6: Expanding Our Circle of Concern

6.1 Enhancing awareness of our unconscious biases, assumptions, and judgments of others
6.2 Connecting to others by making our similarities visible
6.3 Expanding our ingroup through awareness that everyone shares the fundamental desire to be well and to avoid harm
6.4 Increasing our capacity for acceptance, understanding, and forgiveness
6.5 Appreciating and respecting diversity and differences

Module 7: Deepening Gratitude and Tenderness

7.1 Seeing that we depend on others for our needs
7.2 Expanding feelings of gratitude and tenderness toward the many who benefit us, directly and indirectly, through the awareness of interdependence
7.3 Appreciating the benefits of other-oriented attitudes and seeing the drawbacks of excessive self-focus

Module 8: Harnessing the Power of Compassion

8.1 Deepening awareness of the predicaments of those we hold with warm-heartedness
8.2 Engaging the wisdom of systems-thinking to guide our compassion toward effective action
8.3 Sustaining compassion in our hearts and through action

12

STANISLAVSKY'S WORK WITH THE ACTOR – FROM MEDITATION TO MINDFULNESS

Gabriela Curpan

As mentioned in some of my previous publications,[1] when connecting Stanislavsky's work with certain spiritually originated ideas such as 'meditation' and 'mindfulness,' it is important to start by reminding the reader that no explicit and direct connections can be found in any of Stanislavsky's published writings that could prove his deliberate and conscious use of such concepts. Clearly, Stanislavsky's only direct advice on accessing the artistic creation that arises from the superconscious mind is to explore the practices of the 'Yogis of India, who perform miracles in the realms of the subconscious and superconscious,' offering a wealth of practical guidance (Stanislavsky, 2008, 83). Yet, it is vital to recognize that both the yogic and Buddhist paths rely on meditation and on the silent contemplation of the inner divine nature within the higher self, as well as on practicing 'mindfulness' (being present in the moment every single second). Maybe Stanislavsky's argument that 'an actor cannot be merely someone, somewhere, at some time or other' is not a coincidence. According to him, on the contrary, actors must embody 'I, here, today' at all times while on the stage (Stanislavsky, 1989, 76). Moreover, there are several uncanny similarities between crucial acting principles such as, for example, the 'creative state', 'experiencing', and 'I am'/'being' (rather than 'acting'), including 'I, here, today'/being present in the moment, and principles found in many spiritual practices that aim to attain and maintain 'mindfulness'.

Although it is a practice deeply rooted in ancient spiritual traditions, in the last decades, due to its positive impact on mental health and well-being, mindfulness has gained significant attention from a medical/psychological perspective. However, in many aspects, when we search the past, both in major spiritual practices and in creative fields, spirituality does not seem to be

DOI: 10.4324/9781003517856-13

completely divorced from science or vice versa, and this clearly becomes more and more visible with the new evidence brought forward in relation to Stanislavsky's work.

For example, as explained by David S. Black, the 'term "mindfulness" in the area of contemplative science [...] stems from Eastern introspective psychological practices, specifically Buddhist psychology [...]' (Black, 2011, 1). Its meaning appears to come from two combined words *Sati* and *Sampajana* – that translate into 'awareness, circumspection, discernment, and retention' (Shapiro & Carlson, 2009, cited in Black 2011, 1). Starting from 'these linguistic renderings', mindfulness was defined as a way of paying 'attention to what is occurring in one's immediate experience with care and discernment' (Shapiro & Carlson, 2009). Nevertheless, as argued by Joseph Goldstein, mindfulness seems to derive directly from the Buddhist spiritual concept of '*Sati*' that involves cultivating an attentive awareness on the present moment to reduce suffering and enhance personal spiritual growth,[2] which is known as the most important tool on Buddha's Noble Eightfold Path:

> The predominant iconic image of the Buddha is of him sitting in blissful meditation. This results in the popular conception that meditation is at the center of Buddhism. But, as is evident from the first six components of the Noble Eightfold Path, at the center is how one goes about one's life. This is evident in Right View, Right Intentions, Right Speech, Right Actions, Right Livelihood, Right Effort and Right Concentration.
>
> *(De Castro, 2017, 1)*

However, De Castro argues that 'the real center of Buddhism is contained in the seventh component on this path, being also the basis for all of the other components', known as 'Right Mindfulness' (De Castro, 2017). As pointed out by Thich Nhat Hanh, mindfulness becomes 'the energy that helps us recognize the conditions of happiness that are already present in our lives' (Nhat Hanh, 1999, 78). According to James H. Austin, 'mindfulness' also appears to be imbedded in the spiritual Zen Buddhist practice, crucial to reaching Enlightenment, known as 'receptive meditation', as in 'an "unfocused" but highly sustained attention that "opens up to whatever experience is available, neither overreacting, nor interpreting it"' (Austin in Curpan, 2021, 146–7), as opposed to the 'Concentrative meditation' that mostly applies to the Zen practice of seated meditation (*Zazen*) and which consists of a focused attention on a specific object (inner such as the breath or outer such as a candle or a flower) 'until one tends to become more or less absorbed in it' (Austin, 1999, 72).

In a similar manner, Jon Kabat-Zinn (2003) connects mindfulness with spiritual Buddhist meditation practices that emphasize the idea of being present in the moment while becoming aware of one's thoughts or surrounding experiences without any type of judgment being involved.[3] Kabat-Zinn is known for creating the Mindfulness-Based Stress Reduction (MBSR)[4] technique as a medical tool, 'initially developed for stress management,' but which 'has evolved to encompass the treatment of a variety of health-related disorders' such as 'anxiety, depression, skin diseases, pain, immune disorders, hypertension and diabetes' (Khan Niazi and Khan Niazi, 2011, 20). Yet, as it appears, although MBSR 'employs mindfulness meditation to alleviate suffering associated with physical, psychosomatic and psychiatric disorders' (Grossman et al., 2004, 35), it might actually draw its inspiration from non-scientific, spiritual knowledge.

It is important to mention that, to attain 'mindfulness' (*sati*), defined 'as a function or quality of mind [...] often described as something to be practiced or cultivated' (Kuan, 2008, 1), as well as for maintaining continual focus on each task of the day, both during meditation and in normal life, Zen Buddhist monks or devoted practitioners are constantly blending meditation dedicated to observe/become aware of simple day-to-day activities, with seated (*zazen*) and (*kin-hin*) meditation, 'a "walking exercise" that helps the practitioner to relax the overstressed limbs, without interrupting the inner concentration,' which is mostly 'practised during the sessions of seated meditation' (Curpan, 2021, 142). According to Henry Dumoulin, at 'the heart of the religion of Buddha' (Dumoulin in Curpan, 2021, 157), especially in the Zen school, we can find various meditational processes that clearly involve an underlying state of 'conscious mindfulness' as 'exercises of concentration emphasizing attention of the mind or mindfulness' (Dumoulin, 1974, 133). Being mindfully aware of normal daily activities can lead to '*zanmai*,' a state of mind reachable outside the practice of meditation, when the practitioner aims to become 'completely absorbed and concentrated' (Enomiya-Lassalle, 1995, 40) in all their tasks, and which can lead to Enlightenment. According to the Zen Master Hugo Enomiya-Lassalle, 'after failing over and over through *zazen* (meditation), many Zen practitioners achieved enlightenment by experiencing *zanmai* when simply involved in their daily activities' (Enomiya-Lassalle in Curpan, 2021, 105).

This particular type of mindfulness practiced in everyday life can be linked to 'Stanislavsky's idea of experiencing the life and soul of the character' (Curpan, 2021, 106) naturally, in every aspect, and in the present moment, as in 'I, here, today' (Stanislavsky, 1989, 76), while using the 'I am' concept, which is also observed in Zen as an active way of meditating known as 'meditative doing' (Curpan, 2021, 106). According to Enomiya-Lassalle (1995), this involves complete concentration on every activity, no matter its simplicity or normalcy, while constantly maintaining full mental alertness and presence every single moment and in every situation. Moreover, the creative state of the actor, envisioned by Stanislavsky as functioning 'on a continuum of mind, body, and spirit' (Carnicke, 2009, 180), could be described as a creative mindfulness in which the actor is aware of themselves, living the life of the character, without trying to control the creative process in anyway, and thus becoming a silent witness/spectator of their own performance. This creative awareness was coined by Michael Chekhov as the 'double consciousness' experienced by the actor during the creative state, and which represents 'the fourth level of the creative process' (Chekhov, 1991, 155). For Stanislavsky, this artistic mindfulness can be translated into the 'theatrical reality' that 'is created by the actor experiencing the circumstances and events of the play as if they are real' (Gillett, 2012, 10).

Yet, for Stanislavsky, as he constantly advises the actor to learn from everything, this type of mindful awareness does not appear to be related only to performance, in so far as he clearly asserts that the actor must maintain constant concentration both on and off the stage, always being aware of their surroundings, and this is not necessarily different from the Zen practices 'of mindfulness, leading to *zanmai* and enlightenment' (Curpan, 2021, 106), noted above. Although clearly situated within the context of performance rather than being constantly related to the everyday life of the actor, Stanislavsky envisions the creation of the character as a step-by-step process of discovering and creating the 'through line of actions' as a continuous, uninterrupted, and logical series of events that must be constantly and actively embraced on the stage, from all aspects, not only mentally and physically, but, most importantly, spiritually. While Zen practitioners may contemplate the unity of life in routine tasks by means of practicing mindfulness, the actors pursuing Stanislavsky's creative state should immerse themselves in the life of the stage, while contemplating the imaginary world of the performance and silently witnessing the characters' existence, in a mindfulness type of creative awareness – the creative state. But what is this 'creative state' and how does it relate to mindfulness or meditation?

Unfortunately, there is little research on the subject. Even Stanislavsky's writings do not seem to fully explain it. In Nicolai Demidov's thoughts, this creative state comes in 'flashes of enlightenment.' He asks his readers: 'haven't you ever seen these flashes of enlightenment, when all of a sudden, you got this inkling – that's "IT"...this is "IT!"...Of course, you have! It's for these moments that you threw yourself into theatre in the first place' (Demidov, 2016, 29). Maybe it is not a coincidence that Demidov associates the art of the stage with the spiritual phenomenon of Enlightenment. Even Zen practitioners tend to describe Enlightenment in a very similar manner to actors.[5]

In my personal experience, the creative state can be neither willed nor controlled. The only way to get into it is by being ready and letting go. It comes with significant changes in how time and space are perceived, as well as with heightened senses. Moreover, the consciousness of the actor appears to make room for the consciousness of the character to surface, while the former becomes its own spectator, in a state of awe, with no comment or tendency to control the creative act. It is also transformative in the sense that the actor grows and evolves both spiritually and mentally. The creative state seems to be related to mindfulness because it happens only in the present moment, while the actor becomes mindfully aware of everything around. Yet, at the same time, due to being present in the moment, every single second, the actor (after experiencing it) has fragmented memories, being able to remember only flashes of what happened during it, and how that particular scene/play/exercise went. Of course, this description relates to the highest levels of the creative state, the lower levels being similar but maybe not as strong. To my knowledge, the 'mirror' exercise used during my workshop can be one of the most efficient ways to enter the creative state and to become mindfully aware of both the partner and the environment.

The 'Mirror' Exercise – A Practical Exploration of Creative Mindfulness

It remains unclear who initially developed this exercise. According to Mel Gordon,[6] Evgeny Vakhtangov was using it in his early approaches. It might be that he was the one to actually create it. Yet, we do know that this exercise was extensively used by Stanislavsky in his late sessions as an etude that was focusing on all the five senses.[7] Chekhov also used the 'Mirror' in his teachings, further developing it by introducing a third actor.[8] The original exercise appears to be very simple, and it starts in pairs. As Jean Benedetti describes it, 'two students stand opposite one another. One performs a series of movements. The other acts as his [her] "mirror", reflecting back what he [she] does' (Benedetti, 2008, 34).

The practical stage of my participation in the Stanislavsky and Mindfulness Symposium (London, 2023) was covered with a workshop using this apparently simple and well-known exercise, but extended to three different stages that were developed during my own research. It starts with pairs, it continues in groups of three actors, and it ends in what I called an 'ensemble' mirror. It might be interesting to mention that, in my initial proposal for the symposium participation, I planned to start with a series of meditative practices and then to continue with this acting exercise. However, somehow following Stanislavsky's advice to be present in the moment, because the researcher conducting her workshop before me already had a meditational approach, and keeping in mind that I had the same participants for my own workshop, I decided to go straight into the exercise, which, in my opinion, already contains clear elements of meditation leading to mindfulness. Also, I invited both participants and observers in the room to engage, thus ending up with a much larger group than usual.

Whenever I teach this exercise for the first time, I normally start by describing it to the participants in simple terms (basically following Benedetti's directions noted above) and then I allow them the liberty of engaging in their own way, without getting into any details involving a spiritual type of thinking. Most of the time, when left to the minimum instructions, the exercise does not seem to work. There is not much concentration going on, and the tendency for the actors/students is to challenge each other rather than to work together. In this situation, the exercise might be fun, but it does not really help apart from maybe generating a good physical warm-up. As such, after a while, I usually inform my students that this is not a movement exercise, and that the most important thing is to start by establishing an inner connection between partners through constant eye-to-eye contact. Gently, I encourage them to breathe together while also significantly slowing down the motion. Finally, I remind them that they need to work for and not against each other.

Everything seems to change completely after being introduced to the subtleties of this exercise and constantly guided to maintain such inner connection and communication. It appears to become a meditation in motion while automatically bringing the actors into experiencing the creative state which, as previously explained, is mindful in its essence. However, due to limited time, I skipped directly to guiding the participants towards approaching the correct form straight from the beginning. Ideally, it would be to start the 'mirror' from the basic form noted above, simply because this allows participants to experience the huge difference for themselves, especially when the goal is to guide them towards working with a spiritual understanding/connotation in mind.

As a short parenthesis, I think it is important to explain how I discovered the hidden subtleties of the 'mirror' exercise. Years ago, during my PhD, I began to look into it while working with the group of actors involved in my project. For a while, nothing much happened between my actors. Yet, I was feeling that something might be there; I just could not put my finger on it. Being an actor myself, I decided to engage in it rather than to continue observing from the side. That was when I finally understood how incredibly powerful this little exercise can become. I remember that I started as the partner in charge of the motion first. Soon, I realised that all I was doing was trying to come up with some smart movement that might challenge the mirror, and this clearly could not have been the correct way. In that particular moment I suddenly understood that, in fact, I was only allowing my ego to guide my work, thus going against all Stanislavsky's principles. In his advice, the actor's ego/smaller self needs to be renounced for the higher self to take over. Undoubtedly, for Stanislavsky, 'in the theatre there is no room for an inflated ego. "Leave your ego at the stage door as you come in", he urges the artist. If the actors are to grow artistically and spiritually, inevitably, first and foremost, they have to learn how to let go of their own egotistical desires and to cultivate precious spiritual values' (Curpan, 2021, 89).

By renouncing my egotistic thinking there and then, I was able to understand that what I was trying to do before was wrong, and this understanding generated an increased need to help my partner with their task of mirroring me. As such, I started to slow down my motion while mentally I was there for my partner, encouraging them to be with me, rather than to follow. This allowed a deep connection to be established between us, and that was exactly the moment when we both naturally and effortlessly slipped into the creative state or, more precisely, into a state of mindfulness in motion, in which the need of seeing each other's feet or hands (to be able to follow) or the tendency of controlling, were no longer necessary because we were both effortlessly synchronised. Moreover, the idea of either leading (initiating the movement) or following (mirroring) seemed to disappear, being instead replaced by a mutual sense of collaboration.

To continue my description of the workshop conducted during the symposium, I firstly started by asking participants to spread into the space and to choose a partner.

We established together who was the mirror and who was initiating the motion for each pair and allowed them to engage in the exercise while guiding gently towards slowing down. Additionally, I instructed them to establish and maintain a constant and uninterrupted eye-to-eye contact with the partner, as well as a coordinated breath, while also suggesting that the motion should be constantly flowing, in a very similar manner to the Tai Chi style. (See Figure 12.1) The results were immediate and stunning. I was looking at a large room full of people working together in a beautiful, highly concentrated dance that followed a silent inner tune, while the energy levels increased exponentially, becoming almost tangible. After a while, when all were experiencing this clear communion, I stopped

FIGURE 12.1 Symposium workshop participants mirroring in pairs. Photo by Jean Bravo, London South Bank University.

the first stage of the exercise to have a brief talk about what just happened and why. Next, we moved on to the second stage, using Chekhov's style, with groups of three, rather than being in pairs. For this second stage, I worked with one group at a time as opposed to all together.

In the middle of the room, we had a pair volunteering to start with the first stage as experienced before, while the rest were observing from the side. Because this stage necessitates light physical touching from my part to guide them, I started by asking for the participants' consent. The idea behind this second stage is to add a new partner to the initial pair while constantly and sequentially replacing one of them by guiding new additions, followed immediately by retractions. As such, a fluid working team is maintained, with everyone either engaging (one at a time) or observing. Due to this constant replacement, the distance between the central partners keeps changing while the consciousness of who is leading and who is following tends to completely disappear. When everyone had their turn, without any further interruption, I continued to guide them through the third stage which gradually adds on to the central pair without replacing any partners, as done during the second stage.

I originally developed this third stage of the exercise with my PhD research group and, as previously noted, I named it the 'ensemble mirror'. In a similar manner as occurred with the second stage, this one starts with an initial pair in the middle, while another one (with a separate motion) is placed diagonally to them, thus building up either a cross or an x shape. One by one, the rest of the participants are directed to join while mirroring either one or the other of the two pairs in the middle, until all are engaged. The effect is highly interesting to witness.

The exercise becomes a performance in itself and a clear demonstration of collective deep concentration and focus, with the entire group breathing and moving together in an amazingly coordinated abstract dance while experiencing a multiplied effect of a mirror in a mirror. Although each one is focusing on the partner they chose to mirror, there is an interesting element of group mindfulness in which the communication goes beyond the five senses, with a feeling of knowing what happens in the room, without a need to change the attention in different directions. Moreover, most of those engaged appear to experience various levels of the creative state. Because of the large number of participants in this workshop (probably over 30), the experience was unique and memorable, not only for me as the facilitator, but also for the participants, as clearly visible from their excited reactions and the many questions addressed at the end.

The participants were keen to confirm the deep sense of communion experienced, and to describe the ways in which they could feel the energy in the room changing. Moreover, they wanted to find out more about the 'mirror' exercise and what makes it work in this manner. Finally, there were some questions around the creative state, the sense of double consciousness of the actor (as being both the character and themselves at the same time), and how this connects with the idea of mindfulness. Based on my entire experience, both during research and when teaching, the 'mirror' is one of the most efficient and powerful acting exercises, for several reasons: 1. It is the fastest and easiest way to enter the creative state; 2. It works with inner communication and energy/*prana* exchange; 3. It builds up skills and artistic prowess fast; 3 It teaches a deep sense of communion within the group; and 4. It is also one of the best ways of creating a strong and cohesive ensemble that may become mindfully aware of the entire artistic act.

Notes

1 Curpan, 2019, 2020, 2021.
2 Goldstein, 2013, 44.
3 Kabat-Zinn, 2003, 145.
4 Mentioned in Ingleson, 2022, 162.
5 For further information on such similarities, please see my book – Curpan, 2021, 104–107.
6 Gordon, 1988, 103.
7 Benedetti, 2008, 33.
8 Zinder, 2009, 114.

References

Austin, H.J. (1999) *Zen and the Brain—Toward an Understanding of Meditation and Consciousness.* Cambridge, MA and London: MIT Press.

Benedetti, J. (2008) *Stanislavski and the Actor: The Final Acting Lessons.* London: Methuen Drama.

Black, D.S. (2011). *A Brief Definition of Mindfulness.* Mindfulness Research Guide. Accessed from http://www.mindfulexperience.org

Carnicke, S.M. (2009) *Stanislavsky in Focus: An Acting Master for the Twenty-First Century.* Abingdon: Routledge.

Chekhov, M. (1991) *On the Technique of Acting.* (M. Gordon, Ed.). New York: Quill - A Harper Resource Book.

Curpan, G. (2019) 'The influence of Christian Orthodox thought on Stanislavski's theatrical legacy', *Stanislavski Studies*, 72. 201–217, https://doi.org/10.1080/20567790.2019.1644747

Curpan, G. (2020) 'Stanislavski's creative state on the stage. A spiritual approach to the "system" through practice as research', *Stanislavski Studies*, 81, 71–85, https://doi.org/10.1080/20567790.2019.1710057

Curpan, G. (2021) *In Search of Stanislavsky's Creative State on the Stage, with a practice as research case study.* London and New York: Routledge.

De Castro, J.M. (2017) 'The Noble Eightfold Path – Right Mindfulness', *Contemplative Studies*, http://contemplative-studies.org/wp/index.php/2018/03/11/the-noble-eightfold-path-right-mindfulness-2/ (Accessed 20.11.23).

Demidov, N. (2016) *Becoming an Actor-Creator.* (A. Malaev-Babel, M. Laskina, Eds.). London and New York: Routledge, Taylor & Francis Group.

Dumoulin, H. (1974) *Christianity Meets Buddhism.* (J.C. Maraldo, Trans.). La Salle, IL: Open Court Publishing Company.

Enomiya-Lassalle, H. (1995) *The Practice of Zen Meditation.* (R. Ropers, B. Snela, Eds.). (M. Bromley, Trans.). London: Harper Collins.
Gillett, J. (2012) 'Experiencing or pretending – are we getting to the core of Stanislavski's approach?,' *Stanislavski Studies*, 1 (1). doi:10.1080/20567790.2012.11428584
Goldstein, J. (2013) *Mindfulness: A Practical Guide to Awakening.* Boulder, CO: Sounds True.
Gordon, M. (1988) *The Stanislavsky Technique: Russia—A Workbook for Actors.* New York: Applause Theatre Book Publishers.
Grossman, P., Niemann, L., Schmidt, S. and Walach, H. (2004). 'Mindfulness-based stress reduction and health benefits', *Journal of Psychosomatic Research*, [online], 57(1), pp. 35–43, https://doi.org/10.1016/s0022-3999(03)00573-7
Hanh, T. N. (1999) *The Miracle of Mindfulness: An Introduction to the Practice of Meditation.* Boston, MA: Beacon Press.
Ingleson, D. (2022) 'Stanislavski training and mindfulness – being in the moment', *Stanislavski Studies*, 10(2), 161–176, DOI:10.1080/20567790.2022.2094103
Kabat-Zinn, J. (2003) 'Mindfulness-based interventions in context: Past, present, and future', *Clinical Psychology: Science and Practice*, 10(2),144–156.
Khan Niazi, A. and Khan Niazi, S. (2011) 'Mindfulness-based stress reduction: a non-pharmacological approach for chronic illnesses, *New American Journal of Medicine and Science*, 3(1):20–23. doi:10.4297/najms.2011.320, https://pubmed.ncbi.nlm.nih.gov/22540058/
Kuan, T. (2008). *Mindfulness in Early Buddhism: New Approaches through Psychology and Textual Analysis of Pali, Chinese, and Sanskrit Sources.* London: Routledge.
Shapiro, S. L. and Carlson, L. E. (2009). *The Art and Science of Mindfulness: Integrating Mindfulness into Psychology and the Helping Professions.* Washington, DC: APA.
Stanislavsky, K. (1989) *Creating a Role.* (E.R. Hapgood, Trans.). (H. Popper, Ed.). New York: Routledge, Theatre Arts Books.
Stanislavsky, K. (2008) *Stanislavsky's Legacy* (E.R. Hapgood, Trans.). (H. Popper, Ed.). London: Methuen Drama.
Zinder, D. (2009) *Body Voice Imagination: Image Work Training and the Chekhov Technique.* Abingdon and New York: Routledge.

13

CONNECTION, CREATIVITY AND COMPASSION

Using Our Inner Lives as a Rich Resource – In Conversation

Polly Teale and Dawn Ingleson

Dawn Ingleson (DI): Stanislavsky asks us to be rigorous in exploring character history and circumstances to understand psychological drives. You link this to self-awareness and the capacity to reflect on our own histories using mindfulness to explore our habitual patterns. You're an arts psychotherapist now but let's start with your theatre work.

Polly Teale (PT): I was always interested in characters that have complex inner worlds, and Shared Experience, the company that I ran with Nancy Meckler, made work that had a potent physical and visual life. (See Figure 13.1 showing an image from Shared Experience's production of *A Doll's House*.). We explored the way that our emotions are a visceral experience in the body. It's often hard to read other people, to know what's going on under the surface. But in theatre, we have this opportunity to make visible what's hidden inside us, and that was at the heart of the work. This possibility that in theatre you can suddenly explode the surface reality and make physical, make palpable the internal experience of the characters. Then you can come back into reality and see this tension between what's being felt, what's happening internally, and what's visible to others. I'm fascinated by that tension between what we reveal and what we hide.

DOI: 10.4324/9781003517856-14

FIGURE 13.1 Shared experience production of Ibsen's *A Doll's House* with Anne-Marie Duff as Nora. Photo by Jonathan Dockar-Drysdale.

Working with objectives and obstacles was always central to the work. The rigour that Stanislavsky applies to given circumstances and understanding the history and world of the characters is key. Our life experiences are carried in our bodies. In order to step inside a character, we need to understand the ways in which they survived their early experience and the beliefs and messages they absorbed. We are often driven by a compulsive need to achieve something: the super objective. Then there are all these obstacles, both external and internal, which create conflict, but can also drive the objective. For example, a super objective of wanting to prove your worth might spring from the fear/obstacle that you will never be good enough.

We did several adaptations of novels, where the writer gives you intimate access to the character's inner world. So, we must find a way to dramatize what's usually hidden. If we focus on the events of the narrative, we're missing what makes the novel so potent and gives us this window into someone's internal reality. With *Jane Eyre*, we used the mad woman in the attic as an alter ego to express everything that a Victorian woman was not allowed to feel or do. While Jane played scenes with all the restraint and formality required by the social codes of the time, we could see her feelings erupting in the body of the mad woman above her in the attic. At the same time, we could see Jane struggling to repress these powerful physical emotional states, these primitive drives and longings. Because Jane was an orphan, a poor governess dependent on her wealthy master, her survival depends upon her compliance and suppression of unruly feelings. Of course that doesn't mean the feelings disappear; they are coursing through Jane's body, threatening to destroy her. It's this tension that fascinates me.

Stanislavsky is rigorous about getting the actor to connect with what is driving the character, that forensic excavation of the given circumstances, the current and historic conditions that formed their understanding of the world and how they have survived. He talks about the psychological and the physical being connected. Bella Merlin talks about how (reading from *The Complete Stanislavsky Toolkit*) 'the emotion-centre is physically associated with your solar plexus, which is the nucleus of nerve endings located anatomically between your stomach and your spine. We talk about butterflies in our stomach, being sick with rage, losing your appetite when you're in love. And the idea of the action-centre coursing throughout the whole body because it's through the actions of your body that your thoughts and feelings can be manifested in the world. The action-centre is very complex; it houses both unbridled sexual energy and restrained formal etiquette' (Merlin, 2007, 163). It is the animal body with all that raw feeling and then all the constraints that exist because of the social context, which are very different, depending on the world you inhabit. That's why Stanislavsky asks us to be rigorous about understanding the world of the character.

In our work we wanted to give audiences an experience where they would viscerally connect with the feelings of the characters. We carry our history in our animal bodies, it's all embedded in the nervous system. That's where I think mindfulness comes in, being able to be in touch with the body mind.

DI: Why did you decide to move into teaching?

PT: About eight years ago, I began an arts psychotherapy training. It was a natural evolution from the theatre work, which was always about the psychology of the characters and complex inner worlds. I didn't know I would end up doing the four-year MA training, but I got hooked.

Towards the end I had a conversation with Guildhall drama school, and they were talking about some of the challenges for young people, the amount of time spent on social media and online and COVID. Young people coming into the training were not so used to being in the room with other people. They were seeing the impact of social media and the pressure to present a curated image of yourself to the world and the anxiety that creates. And on top of that, a drama school training, from nine to six every day in groups learning to collaborate, it's intensive.

Guildhall was interested in a reflective space where students could grow their self-awareness and use that understanding to support their training. I was using the skills that I have as a theatre director but informing it with my arts psychotherapy training.

Designing the course was a real journey, there wasn't a blueprint. The big question in higher education, and drama training especially, is how you get the balance between the Safe and the Brave space. We all naturally want to protect ourselves from going into the unknown, from discomfort, from failure, but these are inevitable if we want to learn and grow.

We teachers are more alert now to neurodiversity, mental health issues and the different needs and sensitivities of our students. Then we've got theatre, which is about stepping into the messy, exploring the complicated, crunchy, uncomfortable, and the shadow parts of ourselves. So, how do we encourage a culture where we know that it's normal for it to feel uncomfortable? We must become curious about ourselves and our resistance. Like the characters we play we are full of conflicts and contradictions.

Arts Psychotherapy is using the arts to explore our inner world. For example, in my room here there is a case full of props: creatures, figures, objects. I could ask you to create a picture of something troubling you that you want to explore, and together we would feel into that image and explore its emotional charge and meaning.(See Figure 13.2 for an example of a student's exploration.)

FIGURE 13.2 A student explores feelings of pressure, competition and judgement through an image created in a session. Photo by Polly Teale.

I had a client, the other day, who took this werewolf with a great big biting mouth and placed it in the middle of their image. It allowed them to capture and share a sense of their depression and what that lonely, scary place feels like. They put other creatures around it, some were hiding, some were buried; there was a Superhero figure trying to conceal the werewolf. All of a sudden, it's a metaphor, rich with meaning. We can feel into the different parts, give each a voice. We recognize that we can have parts that are full of rage, we can also have parts that are joyful, parts that feel frightened and small and want to hide.

The young parts of us are often arrested at different stages of our development, depending on where we experienced challenge or trauma and how we survived. These shadow parts are often repressed and split off from consciousness. In therapy, we seek to own our parts and understand their stories. Stanislavsky understood that one part can take over. Perhaps our perfectionist is trying to keep everything under control, so that the 'bad' parts don't get seen. When this happens, your ability to be in the room, to be open and curious and ready to explore, discover, take a risk, make mistakes, get it wrong, go again, that's going to be so compromised. When I think about Stanislavsky, at the heart of his work, is that desire to free actors up to be in the moment. Super objectives free the actor by asking what in the character's past is driving them to want certain things above all else. What is at their core? What's their wound?

Psychotherapists are interested in how our past informs and sometimes distorts the present. Stanislavsky is saying don't assume you've got it because you've read the script. Excavate the script, the subtext, immerse yourself in research. We're back to empathy, understanding how the conditions, social, cultural, economic, shape the human being.

There's an amazing practitioner called Richard C. Schwartz who's the founder of a movement called Internal Family Systems.

We've got all these parts inside us and some of our parts we might show readily because they win approval, and maybe feel sanctioned socially and culturally, then there are other parts that we hide. The dangerous thing is when they're so shameful that they're completely out of awareness and yet they're driving our behaviours. So, we reenact our trauma and that confirms our negative world view.

For example, if you're harshly disciplined and shamed as a child, you feel a profound sense of powerlessness and internalise that you're bad and unworthy. Because there's such shame you toughen up, you hide that shameful vulnerable part and project it onto others. The person who's been bullied becomes the bully, and shames others for their vulnerability. It's an obvious example but we've all got some of that in us, the part of us that feels small and inadequate, and if it's out of our awareness, we can keep reenacting the trauma in an attempt to feel powerful, so it becomes intergenerational. This is why this work is so important. Mindfulness says, let's sit with the feelings. Let's allow ourselves to be present to all of who we are, what we are, and not push it away, or project onto others.

DI: What kind of challenges do you find acting students face?

PT: One of the challenges that I've recognised is sometimes the students who might most need this work can be most resistant to it. It understandably threatens the way that they've survived, by protecting themselves from vulnerable feelings, so it feels uncomfortable to be asked to engage with these shadow parts.

Some students arrive and think, 'I thought we were going to be given a script and a character but oh, no, you're going to start with *me*? You're going to ask me to think about my history and all the messages and beliefs that I've picked up, and how I might bring those into the room? How do those messages impact my relationship with myself, with others, the world?' This can feel very challenging. However, I believe we need to know our own parts because we will be using aspects of ourselves to create the characters. The character may experience things that touch on difficult things in your own history and trigger your own threat responses. We need to have access to ourselves in a way that allows us to explore a given part, and then step back into our fuller sense of self. In my sessions I hope students can grow their sense of core stability, holding all these younger parts like a compassionate parent.

In drama school you're constantly asked to step out of your comfort zone and expose yourself in some way. We need to understand how the nervous system reacts to perceived threat. I did a session on the amygdala recently, and we were exploring viscerally what happens when we experience fight, flight freeze, fawn, flop. These are primitive reactions that helped us survive when we were in danger of being eaten by predators or dying of starvation. In the modern world the threat is more often an imagined danger that relates to our history and early experience. Developing that curiosity about ourselves and others and how we are shaped by our life experience is key to an actor's skill.

DI: What are your aims when you work with student actors and teachers, lecturers, and/or actors?

PT: I no longer work as a theatre director. I have a therapy practice. I also teach at the Institute for the Arts in Therapy and Education, and I work for an organization called Trauma Informed Schools (TIS), who do wonderful work with teachers. We want to see a seismic change in our education system towards a more creative, compassionate, inclusive culture. The work is incredibly powerful and humbling and I feel very privileged to be part of it.

DI: Where does resilience fit into actor training and the industry, and how do we define resilience?

PT: In Trauma Informed Schools, we're cautious about that word. Of course, we want to empower and equip people to feel more robust. But the danger is that resilience can sound like this quality that you acquire through your grit and determination. But we know, statistically, that the more adverse childhood experiences, deprivation and trauma, the more likely you are to suffer from mental illness. The danger is that we make resilience sound like it's about willpower. What we need is to understand and foster the conditions that create resilience.

Trauma Informed Schools come from the premise that every child should have an emotionally available adult, who is able to understand and empathise with their reality without judgement. TIS talks about relationship not behaviour, because the problems stem from a lack of trust, from not having a secure base, and therefore coming into school, and not being able to trust relationships. If the amygdala is firing off, the nervous system is overactive, we're hyper-vigilant, or we're withdrawn. We can't learn. So, it's using the arts to build this bridge, creating that live connection and attachment to another human being in an age where people can easily become isolated.

One of the biggest challenges to connection we face is screens. I do a session with my acting students that starts by putting our phones together in the middle of the room. I ask what it feels like. Every year somebody says, 'I wish I could throw my phone out the window. But even as I'm looking at it now, I can see a notification, and I'm desperate to look.'

There's good things about phones, but they also fuel our insecurities, create addictive needs and dangerous false narratives.

DI: How can mindfulness help?

PT: I often begin sessions with a meditation/body scan. I ask: what sensation is there inside right now? There's no judgement, just curiosity. I'm wary of mindfulness meaning calm. Because we have these many parts, and each part is an energetic state. It's like the *Inside Out* movies. We want to build a more compassionate relationship with those young parts which are arrested at different stages of development because of our history. Once we're in a relationship with them we recognize their needs. Mindfulness can be the conduit to get to that awareness.

I do a session where we physicalise emotional states, we build it onto the work around the autonomic nervous system, and the idea of objectives and obstacles, because our feelings, our shadow parts, are often an obstacle to the objective.

It's not about emotional recall. You don't need to bring back a painful memory and then go back into the trauma. These are universal feeling states. Everyone from the most privileged person in the room to the most disadvantaged knows what jealousy feels like, or shame, rage, fear or joy. It creates a real connective tissue because it's something that we can all plug into because it's visceral. It's a body memory.

You will see a young child having a tantrum, that's anger, fully expressed, or a child that's feeling afraid might hide, or an excited child will jump up and down. They experience their feelings viscerally. Then we learn to cover that up because obviously we must be socialised, learn how to interact, to collaborate, contain our feelings, but they don't disappear, there's still that tantrum-ing three-year-old in us somewhere. I ask them to forensically think about feelings, because jealousy might have moments of rage, where you want to attack, or shame, where you want to shrink and disappear, it might have deep sadness where you feel heavy and want to writhe and howl, it might have moments of wanting to grasp and take. Virtually everyone can do this exercise because we all know what jealousy feels like. There's something releasing and freeing about permission to express and explore these taboo feelings. These are the exiled parts. We don't want anybody to know that we feel jealous.

I do an improv where somebody will come into the room, they'll say, 'I've just heard I need to leave drama school because I got a lead in a Netflix series' – I choose something the students can relate to. When I clap everyone physicalizes their feelings and there is an explosion of envy, then when I clap again they have to cover it up. We look at how we often cover with the opposite of what we feel, so the students who are envious about the Netflix series will say, 'Wow, that's amazing. I'm so happy for you.'

You can do that with any scenario, like for example being infatuated. We might hide even a relatively positive emotion, because we fear being out of control, being rejected, vulnerable. Students can do it at the drop of a hat because we know what it feels like. When we cover up, the suppressed feeling is still coursing through the body, it's palpably there. For example, I might be super-positive to my classmate when I'm actually feeling devastated that they've got this Netflix role – my best friend's about to go off to become a star and leave me behind. It allows us to explore a part of us that we would not normally want anybody to see. Most of us have been brought up to be polite, and that can mean denial of our feelings. This links to mindfulness because it says, 'Find out what's really going on inside. Let's explore', I think that session is really releasing, because you get to let it out, and realise we all share these universal human feeling states.

The students can then use this directly in their acting. We meet characters when they're in crisis. Drama is about conflict, times when feelings are heightened. And so, they're going to use all their parts in the work. Therefore, the more that you are in touch with all those parts of yourself, the better.

For example, if your anger is something that you are afraid to acknowledge, because it's too scary and unacceptable, then that feeling is out of your awareness. You might say you never get angry, but these feelings probably leak out in other ways – for example, I project onto others. I might be highly critical of others if they get angry, maybe, because I can't own that part of myself. So, the more that we can have all this in our awareness, the more we know that it is human to experience powerful feelings.

DI: To be aware, do we have to be alert?

PT: When I set up our body scan at the beginning of each session students often ask, 'Can we lie down?', but I want there to be an ease ***and*** an alertness. When we're listening, which is key to any kind of collaborative endeavour, we must be alert to ourselves and one another. It's about being present and responsive. We need some healthy adrenaline – if we stay in our comfort zone, we stay in a place that's safe and familiar, but we might lack that curiosity and attentiveness to what's new in this moment. Bringing our attention to the moment. Noticing the sense data. That's at the heart of mindfulness. Perhaps curiosity and attention are better words than alertness.

DI: How do we create, nurture, enable a brave space as theatre practitioners, especially in a training environment?

PT: With Shared Experience, we had always worked with experienced actors that I'd chosen, who were keen to work for the company. It was quite a culture shift going into drama school and working with first years who've just arrived, in so many ways.

I've come to believe, so much of this is about communication.

You have a student who gets anxious and wants to leave the room, or who becomes overwhelmed with feelings. My sessions are all about encouraging them to get curious about what's happening. Is it something that's real now or something you're carrying from a long time ago? What beliefs are fueling the feelings? Crucially, it's about dialogue and agency, knowing that if you need to, you can sit out for a bit, the same way that you would if you're nursing a particular injury, but if you can stay in the room that would be great, because then you're not missing out on the learning. We know the experience of trauma is about feeling isolated and powerless, so when we feel we've got some agency and choice, and we're in a dialogue, the anxiety lessens. In Reflective Practice, we encourage students to share their fears, and so often others have the exact same anxiety. So, it's no longer something you're hiding in a place of shame. It's shared and understood that a student can leave if they need to, but please come back as soon as you're ready. Because the exiled parts can make you feel, 'Once I've gone, I can't go back. What I'm hiding is too shameful.' Therefore, I've come to believe that a lot of it is about communication, about naming and sharing what's in the room.

I ask the group the question, 'How are we going to manage when one of us feels like the work is too challenging?' It's naming some of the things that we fear can't be talked about and building that trust.

I try to model when we talk about inner critics, I say, 'Is anybody like me? I've got a harsh inner critic and once it gets going, oh, my goodness!' I'm modeling that we're all in this together, it's a lifelong journey. I think there's a longing for something to magically transform us so that we don't have to feel anxious anymore. But it's more about our relationship to our anxiety. We can change our response to it. It's important to know that a level of anxiety is a sign that you're learning and growing and putting yourself out of your comfort zone and taking a risk. Even having that message is helpful.

We've all got perfectionist thinking, because we think it will keep us safe from rejection or failure. We think it will protect us, but it actually triggers our threat system and makes us react from the amygdala and a place of fear.

DI: In your therapy you encourage spontaneous expression, which can foster a growing sense of agency, aliveness and authenticity. These qualities can be transferred into Stanislavskian acting.

PT: Yes, most of the time, when we're responding from a reflex, that's an old pattern, an old 'script'. I always use the example of being bitten by a dog when I was little. And so, every single dog I met, I thought was going to bite me, no matter how friendly or gentle they were. I brought my old script to every new situation and reacted to the dog as if it were dangerous. Then, of course, the dog experiences this jumpy, unpredictable person so they start barking and before you know it, you've fulfilled your expectation and the frightened dog snaps. So, supposing we had a scary dad, every male authority figure might evoke that transference. We think he's going to diminish and frighten us like our dad did when we were little, when we had no power or agency. So that's one of the key learnings in therapy: that was about something that happened then, it's no longer your reality now.

That frightened part inhibits spontaneity, so that I'm not able to enjoy the dog, but then I remember somebody saying to me, 'Just put out your hand so the dog can smell it.' And that meant there was an interim stage. It's like a student who needs to develop trust because relationships haven't felt safe. So, the dog would come and sniff. And they would get to know me, I would get to feel the dog's soft nose and warm mouth and then, slowly, we communicate. Because trust builds incrementally. We relearn. We come back from trauma through new experiences. It's a gradual building of trust as the nervous system learns that this is safe now. Over time I learned to be able to enjoy touching a dog and finally playing with a dog. When I meet a new dog, I still experience some fear, but I can override it.

The idea of spontaneity relates to our concept of time too; time shifts. When we're in our animal body that 'React' energy is actually taking us out of the moment. We're in an old pattern, an old script. It's only when we realise, for example being with a dog, that we don't have to react in that way because that was to do with a particular set of given circumstances and one particular dog. Ultimately, we want to be open, curious, ready to experience what's here now rather than defending against past injuries, we can think about stepping towards a feeling, holding that fearful protective part in awareness as we encounter the present.

These young protective parts might not any longer be serving our best interests, but we can hold them with compassion. I can feel into that anxious young me that was so afraid of getting into trouble because my dad was scary when he got angry and remember how I would try to do everything I could to avoid that, and then you're holding that anxious part in a tender place. It's not our enemy. In mindfulness, we can hold it and feel connected to it, and alive to the present moment. Alive to new possibilities.

Reference

Merlin, B. (2007). *The Complete Stanislavsky Toolkit*, London: Nick Hern Books.

Bibliography

Schwartz, R. C. (2021) *No Bad Parts: Healing Trauma and Restoring Wholeness with the Internal Family Systems Model.* Boulder, CO: Sounds True.

14

MINDFULNESS & STANISLAVSKY IN THE REHEARSAL PROCESS – A DISCUSSION

Dawn Ingleson, Max Harrison and David Gilbert

Dawn Ingleson (DI): What aspects of Stanislavsky's work is useful in your rehearsal room?

Max Harrison (MH): I use objectives, actions and units, although I find units difficult. Bella Merlin once said, 'There's no right or wrong.' As soon as I shifted my view to that way of thinking, I found them useful to give us something more bite-sized in rehearsal. Halfway through a run, it becomes obvious where the units are. I do the act of analysis in rehearsals. I'll do a bit on the text and then we'll improvise it and then we'll add the text. We'll be talking in that process about what the intentions are and using the improv often to explore the objectives more.

I use Mike Alfreds' 'points of concentration' to filter in the given circumstances.

David Gilbert (DG): For me, it's managing what we're doing in chunks. I also work towards a shared language with the company about the world we're working with. So, whether it's a unit, event or change, we chop up the text and give it little scene titles, to start to zone in on our shared understanding and language about how we want to talk about what we're making.

DI: What is mindfulness? Do you practice it?

DG: I don't have a definition, yet. I'm interested in the idea of surrender. How we process our ego. I practice

DOI: 10.4324/9781003517856-15

yoga. My Christian faith is important. The idea of being still which is something that might link into meditation, being still from within. What always comes up is this sense of surrendering to holding on to myself and being open to being open.

MH: Day-to-day, I define it as remaining aware of what you're doing. So that I'm not caught up or entangled in something without being aware that that's what's happening. Not to say that thinking is bad, it's just part of our experience and obviously useful in rehearsals. Mindfulness is about having self-possession, being aware of what's going on in our minds; whether that is a torrent of thoughts or a still, peaceful vista, rather than being caught up in thinking or feeling without realising that we're caught up. It's about coming back to that awareness.

There are four foundations of mindfulness in Buddhism. The Buddha talked about being 'not drunk,' that mindfulness is like being sober, i.e. there's a soberness to it, an awakeness and an alertness that you can't get when you're drunk.

From a Buddhist point of view, the mind is not the brain or computer in the skull that drives us around, the Pali word for heart-mind is Citta. So, the centre for the mind traditionally in Buddhism is more the heart centre in the chest.

That's not to say that the mind is only created with feeling; in those times, however, when you really feel mindful, it's quite an embodied sense, a light coming right back down into the body. When we're cut off from experience, we're not sensing into our sensations, we're not really aware of our emotions. Buddhism is this deeper ground of consciousness between us all. *The master and his emissary*, by Ian McGilchrist, is useful for explaining how the brain works. He is a neuroscientist, but his argument is that you can't boil it down to materialism. He says because we've evolved a brain, we can then receive consciousness in this form.

DI: In the rehearsal room, do you lead mindfulness practice?

DG: I was working with a company, in 2015, of teenagers. We had a summer residency, and we started doing yoga in the mornings. From that moment I knew I would bring this into my work. It was a great way of grounding us. I do stretching and breathing together. I try to lower the stakes as some people might be averse to the practice of it. It's always a very relaxed room afterwards and with mindfulness, there's no right or wrong way of doing it.

MH: Yes, it's just the degree to which you're able to access presence with each other. It's easy to make mindfulness synonymous with meditation. However, you can do things in a meditative way and be more present. A working definition for me, of meditation, is working with the mind on the mind.

I used to use meditation in rehearsals, but I felt it could sometimes slow people's rhythms down to something a bit soporific. But in terms of mindfulness, connected presence, I use that. I use Meisner, bringing people into presence and connection. It emphasizes the compassionate side even though sometimes the work can seem quite impolite, what you are doing is connecting and being mindful of another person and what they're doing.

DI: David, does 'surrendering' happen psychologically in the room because of the physical relaxing? How does mindfulness impact your work?

DG: It impacts the work because we do it together. There's a sense of togetherness; it's about trying to listen to each other, to the room, and what we need. You're also making contact with yourself. This feels uniting. What I'm trying to establish in the room is this 'us' working together. It's not compartmentalized. This is a process where you're trying to weave together. That feels inevitably, organically more authentic, and truthful. The more unified the company becomes, the more unified people become with themselves and with their character.

DI: Are there ethical considerations about bringing mindfulness into a space where people may not have been seeking that or is acting/theatre implicitly a move towards a more mindful/examined Life?

MH: The first thing I want to say is that I led meditation one day at drama school. And one guy had quite an intense reaction, and became quite upset, and had to leave the room. I had assumed that he was psychologically healthy, yet he was really thrown by it and had to leave as he felt quite panicky and anxious.

The second thing was, I was listening to a podcast with Patsy Rodenburg. She said that she doesn't answer questions about her faith, if people ask her when she's being interviewed as a voice teacher, because she feels when she's entering that room, she's entering a specific contract with actors, which is to work on their voice with them, not to bring in other things. I, in the above instance, had people that were in that rehearsal room who had come to me for help on a play. And I've then brought them something that they're not asking for: mindfulness, which as we know, brings us in touch with our emotions much more fully.

If I go to the Buddhist Centre, I'm signing up for that, but I'm not signing up for that experience necessarily in a rehearsal room. I therefore do wonder: what are the ethics of that?

DI: Can mindfulness, instead, give us a toolkit to come into the space with?

MH: Yes, and at the same time, it also feels, to me the work of months and years as well. Proper mindfulness is not like a smash-and-grab raid. Although it can also bring us more awareness within 20 minutes.

DI: What are we asking our actors to do when working on a play, in terms of mindfulness or wellbeing?

MH: Stanislavsky changed at the end of his life, from working with emotional memory to physical actions. In rehearsals, if someone's really accessing something that's authentic, truthful, where you've arrived at it through the *imagination*, the scene ends and they're totally fine. The imagination is a much healthier way to access stuff. It's interesting that Stanislavsky dropped the emotional memory element of his work towards the end of his life.

There's also something around being mindful and self-possessed. I was speaking to quite an established director the other day, and he said, he would never cast someone that was too close to the role, because he felt that there wouldn't be enough distance, he said, they wouldn't be able to know why they were doing so well, they wouldn't often be able to see why it was that the scene was working. That's like them being in a place of unawareness. And what I think he was talking about was that he would cast an actor with more awareness so that he, as director, can then better channel it in a safer way for them. And probably a more convincing way for an audience.

DG: Presence. That's one of the key things, even from a professional standpoint, you have a scene, and sometimes, I don't know where the actors – or characters are. Even in professional settings, some of my notes are literally, 'Where are you? What's going on, you're missing obvious stuff. You are all in a different place, get to where we actually are here!' So, even if you're not doing mindfulness as a tool-based process, in your rehearsal, a lot of the discussion is about how we access the moment, how we see the other person, how we listen, how we receive. So, there is something in there which connects us to mindfulness.

A good exercise is when you ask your scene partner to just say their line, and then you wait three seconds. Then you say your line. So those three seconds gives you time to hear what the person said, before you even think, to then say what your next line is. Slowing down. People discover so much from it. It's about trying to genuinely actively listen.

MH: Another exercise is *active grasp*. You put your hands on each other palm to palm and have eye contact, like a mirror exercise. You move your hand, I follow it, you don't need to do any big movements. You start super slow, and it's quite uncomfortable to hold eye contact like that, because you're in quite a deep connection, you feel in tune with your partner. Therefore, they might see a vulnerability or fear or aggression, or your sexuality. It made me feel wide open. The exercise was also about slowing us all down. And the first time we did a scene afterwards, it was super slow. It was good, like with David's exercise, because you're listening. The director who was leading this made us close our eyes and she read three facts about Masha from *The Seagull* – e.g., I wear black, I drink vodka, I take snuff. She kept reading them very slowly for about two minutes. And you got so much about Masha, like she can probably taste vodka on her breath but it's only one o'clock in the afternoon. She's snorting this stuff up her nose, that's quite sensory and maybe painful at the back of the mouth. If I dressed only in black all the time, it's quite a statement to everybody else around me especially in the middle of summer. So, she got us to slow down and zoom in. Normally, you have a notebook full of facts, but I've not taken any of them in, but if I tune in, there's loads there.

The quality of the attention that you're bringing to it is key when talking about how to make Stanislavsky relevant now, as distinct to turn-of-the-century Russia. There's something about the pace at which we live being so different, our thoughts are so much quicker. We live so much of our lives much more disembodied. Mindfulness is about slowing down and dropping into the body.

DI: Does Stanislavsky and mindfulness help us approach the work inclusively?

DG: As an artist, I've always been curious about what it means to be a black or an African performer. I don't necessarily feel like Stanislavsky talks to me about that. I would have to investigate some of my own history that explores acting theory for black actors, like black acting methods: critical approaches by Sharrell D. Luckett or stages of reckoning: anti-racist and decolonial actor training by Amy Mihyang Ginther.

As someone who's from the diaspora, some of my understanding of my own history needs thinking about. So even things like given circumstances. I'm walking into the room as an artist not knowing parts of my history, so then when I'm now having to apply this way of thinking to a process, I think there's a disconnect I might find. I've been with others who have to kind of force themselves into plays that they don't connect to.

MH: What's lovely about making theatre together is we can keep the real world out of this sacred ritualistic space, which is creating work together as an ensemble, which brings us back to unification.

I often start with the Michael Chekhov Golden Hoop or Circle:

You imagine this golden hoop dropping down and then hold it all together, then you find a time to put it on the floor and you step over it. And you imagine the stuff from your life fading away. Then you're ready to work and at the end of the day, you come back into it or take a step out and throw it back up. It's a really nice way to create that distinction from normal life to then stepping into this braver space. I'd argue that that's mindful practice. We're all focused on one thing, very simple. That's the beauty of mindfulness. It's simple. It's anchoring, getting myself ready. It's quite profound, working out these are the things that I need to put down to enter this room so you're recognizing what's present for you. You've been very deliberate and aware about it.

DI: We're searching for the creative state. How can we define the relationship between creativity and mindfulness?

DG: I think curiosity can help bridge the gap between mindfulness and creativity. Being open. I think there's a relationship there, between being excited about what could be and the will to be curious.

MH: Mindfulness is about allowing whatever's coming up. From a Buddhist point of view, the things that we do that are unhelpful are called cravings and aversion. There's nothing wrong with having pleasant or painful sensations happen to us through thoughts or emotions, the issue comes when we crave after the good ones. If we get something good, we try to grab it and hold it and don't let go and hope that it never ends.

We have that in rehearsal rooms all the time. 'It's not good enough yet.' 'Can we get more done?' The issue is when we try to push any negative feelings that we might be having away. We need to make a distinction between the *reactive* mind and the *creative* mind. The reactive mind does go to craving and aversion. We all have different patterns of thinking, based on our upbringing. Some pattern can be like, 'Okay, I get a good feeling. But I worry when it's going to finish,' and that is a reaction that I'm not even aware of. Whereas a creative thing would then be to simply accept the sensation/feeling. 'This is good. I'm not worried if it's going to leave.'

To give an example, when I came back from retreat once, I felt so creative. I just knew what to say somehow to get the work out of people, I could see and I would stop it much quicker and work on it in a clearer way. I was speaking to one of my teachers about it and he said that often people feel when they come off retreat, or they've been practicing a lot that they're more relaxed. He said, 'You're not more relaxed; what you are is less reactive.' So, you have more time or space. You're not knee jerk, and it feels more relaxed but it's just way less reactive. I think the more we can put actors into that creative place with each other, the richer their work will be because something deeper in them can come up.

Your own tensions have gone so that you can embody something else. Mike Alfreds says *intensity* is vital for an actor, but *tension* is lethal. There's a clarity that that time gives you. If mindfulness practice can get us to that space, I think we come to the work more open and curious.

So, you can turn up to rehearsal knowing certain bits about your character. But feeling that I don't know how I'm going to respond to what you're going to bring as that'll have to happen when I meet you.

DG: I think they're my favourite people to work with. Creative actors are up for a game and are free to play. Choices don't always have to be right. But they feel like they're coming from somewhere. The importance of being playful cannot be underestimated. Auditions are sometimes won by that alone. The creative actor is a playful actor.

MH: Ian McGilchrist talks about what the different hemispheres of the brain do. He states that the right side should be the dominant one. It has greater flexibility and depth. It is more generous than the left side, which is more self-interested and has less of a grip on reality. His argument is because of the society we live in, we're stuck on the left side of the brain. So, we have this skewed vision of the world. At the end of *An Actor Prepares*, the last chapter is called On the Threshold of the Subconscious, which I feel all the work is trying to get us to. I think the balance of knowing and not knowing is super important. And ultimately creativity, I feel, must come from the unknown with the known as a scaffold.

Mindfulness can allow us to see that a scene is going well; there's always that little watcher in the back saying 'Oh, this is really working.'

Listening to these Patsy Rodenburg podcasts, she said the craft is just a scaffold to your creativity. She's making a big case for craft not as an end but as a means to an end. Mike Alfreds is also rigorous. As we know, he asks actors to action every line, do character lists, unit and title the text before you start rehearsals. Then when you get in there, you have, say, six weeks of spontaneity and exercises, because for him, that's the only way to that genuine creativity, to pass it back to the right side of the brain.

DI: So, is it mind or is it soul?

MH: There's another good podcast by Declan Donellan, *Not True but Useful*, where he talks about rehearsal room techniques. He emphasises that nothing he says is true; it's just useful over time, to all these actors that he's worked with, to talk about the predicament rather than the intention. I feel the same with 'soul', whether we call it mind or soul is more a question of how useful it is, to an actor, because they're both metaphors for an experience that we have, personal to every actor. My instinct would be, given the situation that we're in, in 2024, in London, that soul would be a 'one size fits all', maybe to get us away from this feeling of ourselves as computers, which I think is quite ingrained right now. More towards this connection or communion between each other – a meeting of souls.

DG: I think for me, what I'm always looking for constantly is connection. Connection to the work, to the people. So, the audience can connect to it. I think maybe it might not even be about truth and authenticity for me. It's about connection.

MH: Stanislavsky talks about communication and communion, which could be synonyms for connection with your scene partner, with the world of the play, and with the audience. What I like about communion is what a teacher once said to me – what you put on stage must be realer than real life. That is how I feel when I go on retreat. People tend to say, 'Oh, we're going to go back to real life after retreat.' And my teacher would ask, 'What is real about that? Real life is what we're doing here.' There's something about the flavour of the word *communion*. There's something suggestive and evocative about it that I really enjoy.

In Buddhist circles, you're looking to deepen community with each other; part of that is ritual. Theatre came out of religious communities. Stanislavsky was devising his approach in the context of a company that work together again and again, so those deeper conversations can happen. A lot more understanding (through the time a company had been together) was possible in the past because people were working in the context of a proper ensemble and that's been torn apart. I often yearn for that. That's why you often end up working with people repeatedly. You have a shared language, you've got consent, a relationship, a depth of connection.

We can mindfully ask ourselves and others to do as best we can in the moment. Only compassion and understanding will allow people to be the best versions of themselves or go beyond what they think they're capable of. So, I think we have a moral responsibility to push people beyond what even they think they're capable of at the same time as holding that with kindness and understanding. I don't know what that looks like, it feels like that's just a

North Star and then you must work on the ground practically to aim to achieve that.

The most playful, beautiful, creative, provocative space is completely compassionate if you're open with each other. I think some of the best moments in a rehearsal room have come when an actor has pushed back on me and neither of us is reactive. It can be uncomfortable.

David talked about surrender. In Buddhism, it might be particular to the strain that I practice, but they have the three myths of spiritual practice which are three ways that one can conceptualize the path towards enlightenment or, in our case, the path towards good, honest and truthful work. The first one is called self-development/self-transcendence, which is all about putting in the work. The next one is self-surrender, where you surrender yourself to some higher power in our context to serve the play. The last one is self-discovery, which is the idea that you're already enlightened, and you just need to stop stressing, it's all there. Your nature is aware. So come back to that. The great thing about these pathways is that none of them are right or wrong, people can become attached to one. But it's about being intelligent enough to understand which one's going to be useful for us in this moment and being in awareness.

DG: There's an African proverb that says, 'If we want to go fast, go alone; if we want to go far go together.'

Bibliography

Alfreds, M. (2007) *Different every night: freeing the actor*. London: Nick Hern.

Donellan, D. and Ormerod, N., Not True, But Useful Podcast – Cheek by Jowl (Accessed 29/08/24)

Ginther, M.A.,(2023) *Stages of Reckoning Antiracist and Decolonial Actor Training*. 1st ed. Oxon: Routledge.

Luckett, S.D. and Shaffer, T. M. (2017) *Black Acting Methods: Critical approaches*. 1st ed. Oxford: Routledge.

McGilchrist, I. (2009) *The Master and His Emissary: The Divided Brain and the Making of the Western World*. 1st ed. New Haven: Yale University Press.

Merlin, B. (2014) *Beyond Stanislavsky: A Psycho-Physical Approach to Actor Training*. 1st ed. South Yarra: Taylor and Francis.

Rodenburg, P., *Craft: Sweat and Joy*. https://patsyrodenburg.co.uk/podcast/ (Accessed 29/08/24).

Stanislavsky, K. (1989) *An Actor Prepares*. New York: Routledge.

Stanislavsky, K. and Benedetti, J. (2008) *An Actor's Work: A Student's Diary*. London: Routledge.

INDEX

Made in the USA
Monee, IL
14 September 2026

62978580R00103